RUSSIA OFF TRACK

TRANS-SIBERIAN RAILWAY

JARRET SCHECTER

TROLLEY

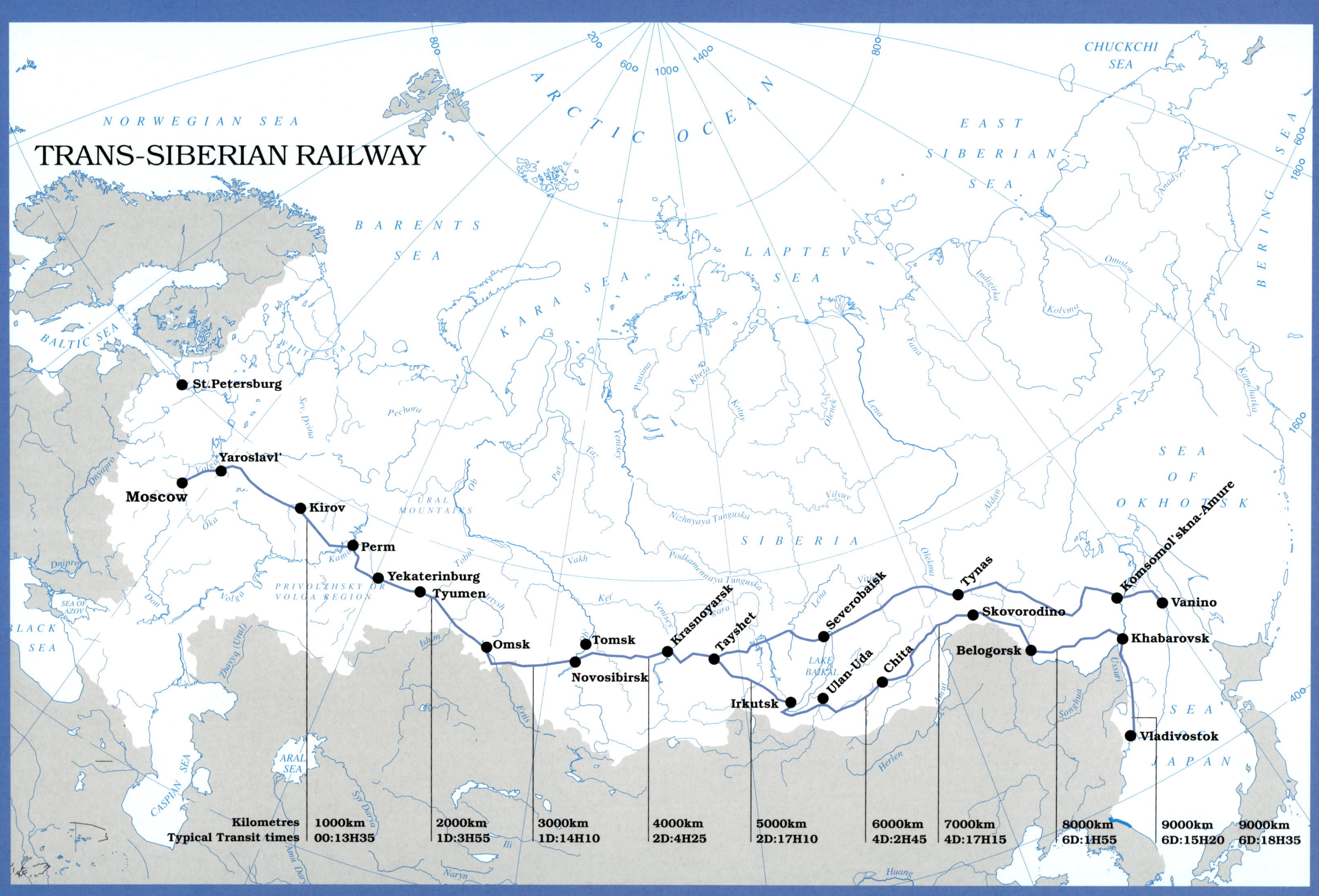

TRANS-SIBERIAN RAILWAY
NORWEGIAN SEA
BALTIC SEA
BARENTS SEA
KARA SEA
ARCTIC OCEAN
LAPTEV SEA
EAST SIBERIAN SEA
CHUCKCHI SEA
BERING SEA
SEA OF OKHOTSK
WHITE SEA
SEA OF AZOV
BLACK SEA
CASPIAN SEA
ARAL SEA
URAL MOUNTAINS
PRIVOLZHSKY OR VOLGA REGION
SIBERIA
SEA OF JAPAN
St.Petersburg
Yaroslavl'
Moscow
Kirov
Perm
Yekaterinburg
Tyumen
Omsk
Tomsk
Novosibirsk
Krasnoyarsk
Tayshet
Severobaisk
Irkutsk
Ulan-Uda
Chita
Tynas
Skovorodino
Belogorsk
Komsomol'skna-Amure
Vanino
Khabarovsk
Vladivostok
LAKE BAIKAL
Kilometres
Typical Transit times
1000km
00:13H35
2000km
1D:3H55
3000km
1D:14H10
4000km
2D:4H25
5000km
2D:17H10
6000km
4D:2H45
7000km
4D:17H15
8000km
6D:1H55
9000km
6D:15H20
9000km
6D:18H35

At 5,753 miles (9,258 KM) the Trans-Siberian is the longest railway in the world and connects Moscow with the Pacific port city of Vladivostok. The Trans-Siberian runs through 7 time zones, 21 regions of Russia, passes by 14 cities of 300,000 or more people and runs across 16 large rivers.

Begun in 1891 and largely completed in 1905 at an equivalent cost of $250 million, the railway aimed to unite both the east and west of the country and to play a pivotal role in the Russo-Japanese war. Unanticipated defeat to the Japanese however, bolstered Japan's imperial appetite in the East, which was a contributing factor in speeding up the demise of Czarism and the rise of the Soviet Union.

RUSSIA: STILLNESS AND MOTION

Looking at the past in the present, we can glimpse the future and the consequences that it may hold. Although purported to be one-dimensional, a rich photograph laden with past stillness and future motion, is multi-layered by time, space and meaningful consequence.

The images that follow were taken of the vast interior of Russia from the Trans-Siberian Railway in the final months of 2009. At 5,753 miles in length, or nearly one quarter of the Earth's diameter, the Trans-Siberian links the frenzied and cosmopolitan capital of Moscow in the West and the ageing port city of Vladivostok in the East. In between these two endpoints is the immense heartland, which besides being dominated by forests and fields, is littered with poor villages, dilapidated industrial plants, and a smattering of non-descript cities. In many respects this heartland, or the body of Russia, is a precarious place, with a no less troubling, unpredictable Muscovite head on top. The images presented here offer a window onto a little seen and overlooked landscape, and hint at a subtle yet tense negotiation between a powerful capital and its boundless interior that is, however, largely filled with nothingness.

As revealed in the prequel *America off Track*, Russia in both words and images is uncannily similar to the USA. The lone superpower is also largely a place of tension and paradox between on the one hand wealth and power, and on the other poverty and weakness. "Towering skylines, seemingly idyllic-looking towns, and inspiring nature", as described in *America Off Track*, often serve as cover for the melancholy and emptiness that also pervade the USA. "Dilapidated and sometimes dangerous, old, bustling city centers, places seemingly isolated to business activity, appear eerily quiet, especially after five... Between communities there is often a string of ordinary-looking, interchangeable townships, or there is frequently just vast nothingness." As in Russia, the scale and vastness exposes not so much a country's strengths, but a void and sense of emptiness.

Despite their historic and cultural differences, the United States and the Russian Federation, the world's largest country in both size and natural resources, seem strangely aligned in the integrated paradox of weakness and strength. Whether in the USA or Russia, the paradox, which in many cases is indistinguishable, can aptly and uniquely be perceived in both places from a window off-track.

Jarret Schecter

Dusk on the Siberian plains

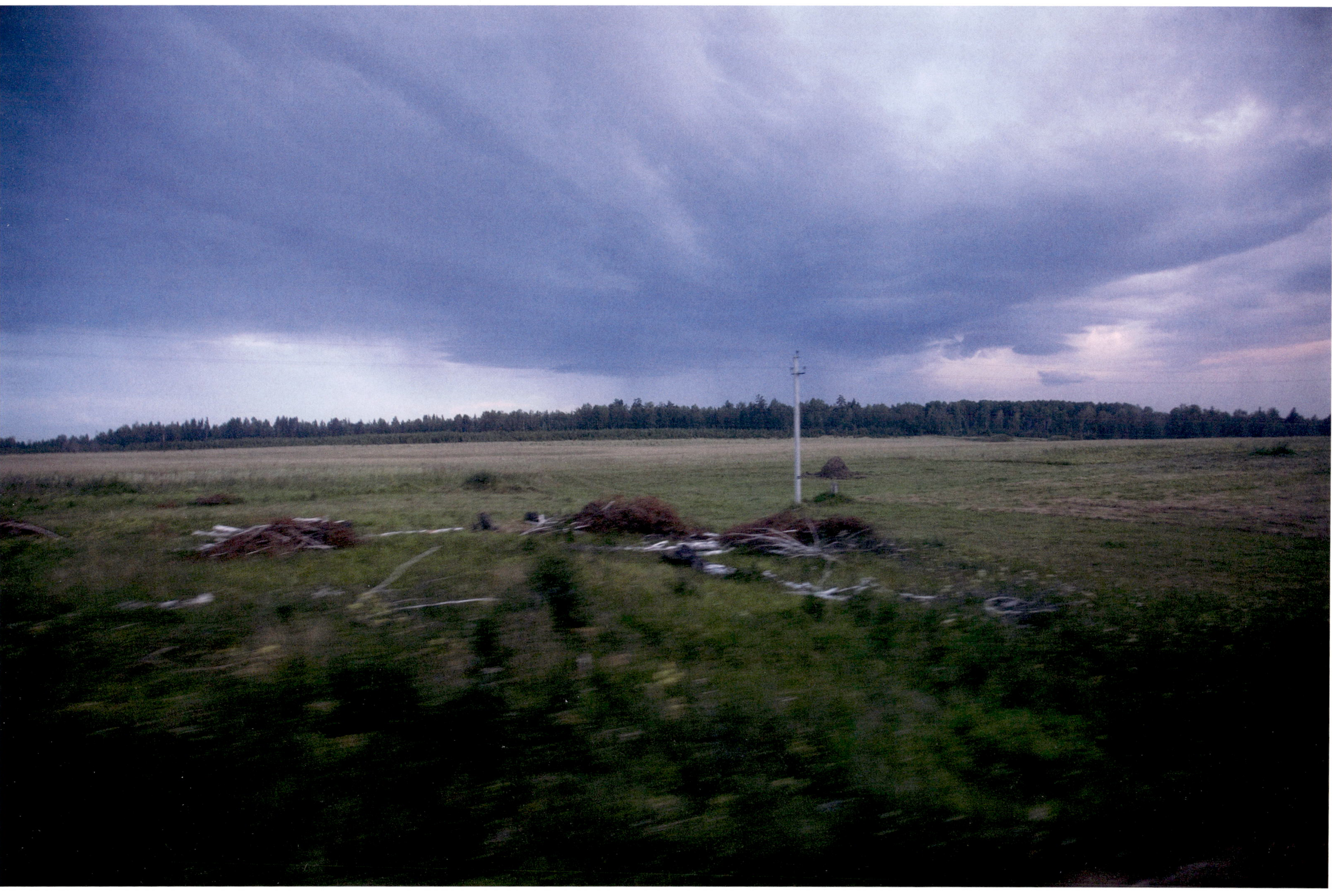

Lake and village in Siberia

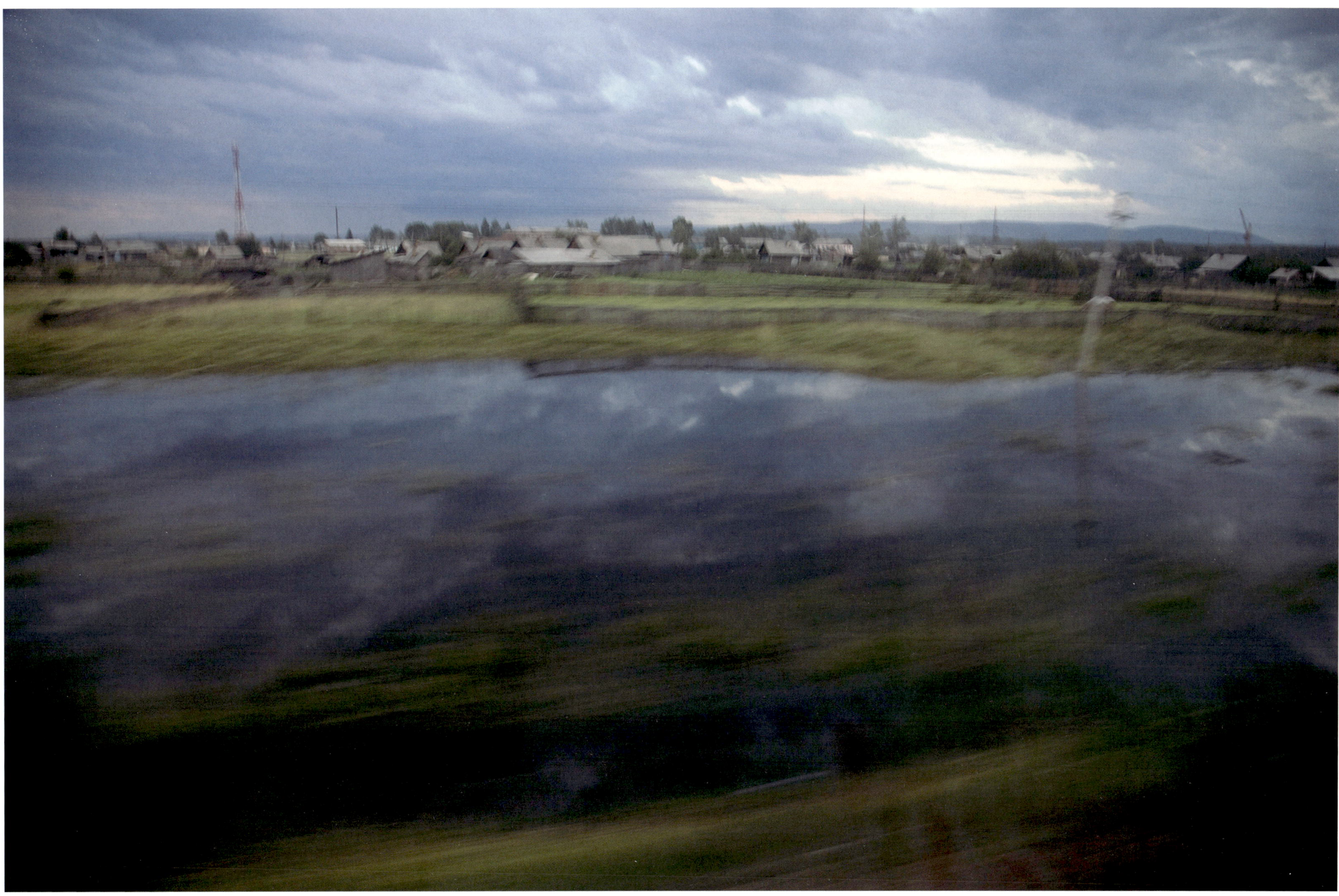

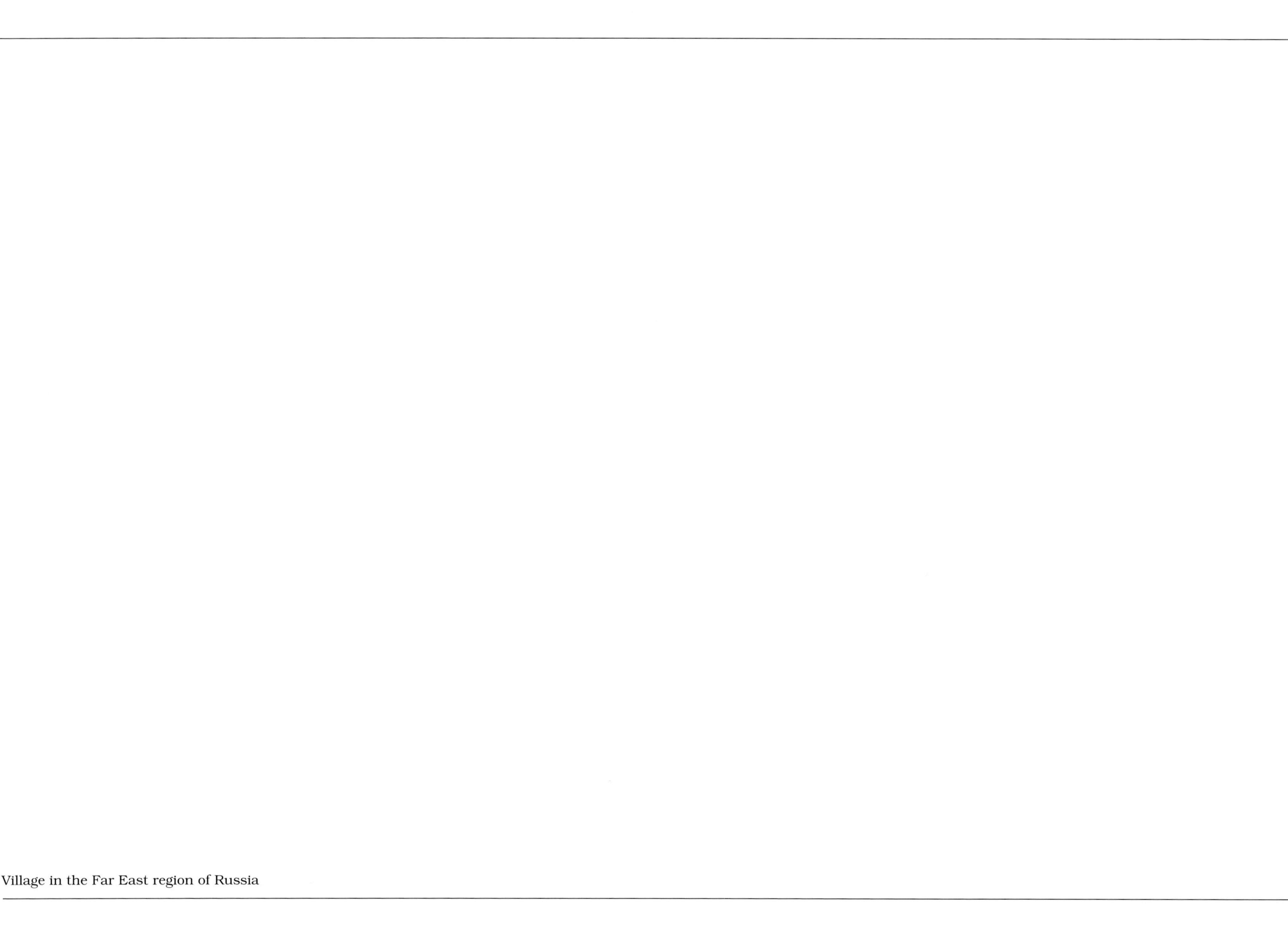

Village in the Far East region of Russia

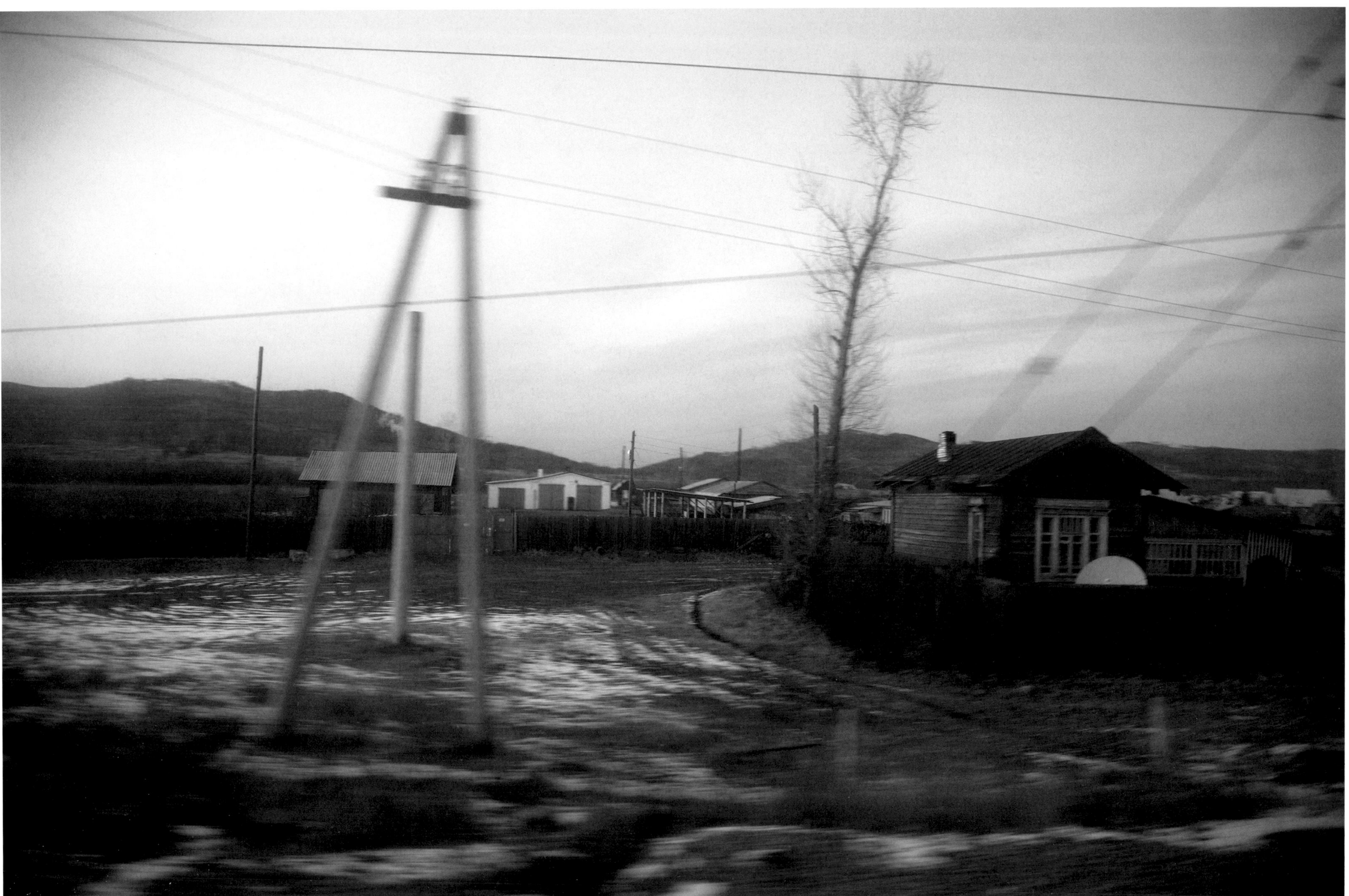

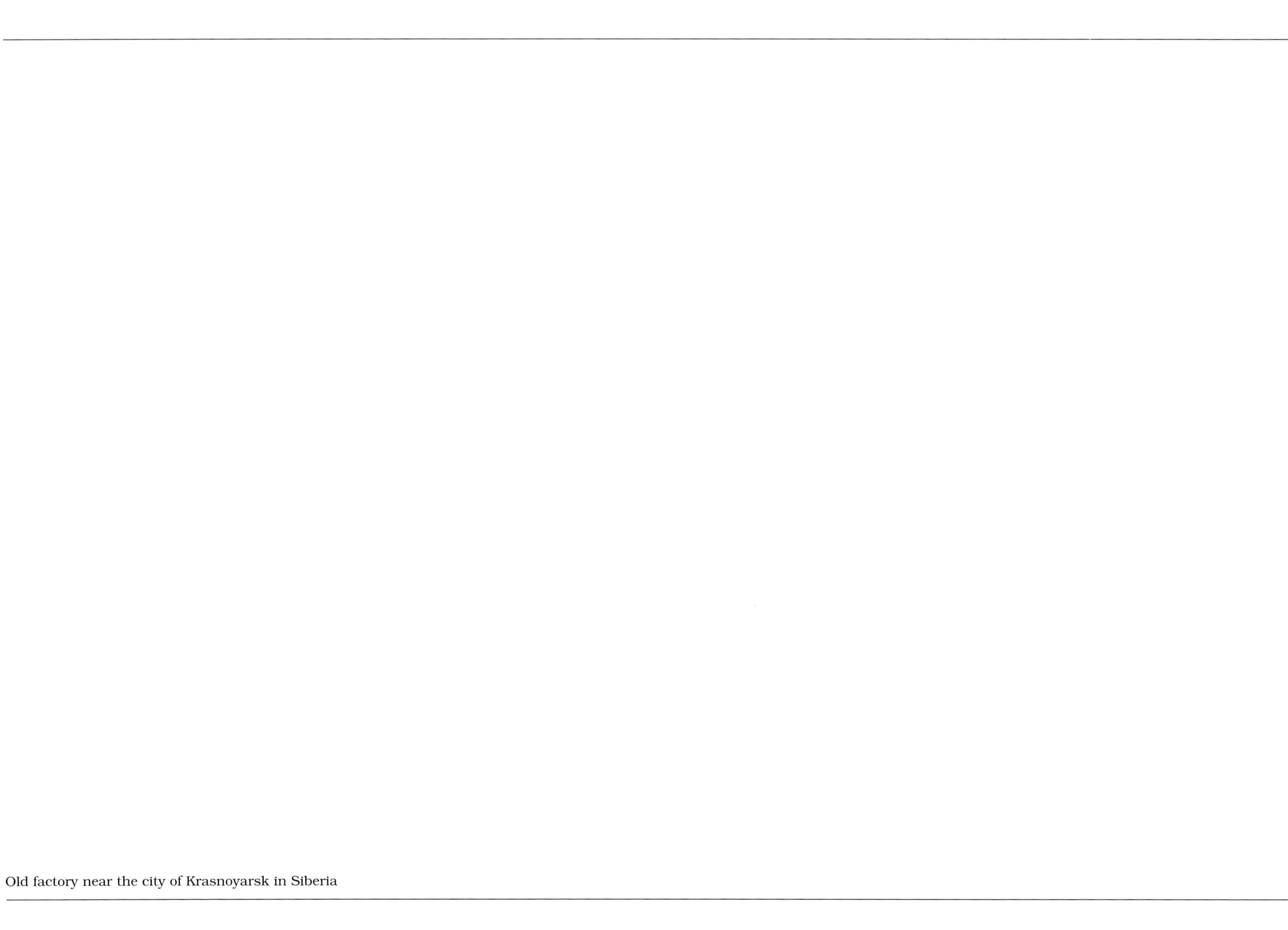

Old factory near the city of Krasnoyarsk in Siberia

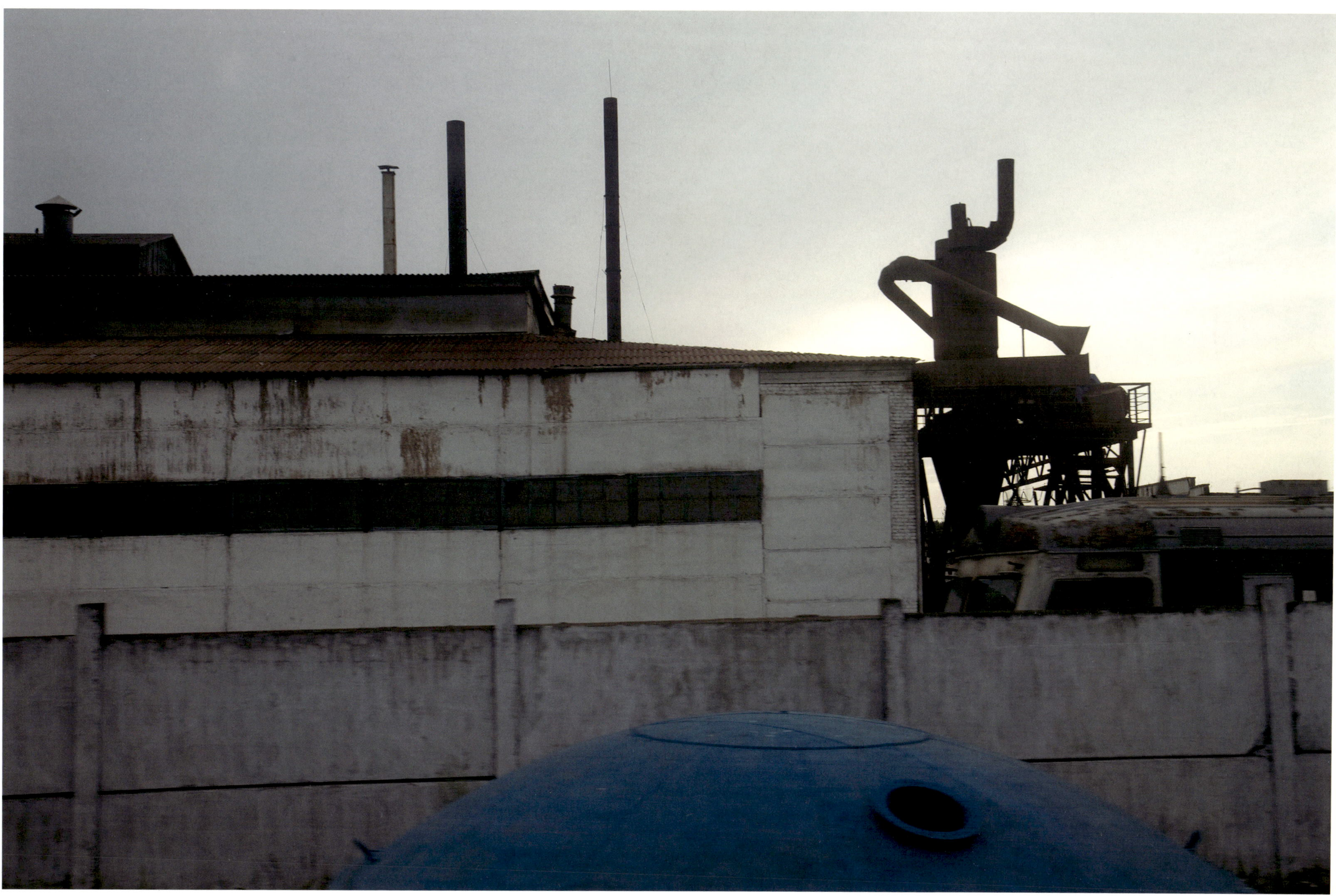

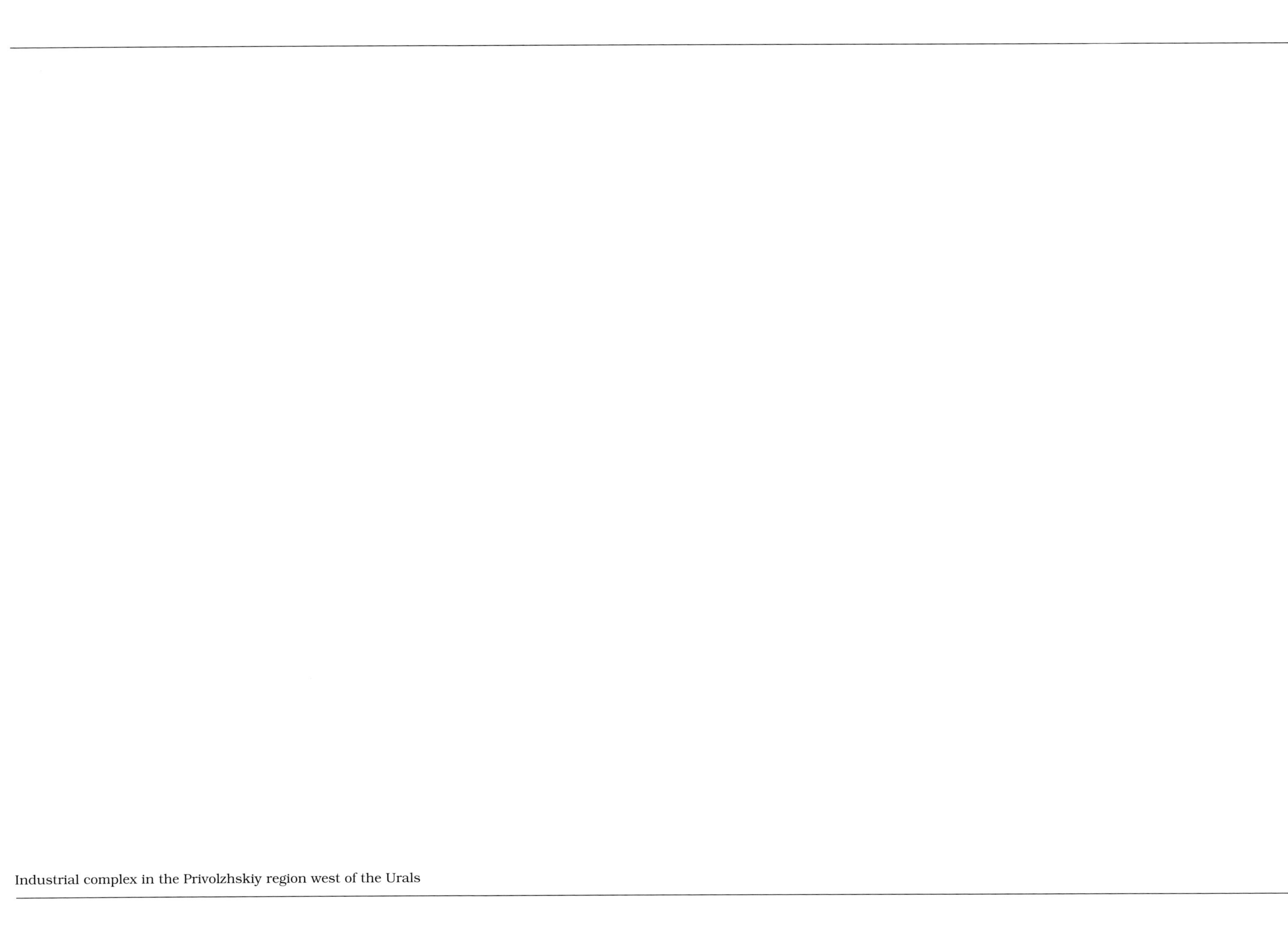

Industrial complex in the Privolzhskiy region west of the Urals

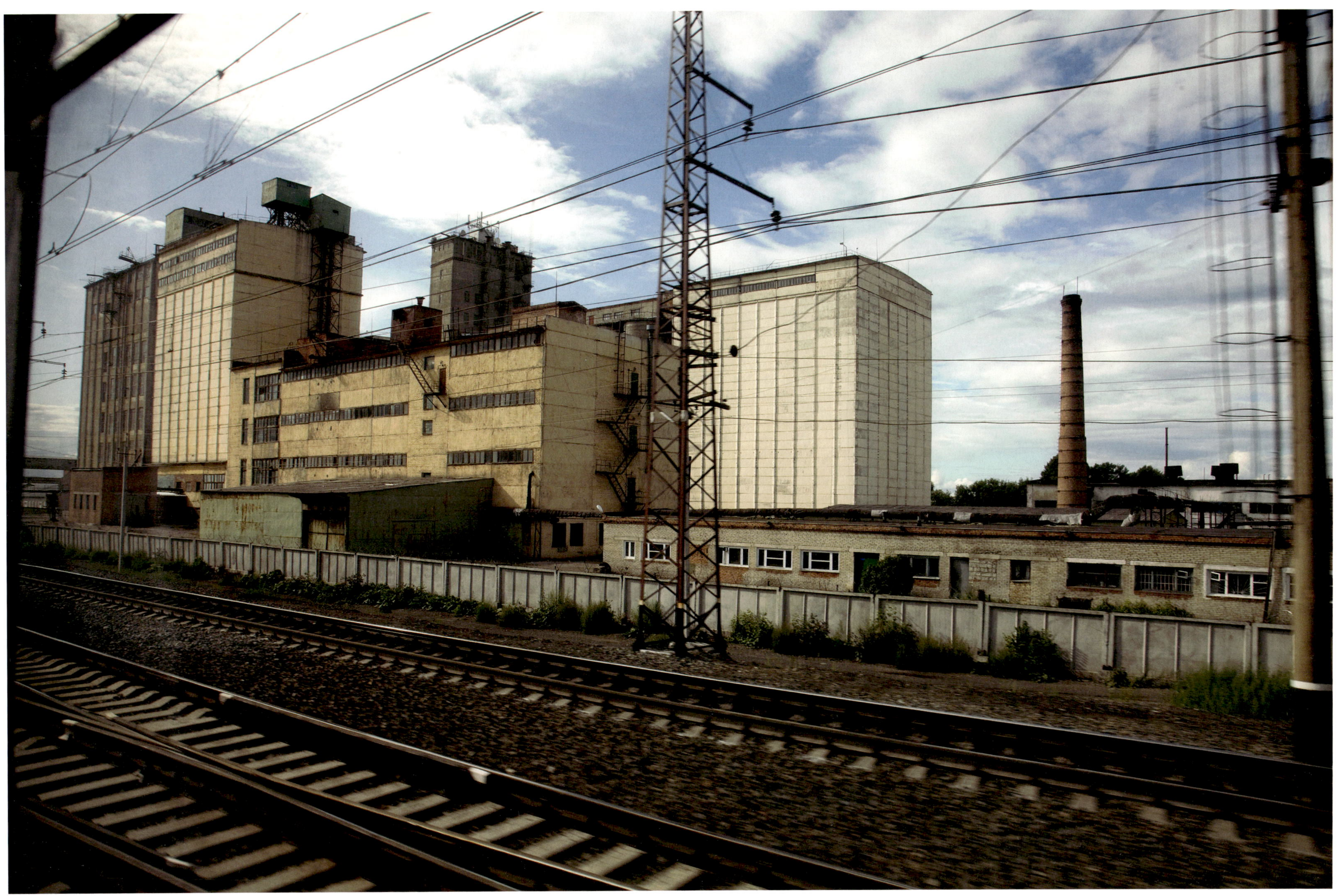

Apartment building in Central Russia

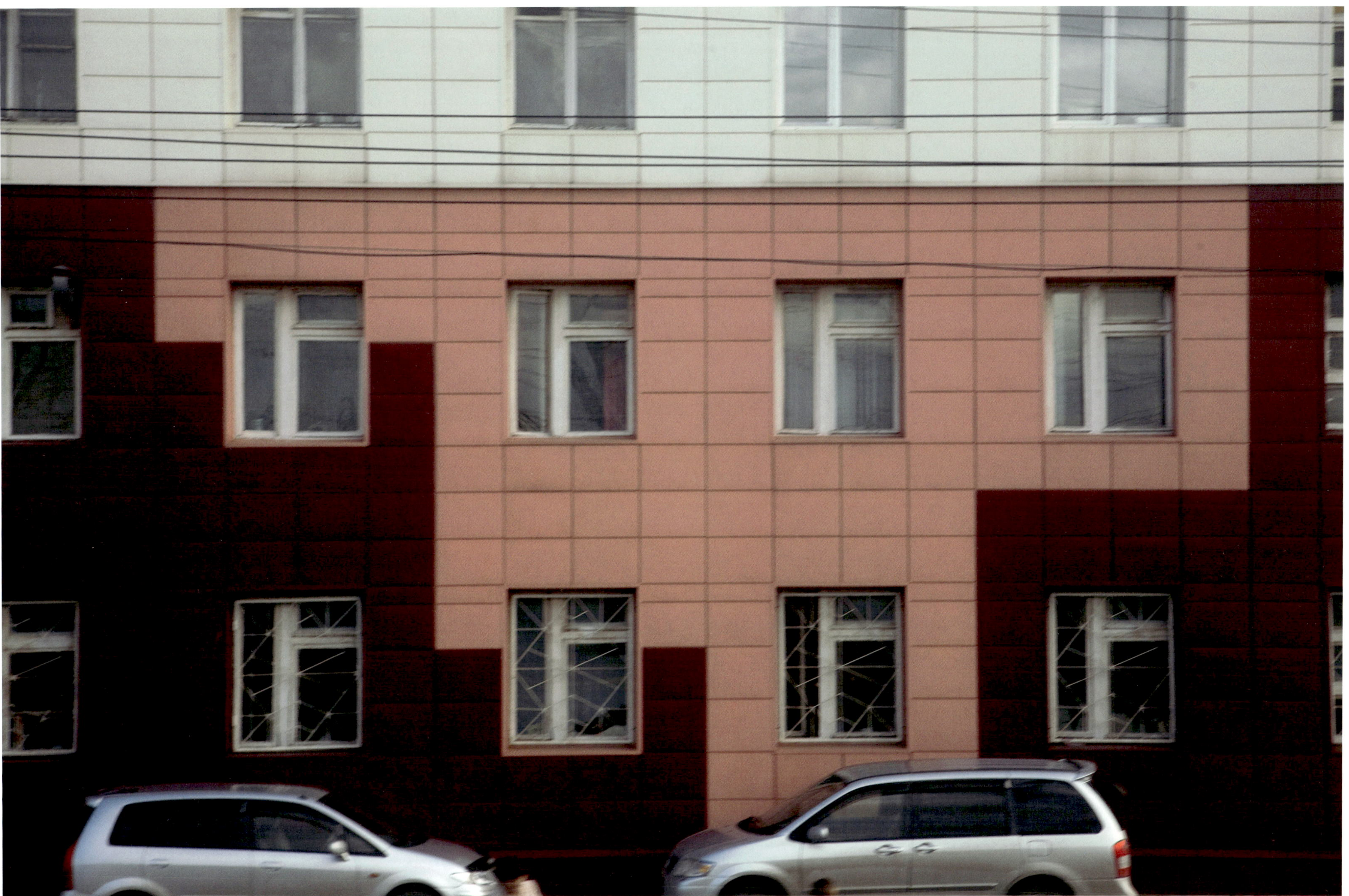

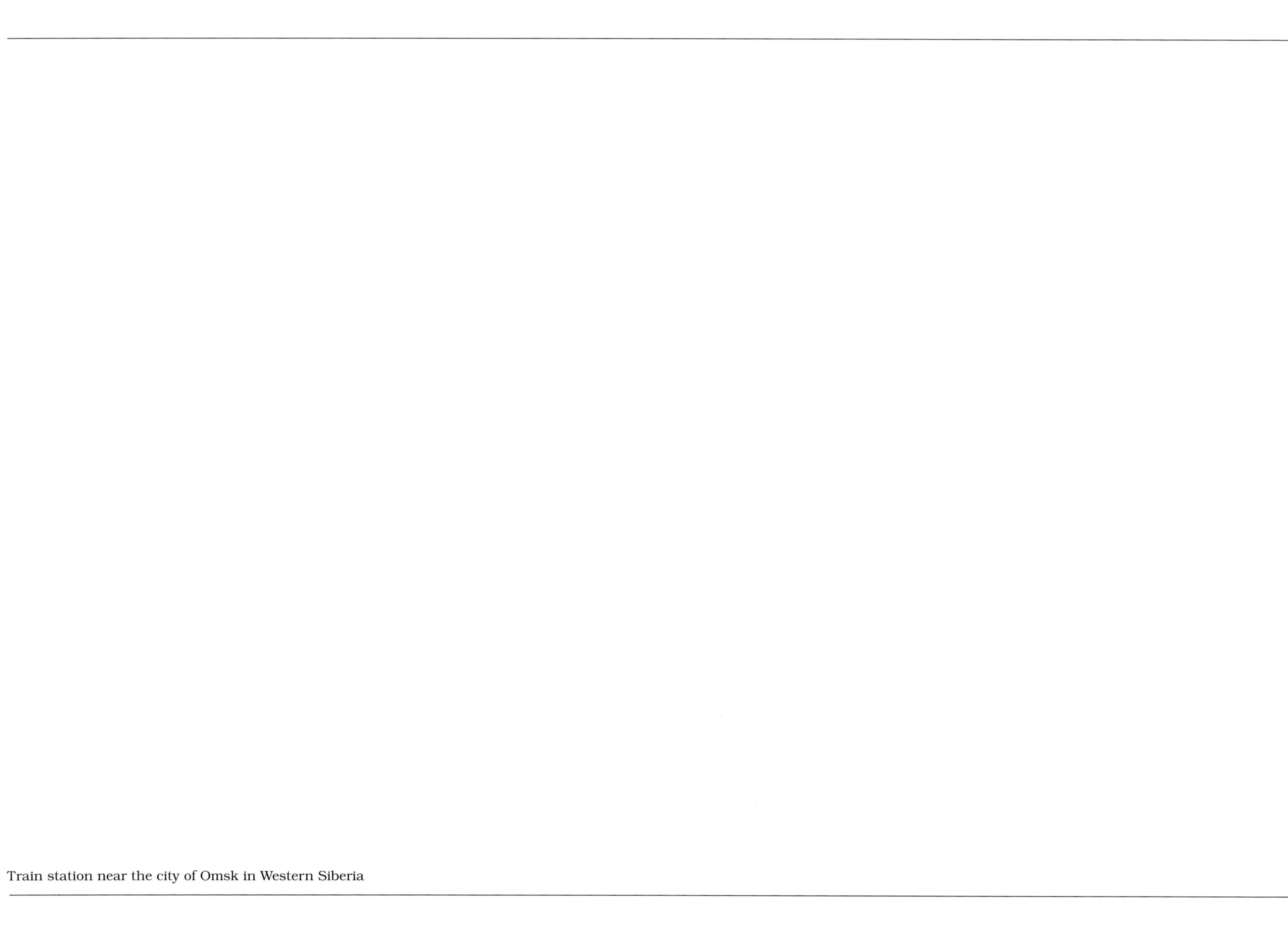

Train station near the city of Omsk in Western Siberia

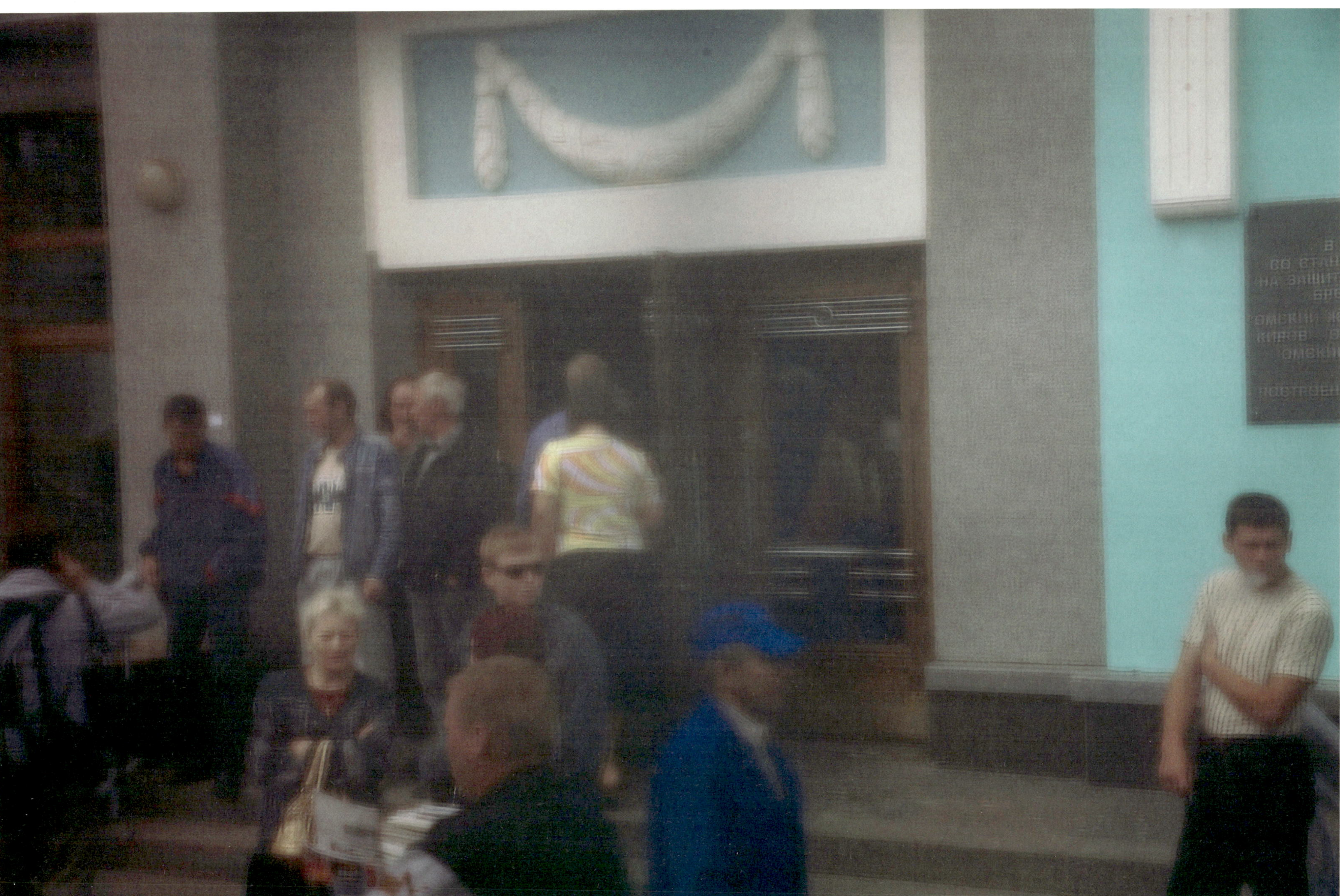

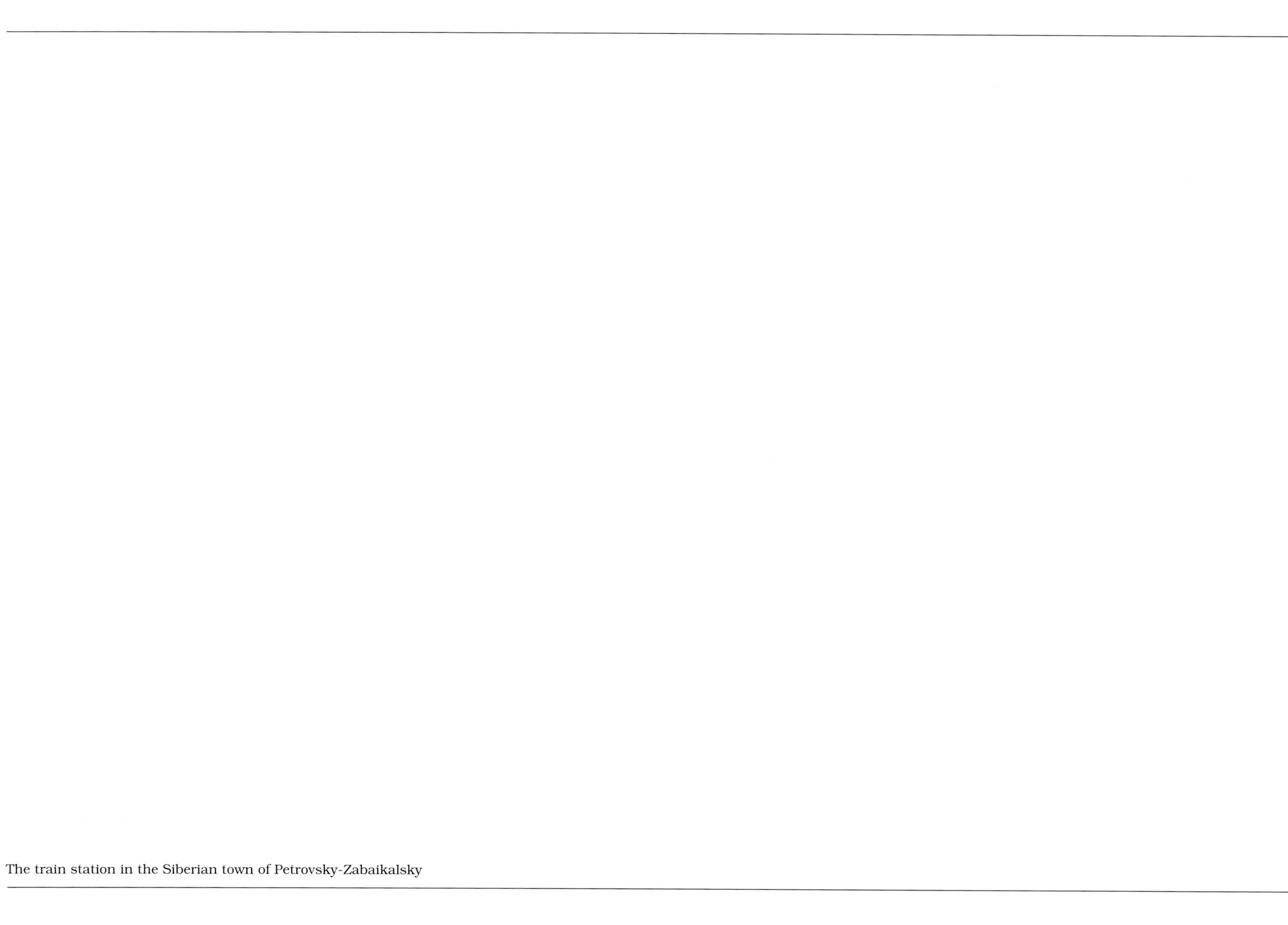

The train station in the Siberian town of Petrovsky-Zabaikalsky

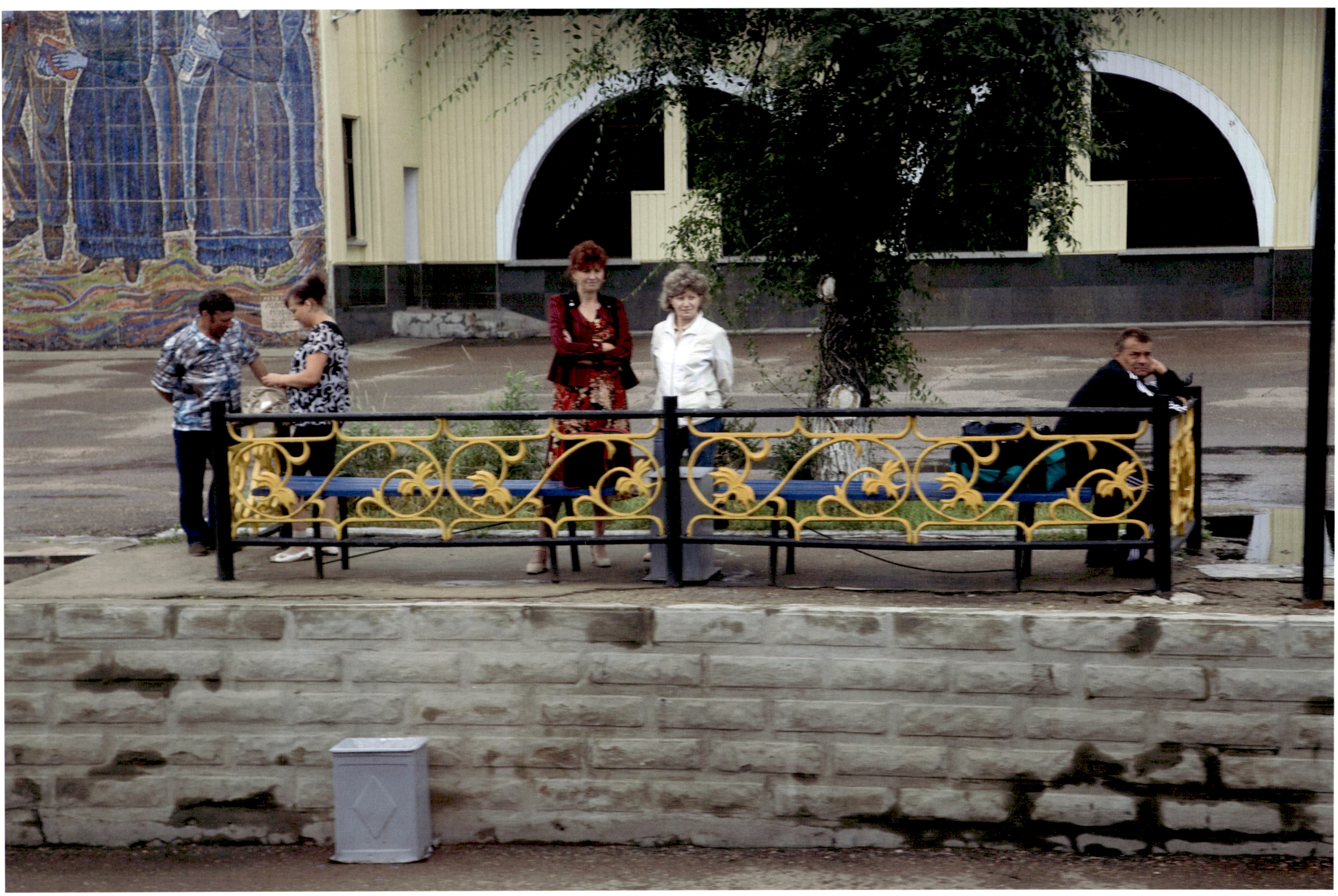

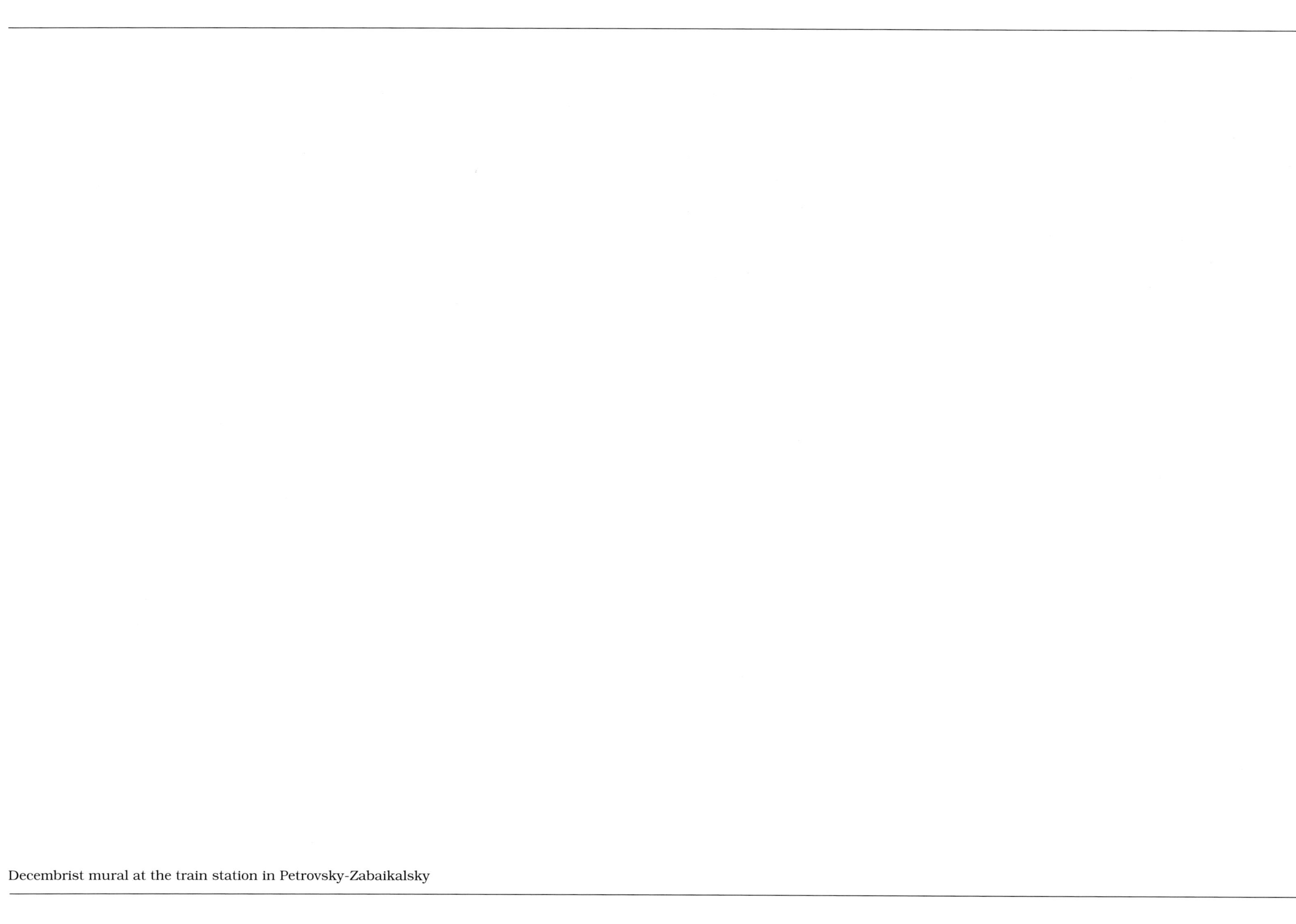

Decembrist mural at the train station in Petrovsky-Zabaikalsky

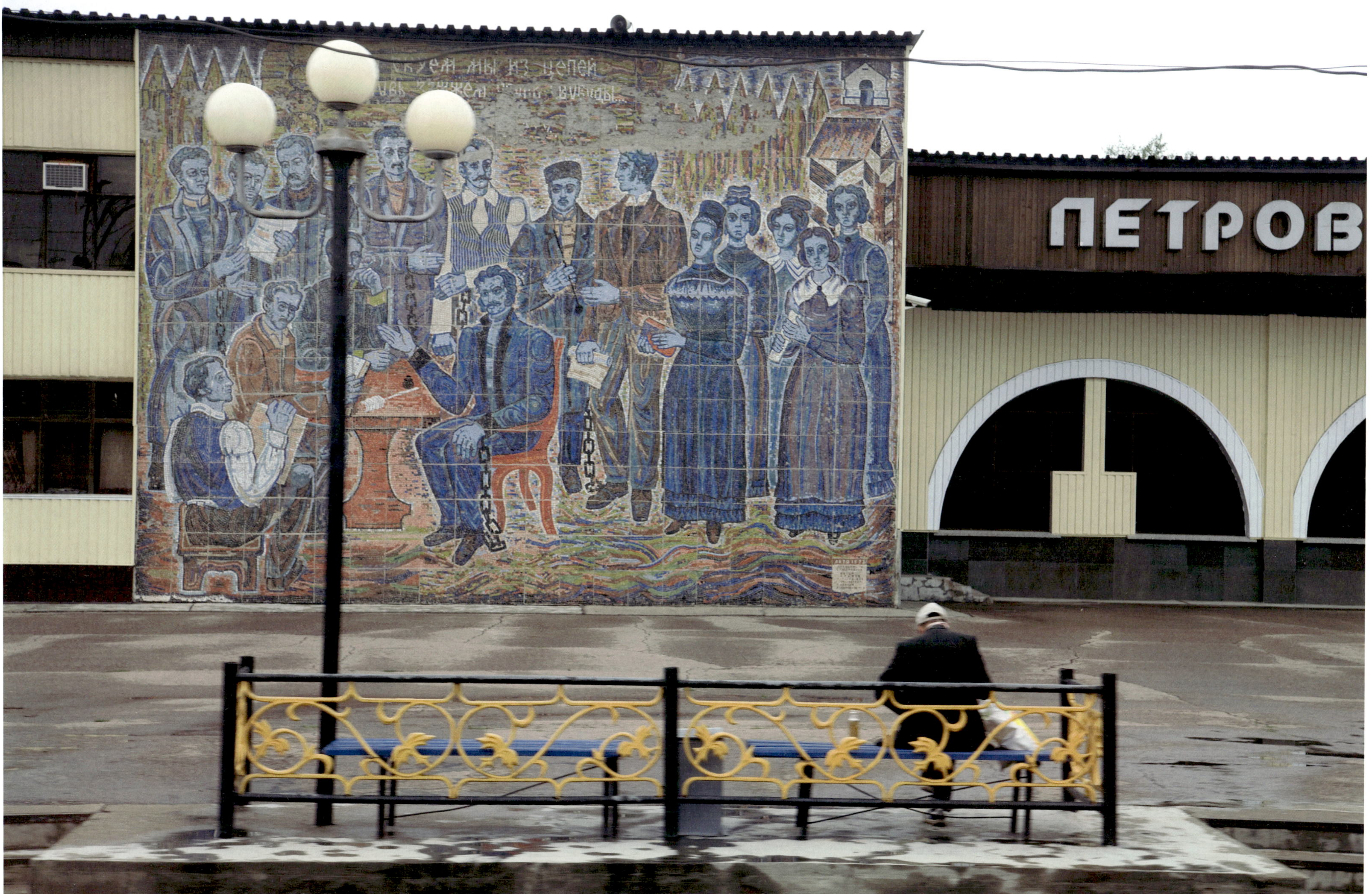
...куём мы из цепей
...вжжём ...вугды...
ПЕТРОВ

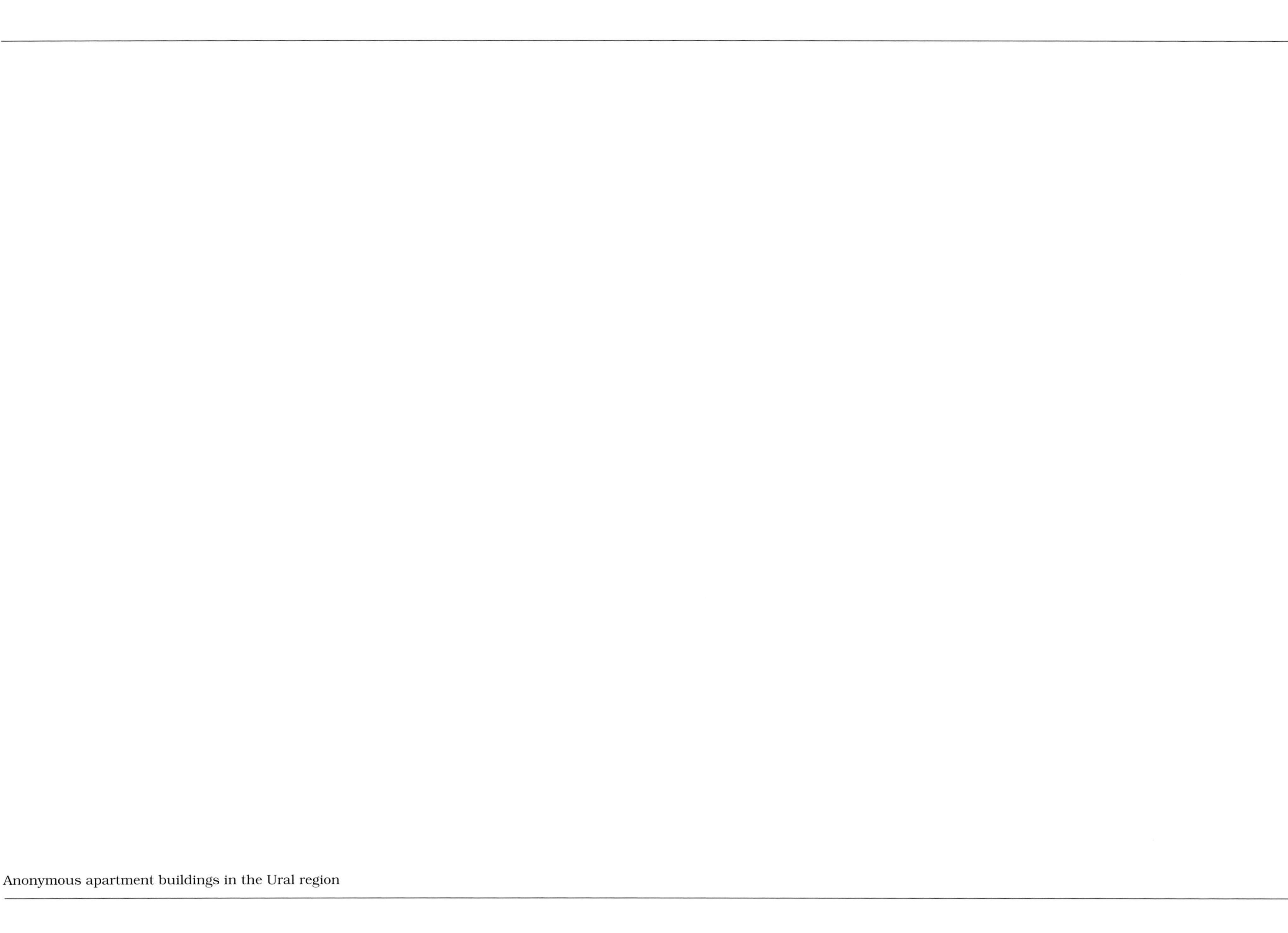

Anonymous apartment buildings in the Ural region

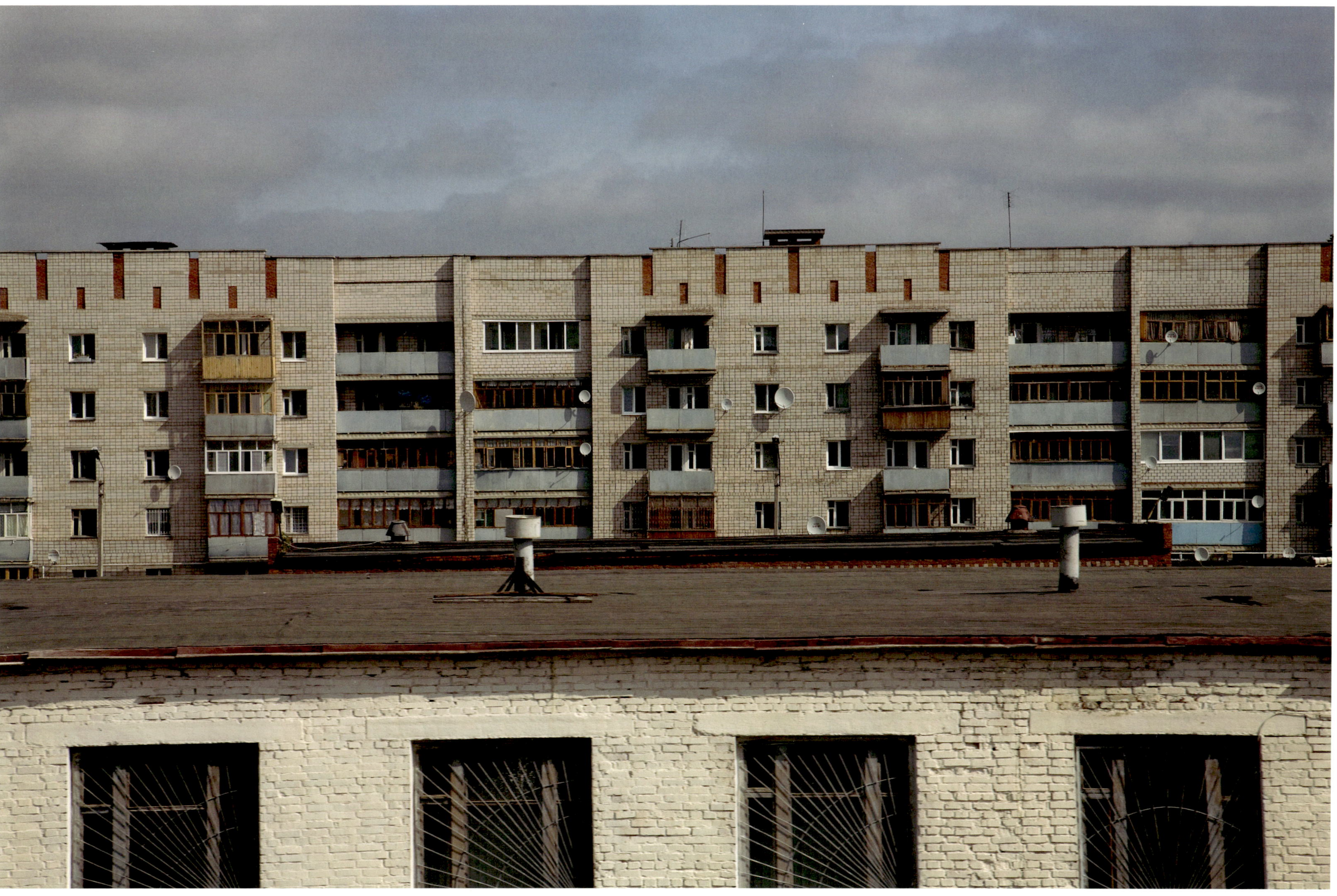

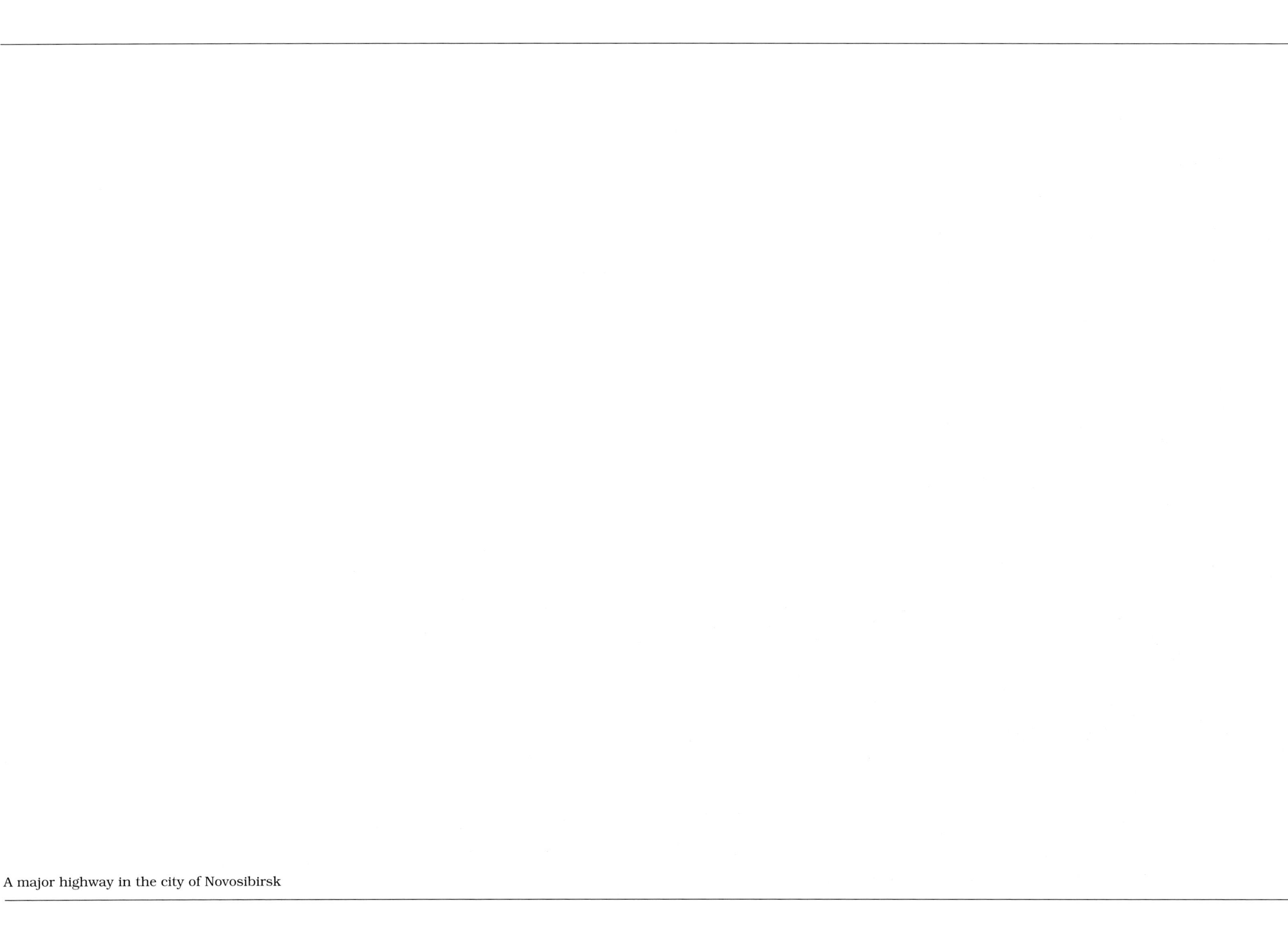

A major highway in the city of Novosibirsk

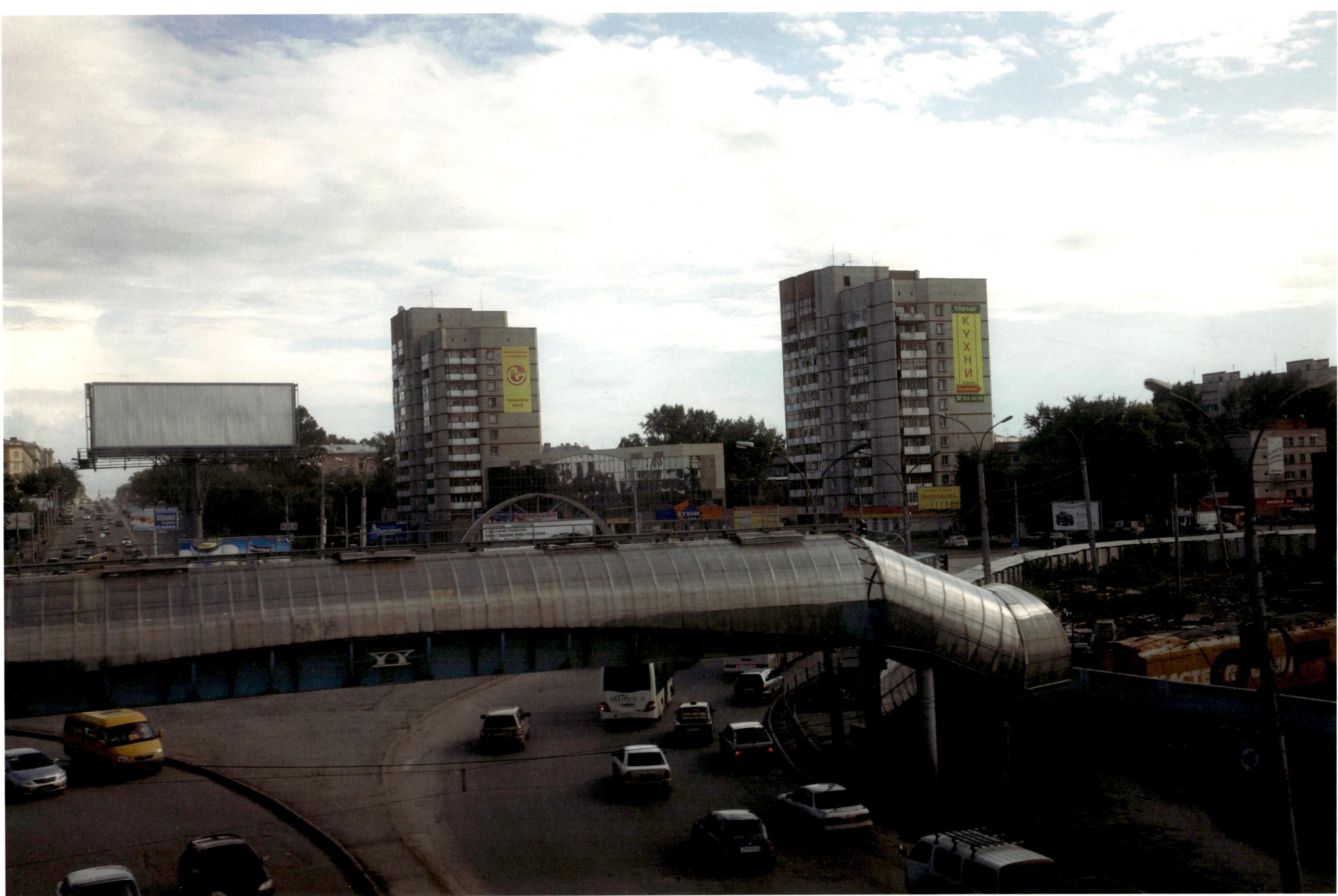

Магнат
КУХНИ
954-52-55
КУХНИ

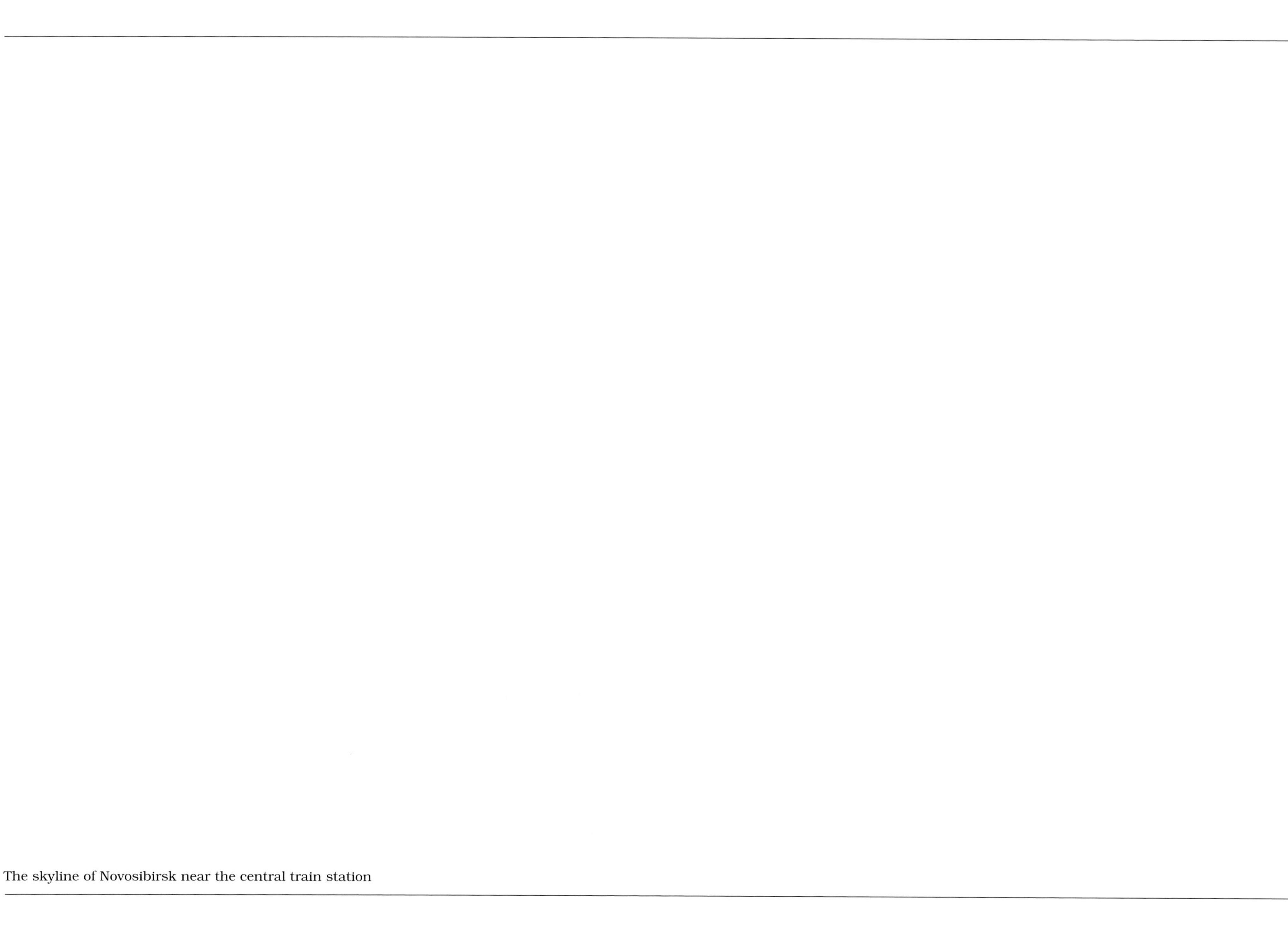

The skyline of Novosibirsk near the central train station

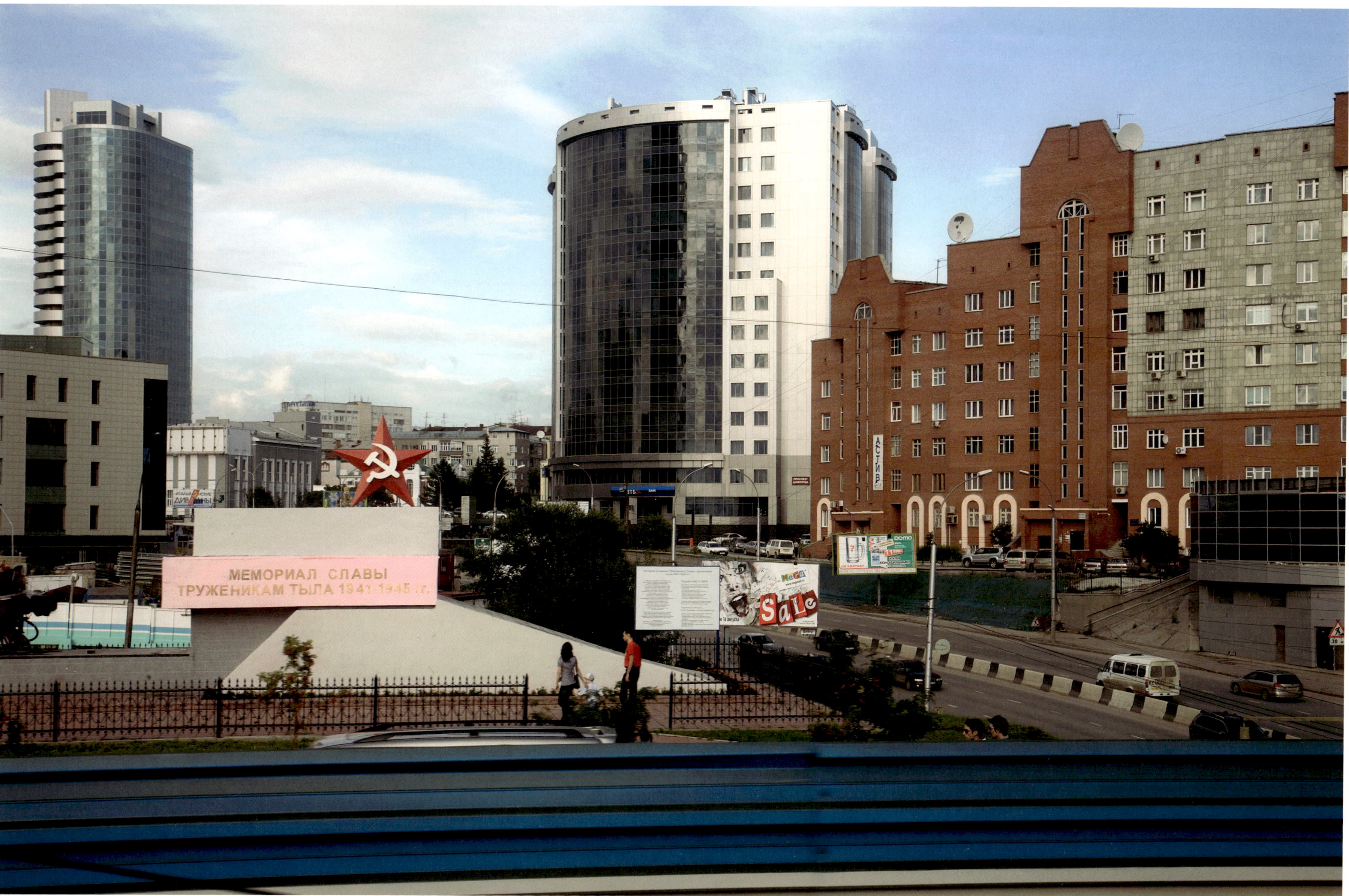

МЕМОРИАЛ СЛАВЫ
ТРУЖЕНИКАМ ТЫЛА 1941-1945 гг.

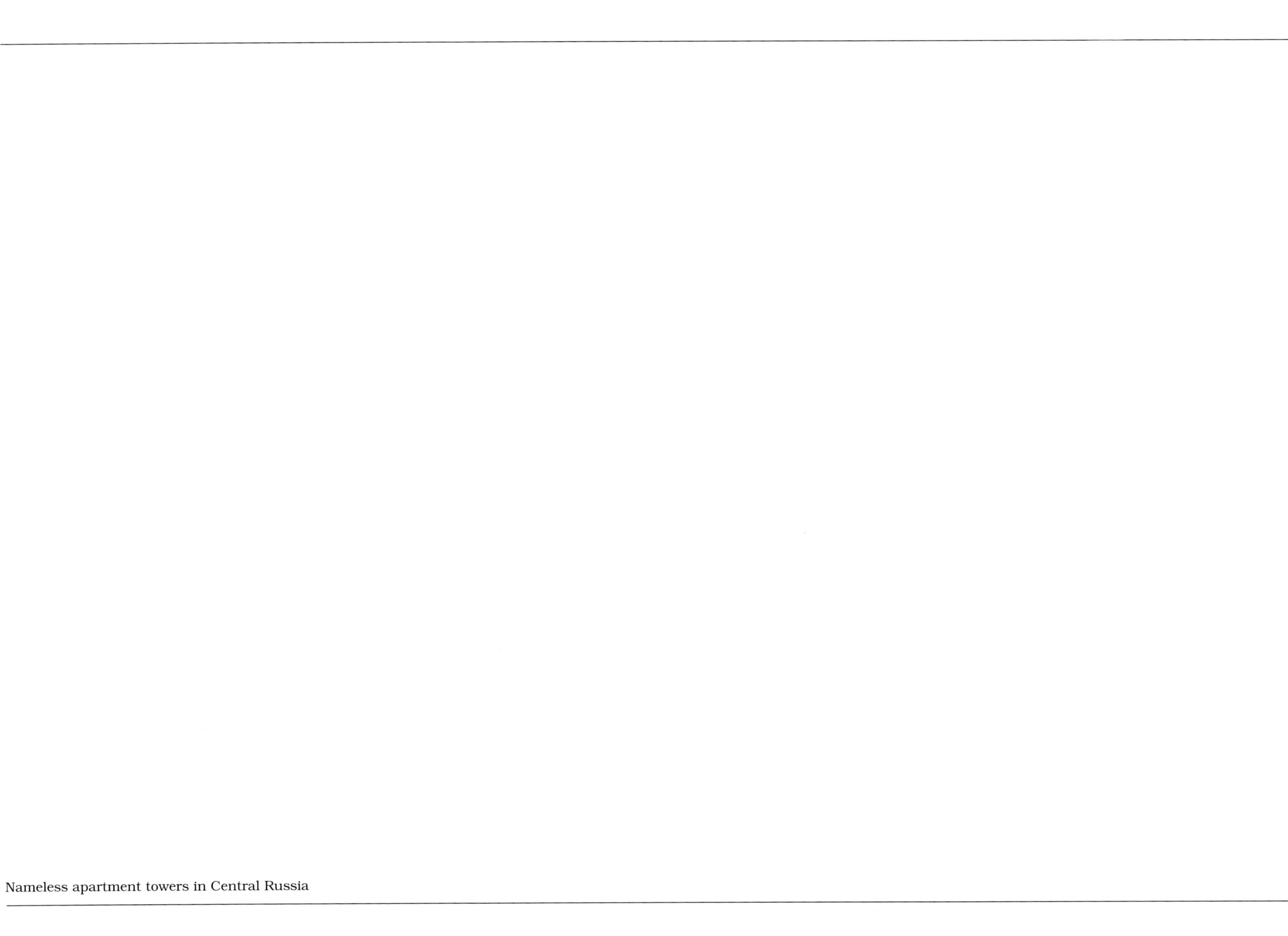

Nameless apartment towers in Central Russia

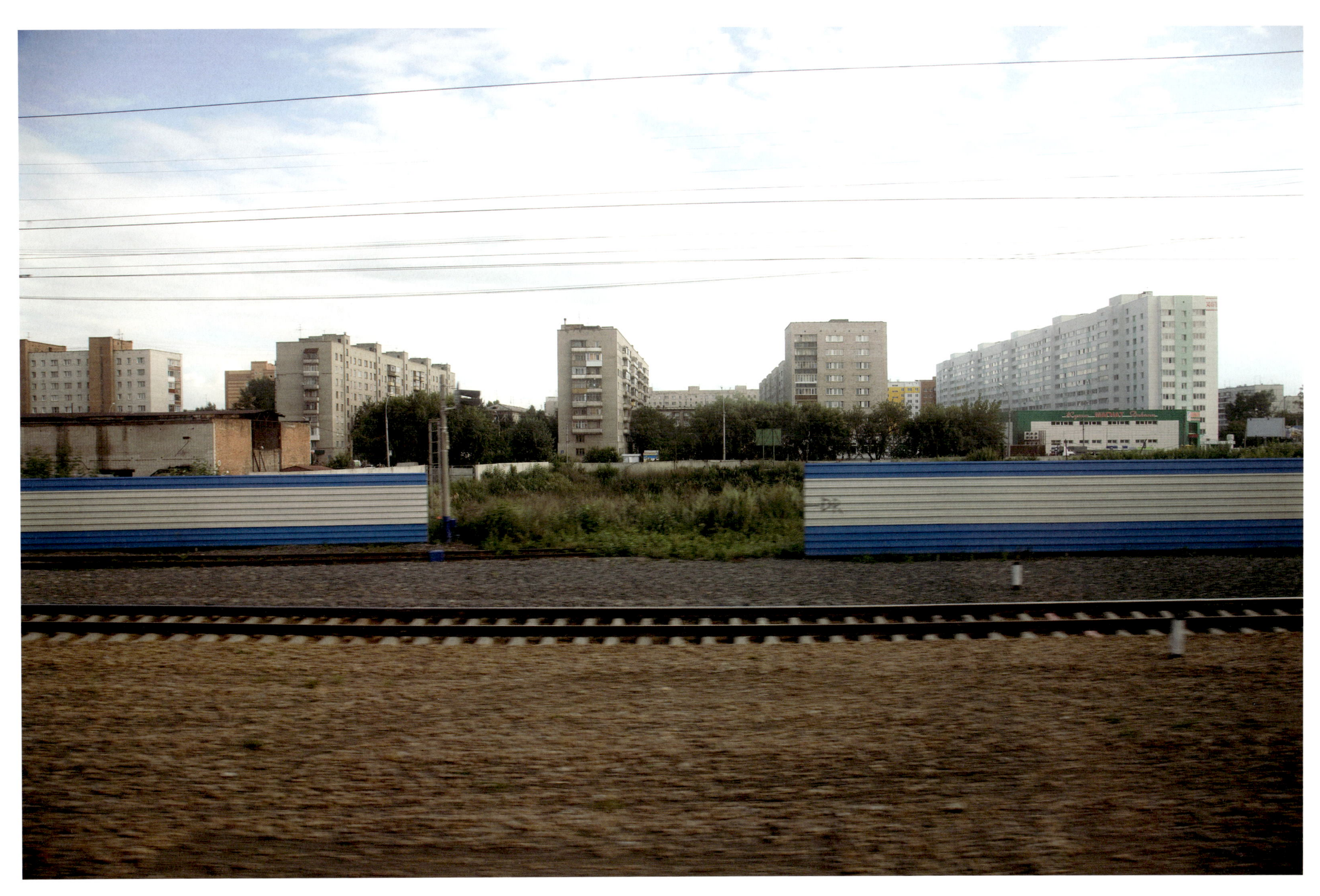

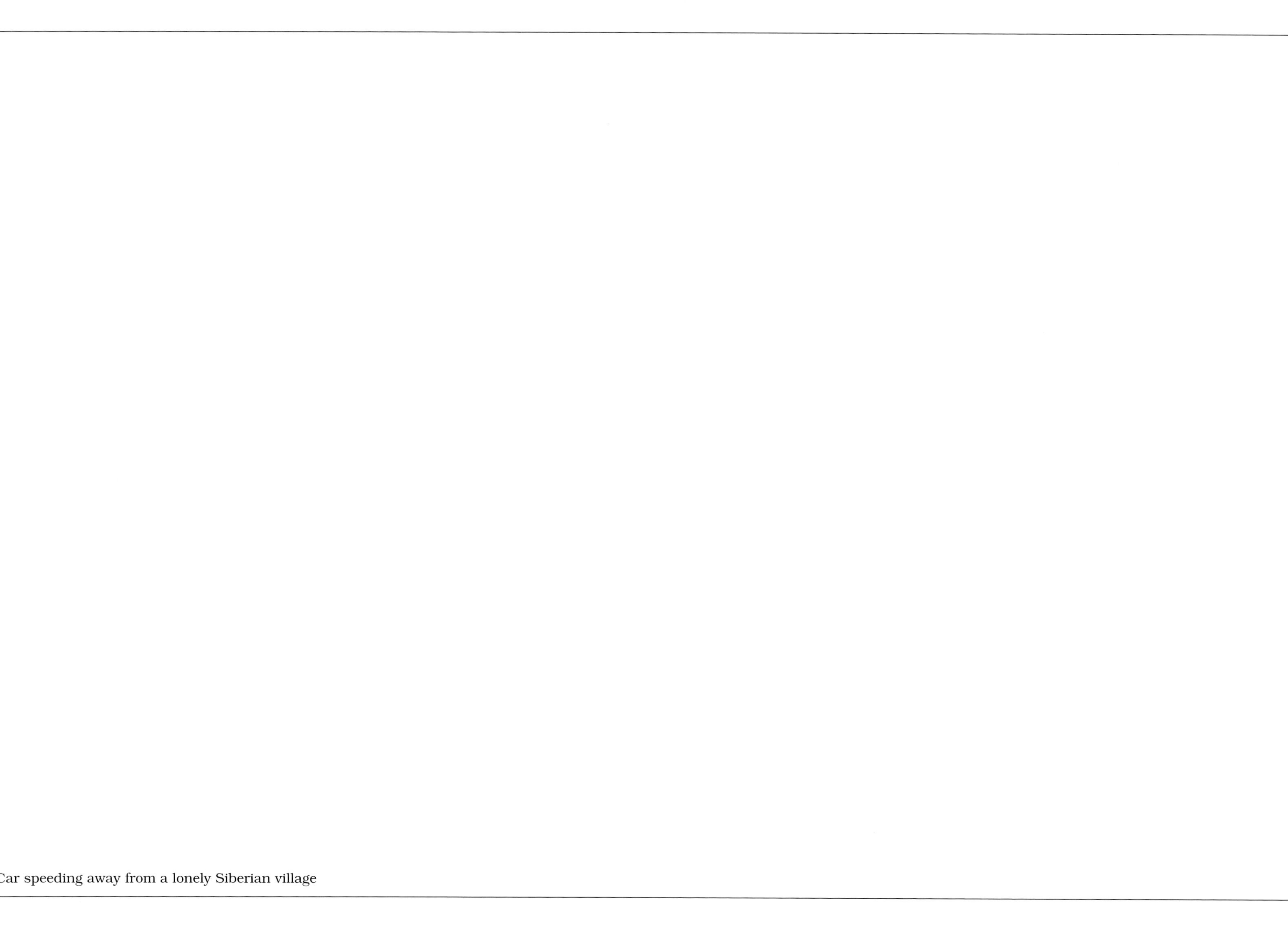

Car speeding away from a lonely Siberian village

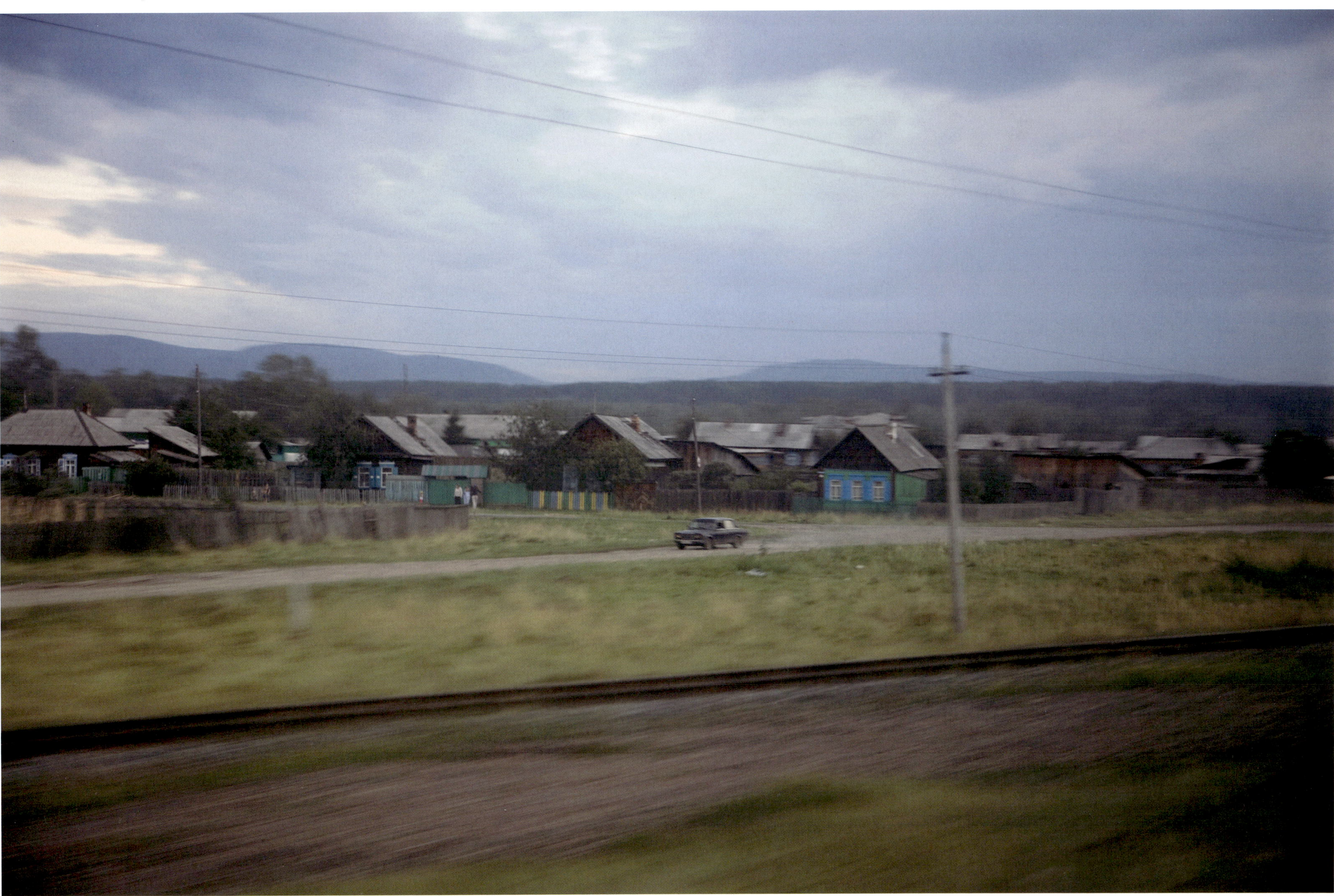

Morning mist in Siberian countryside

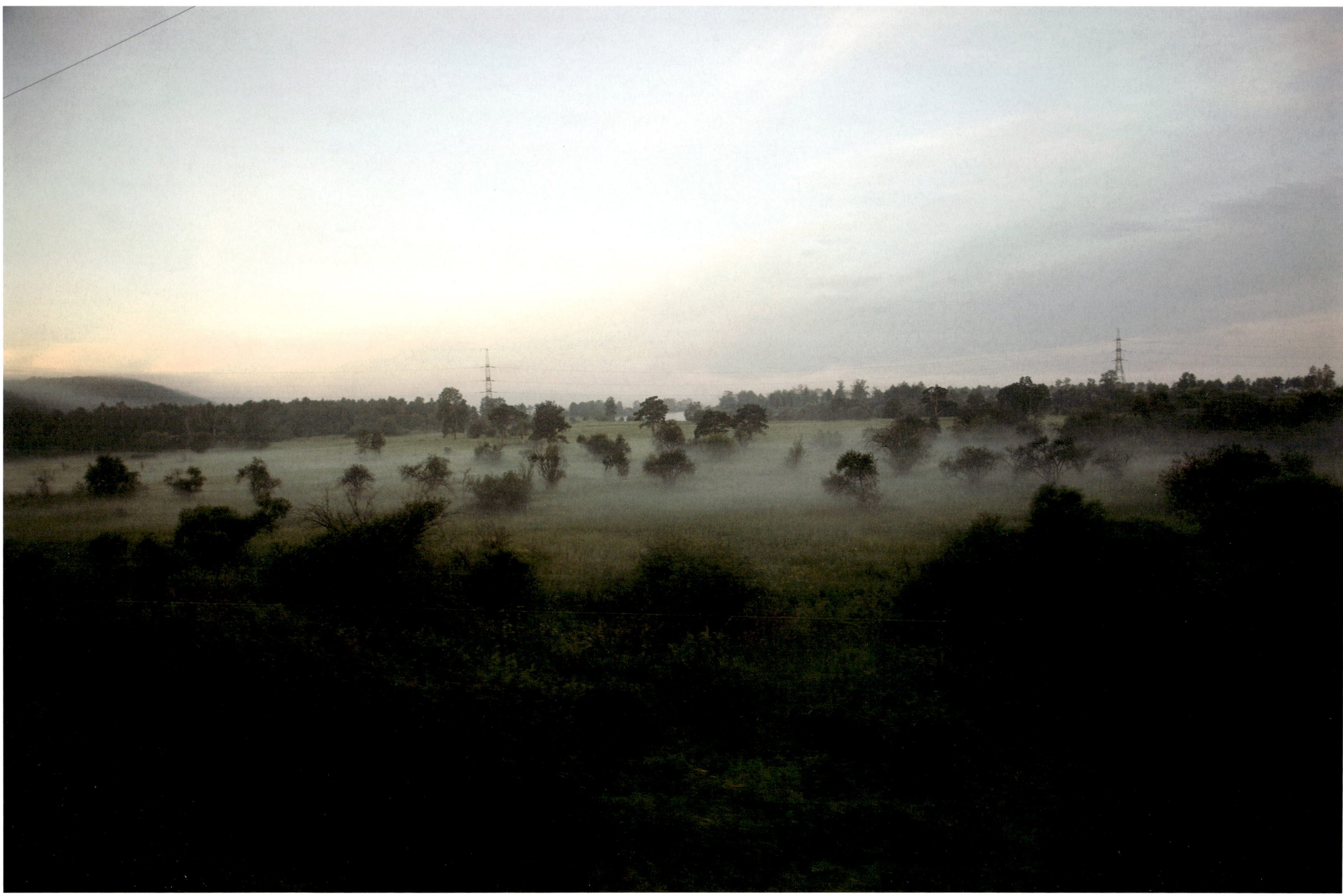

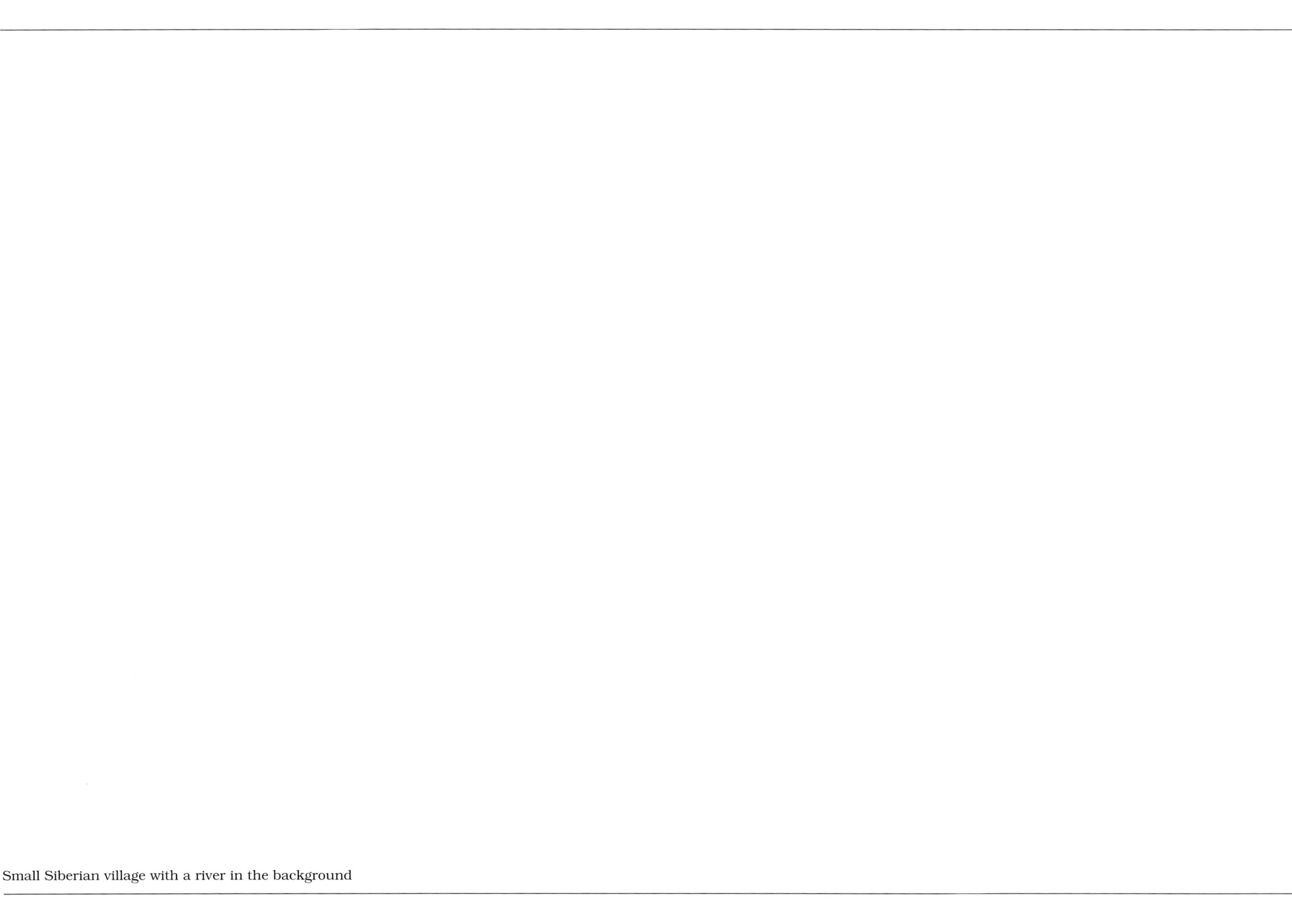

Small Siberian village with a river in the background

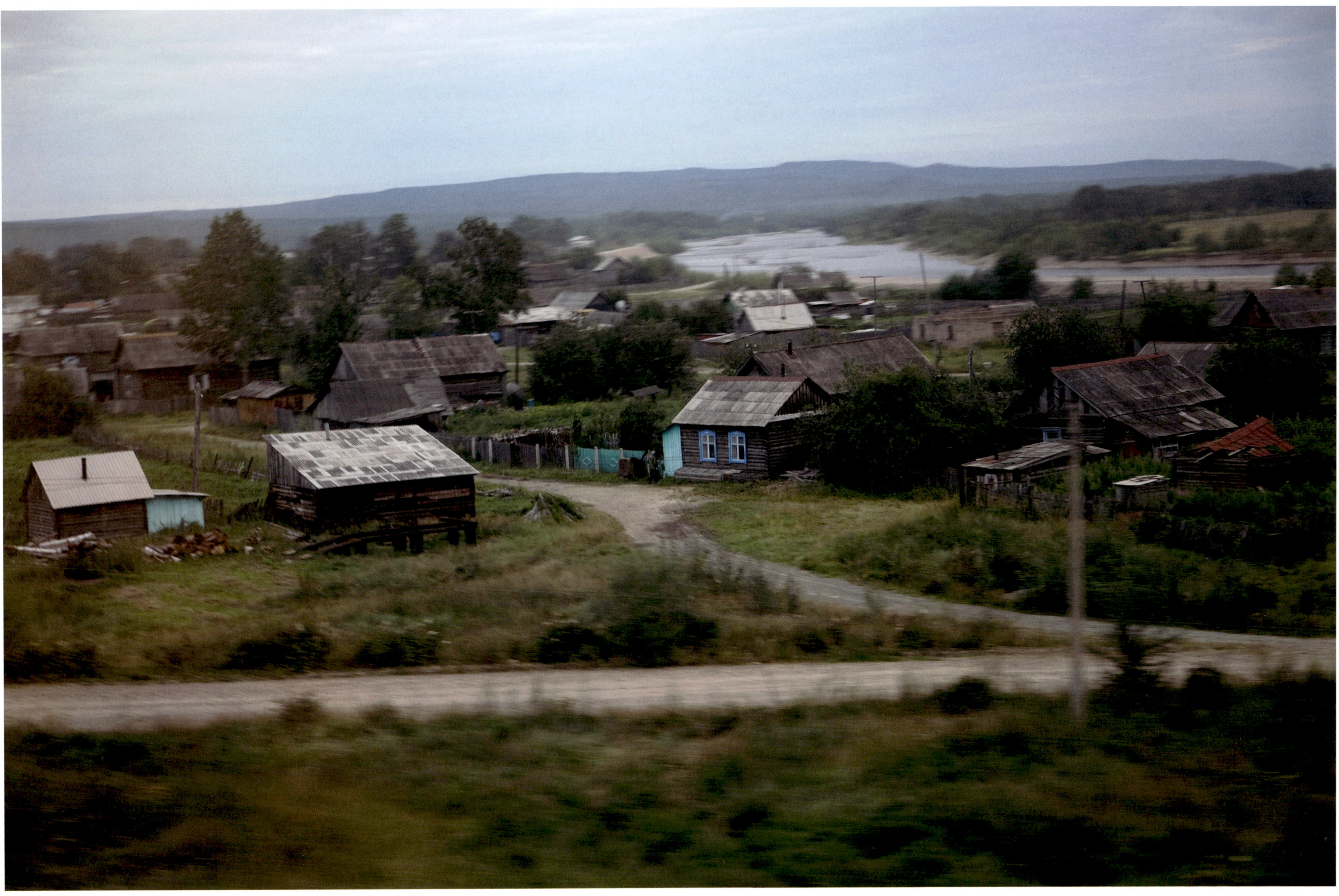

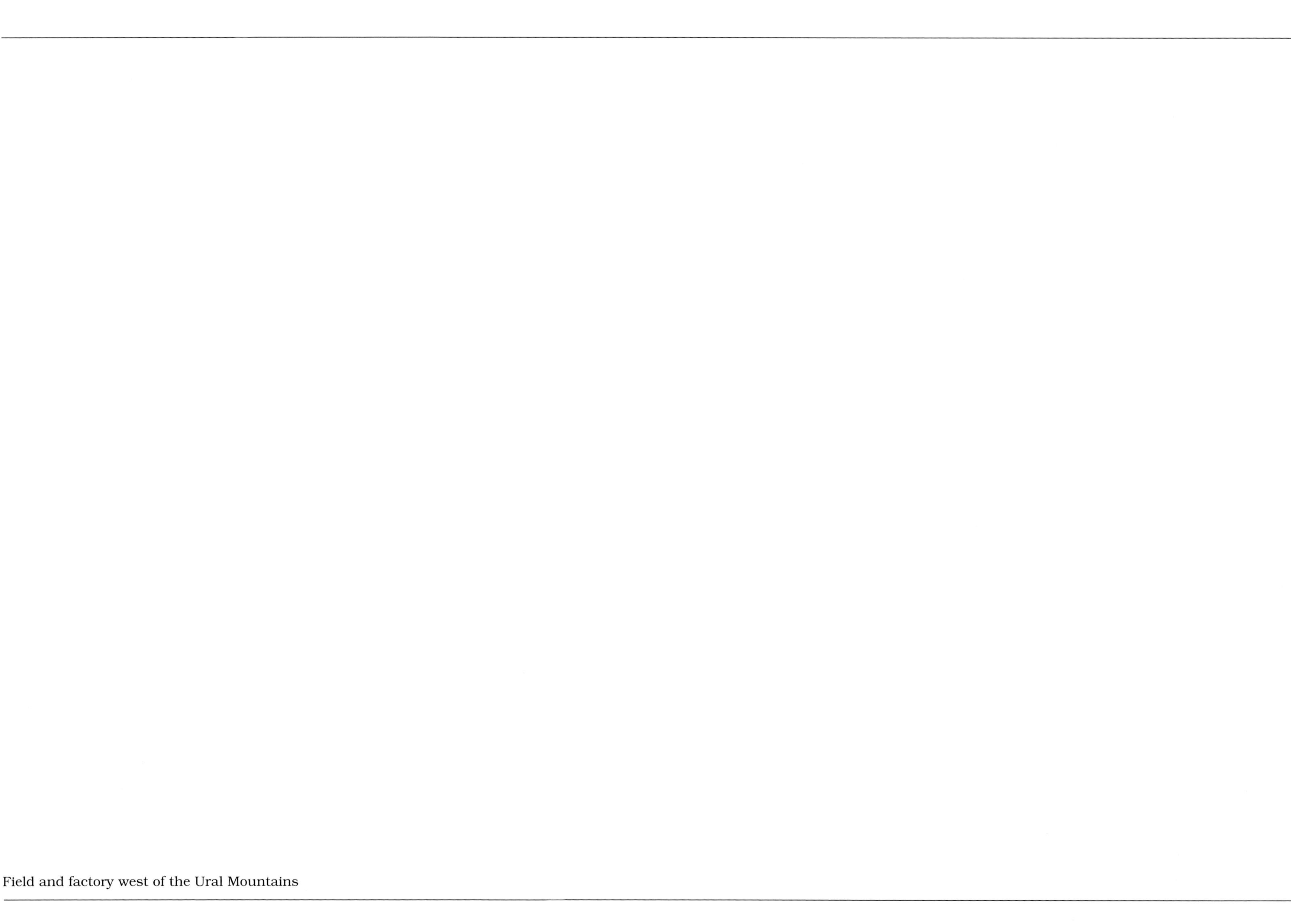

Field and factory west of the Ural Mountains

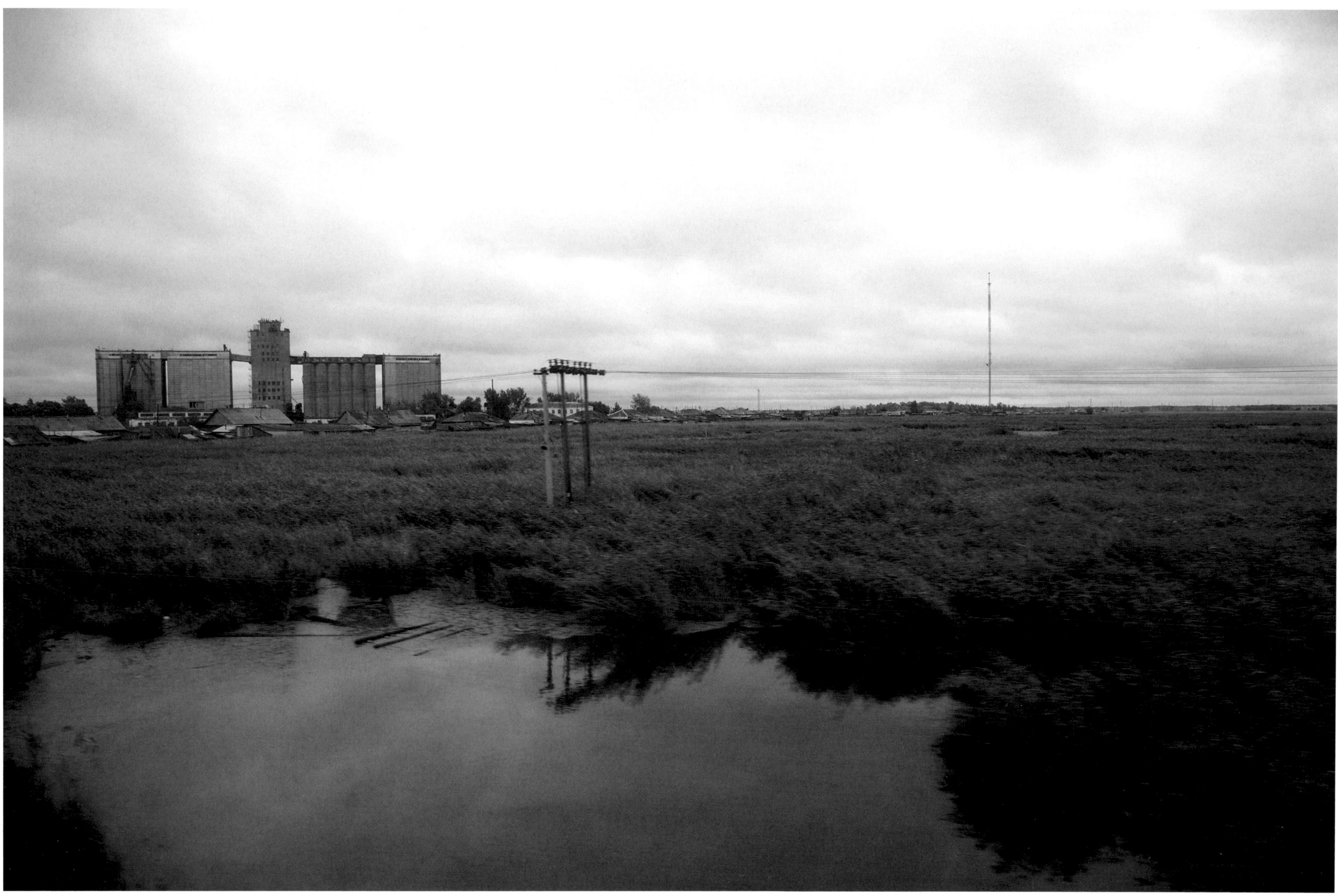

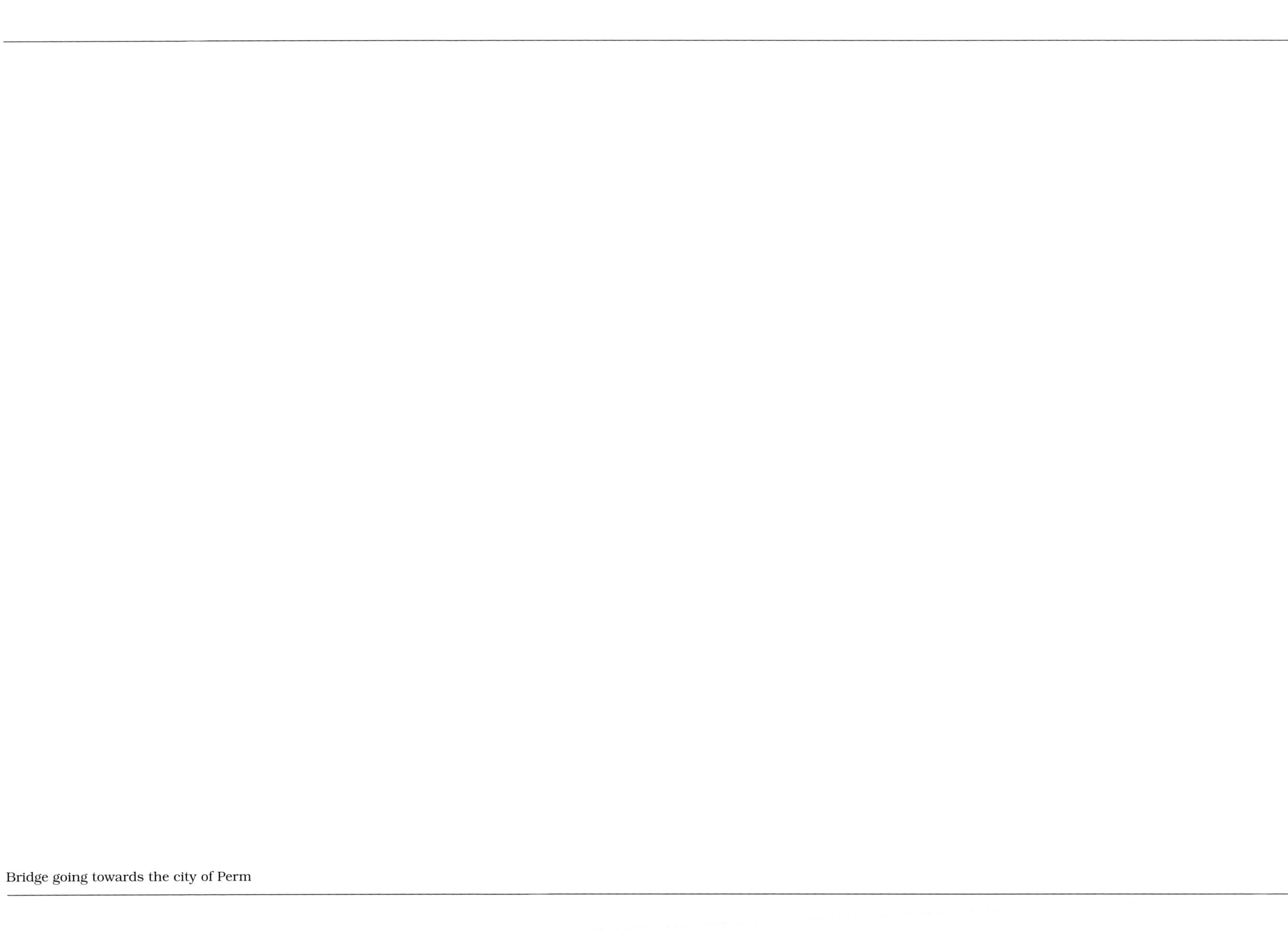

Bridge going towards the city of Perm

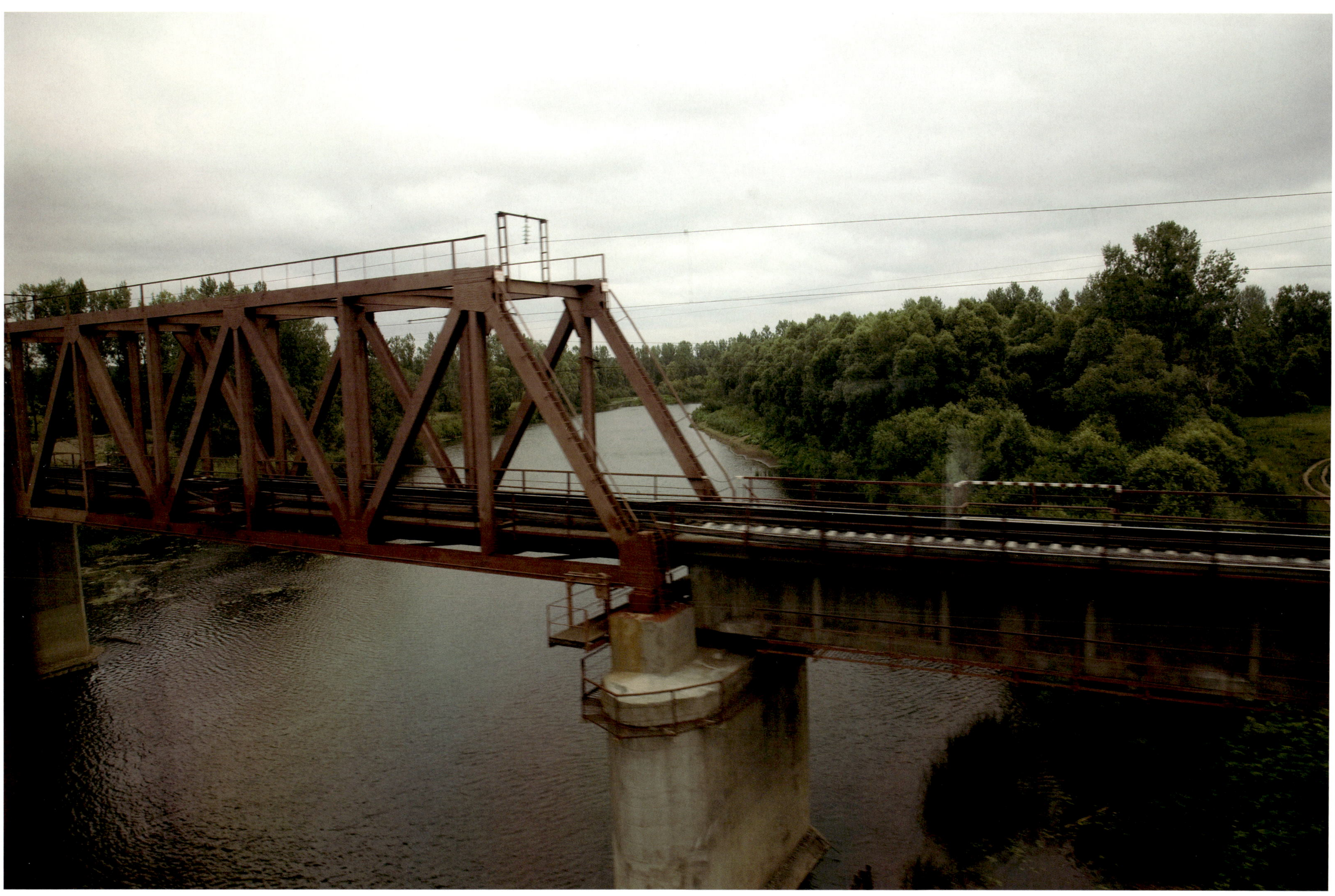

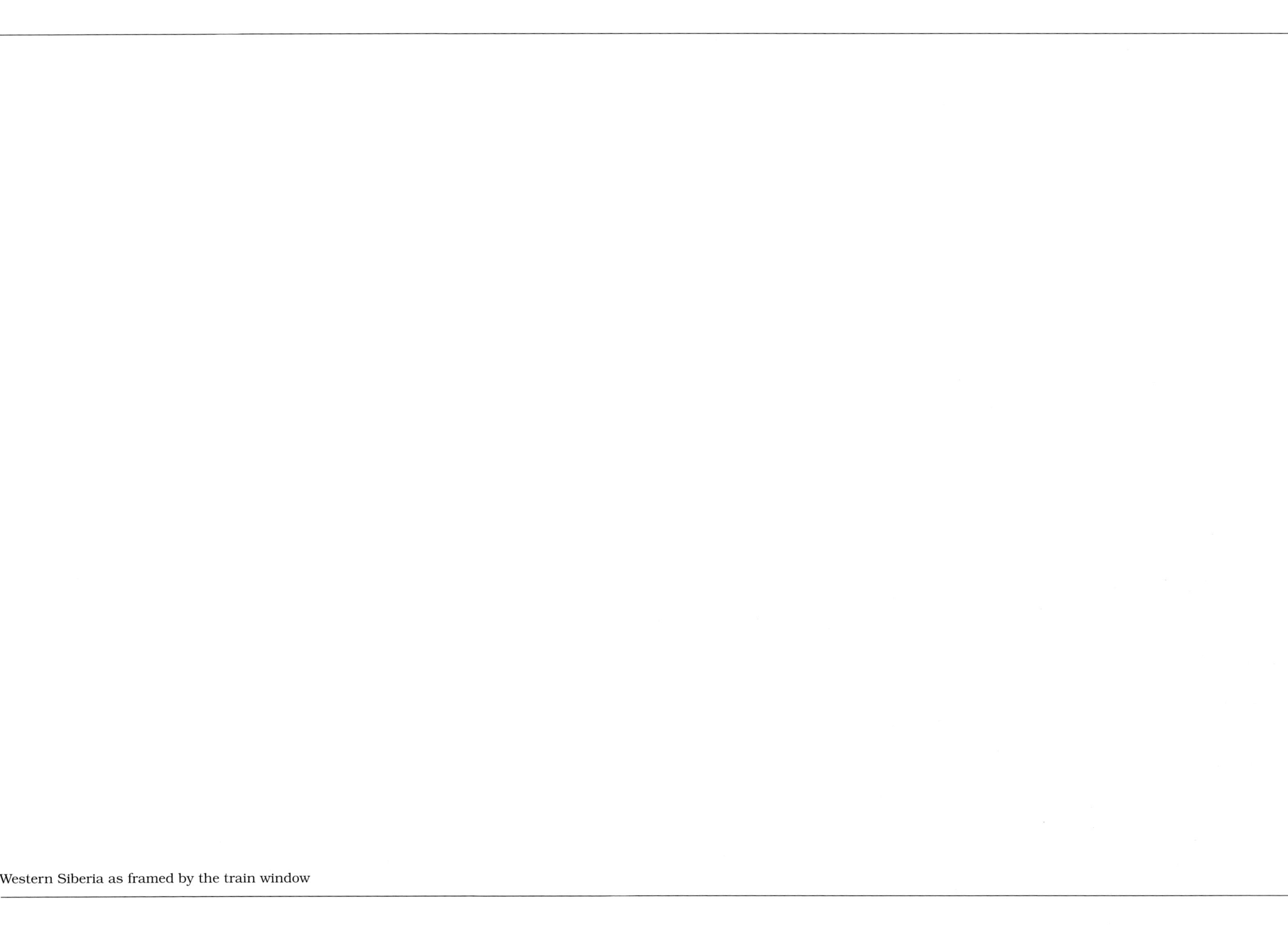

Western Siberia as framed by the train window

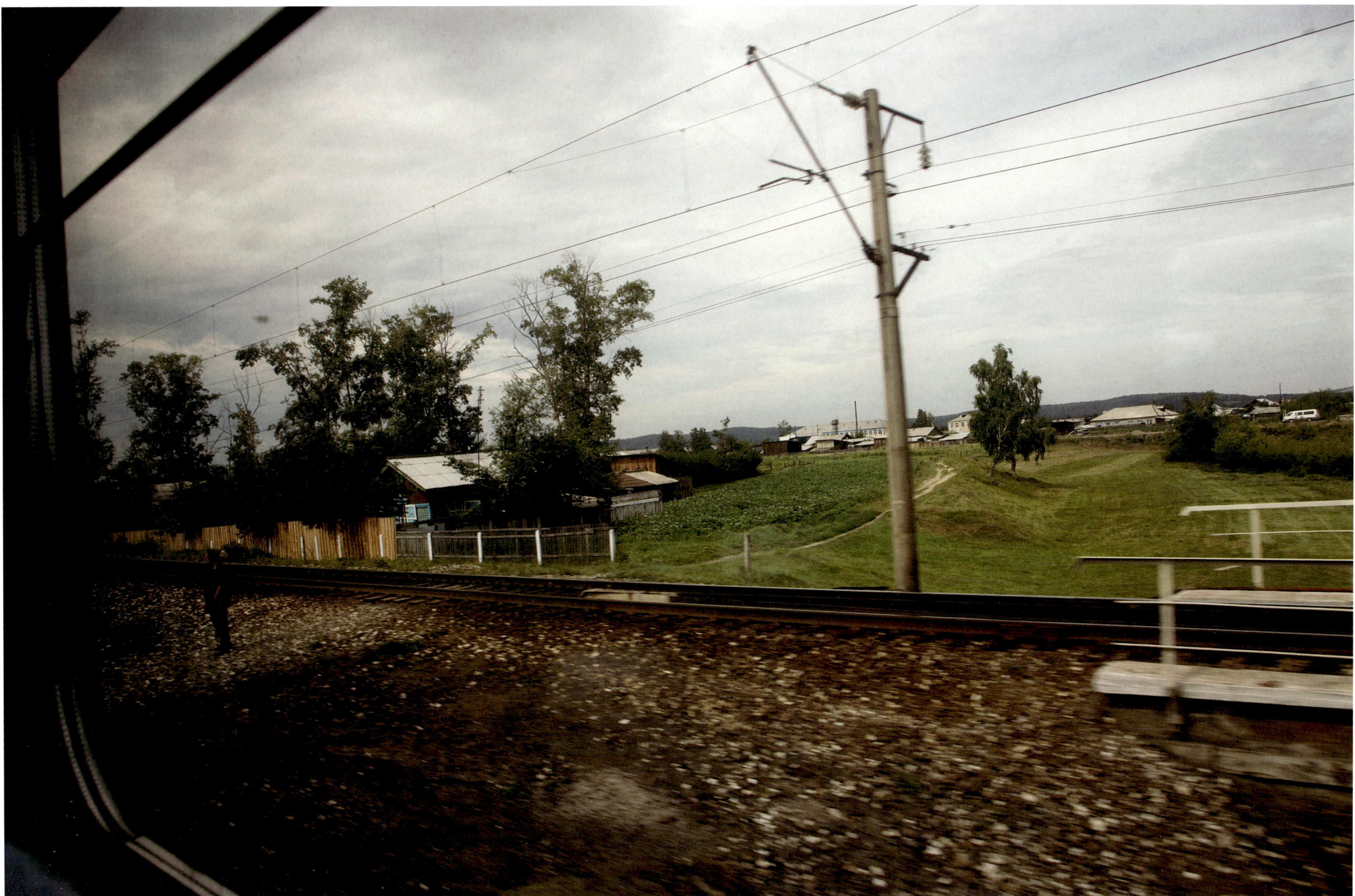

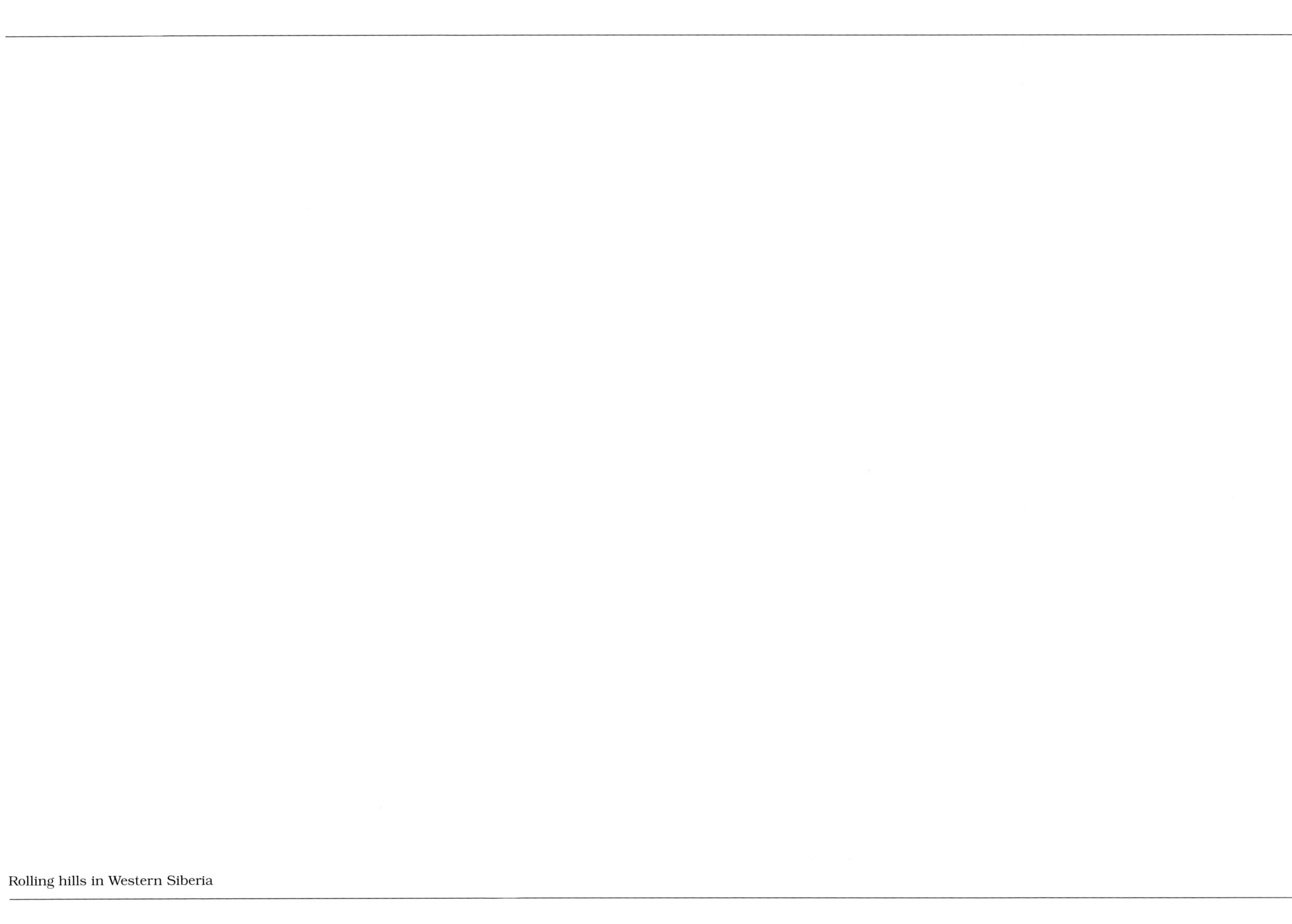

Rolling hills in Western Siberia

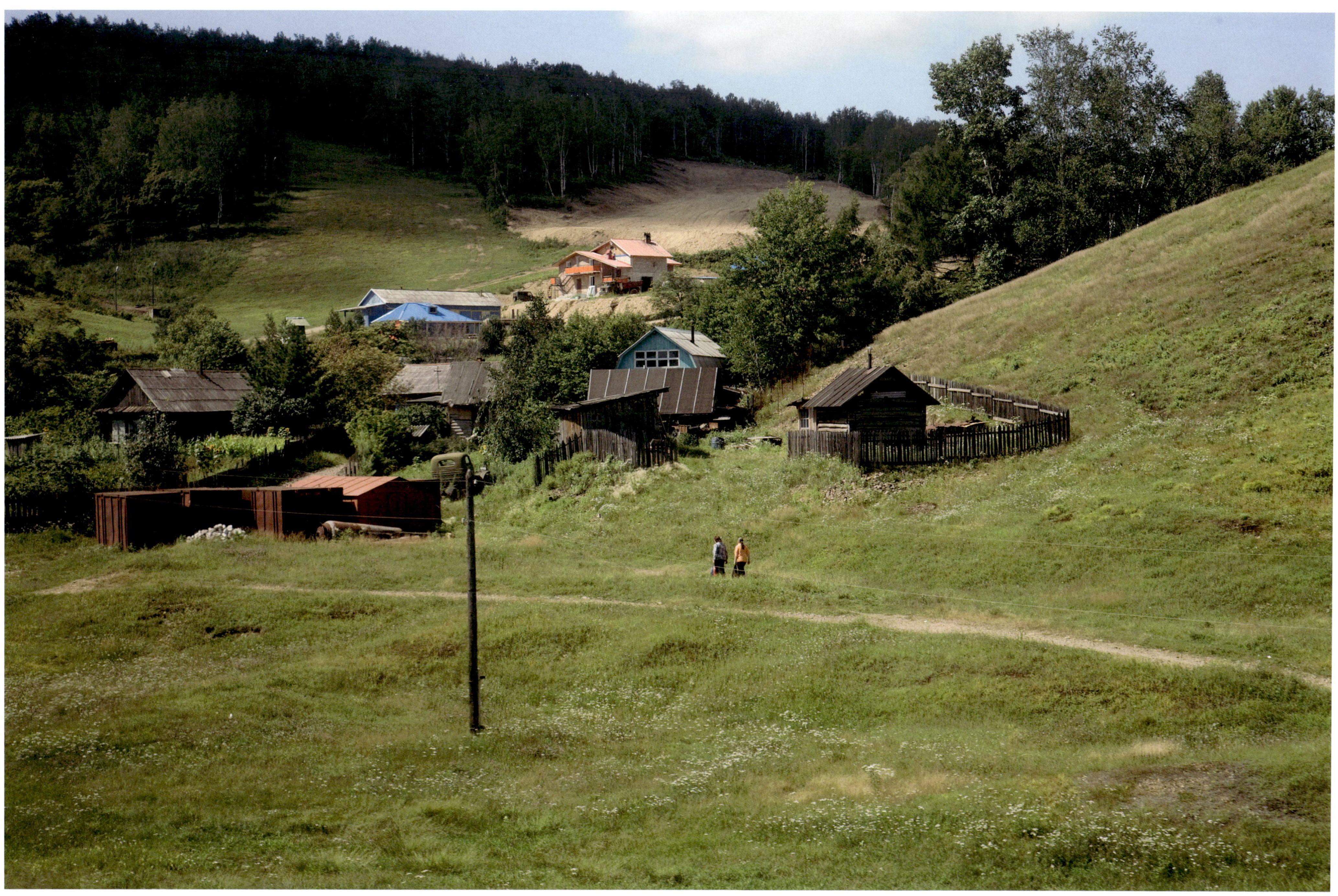

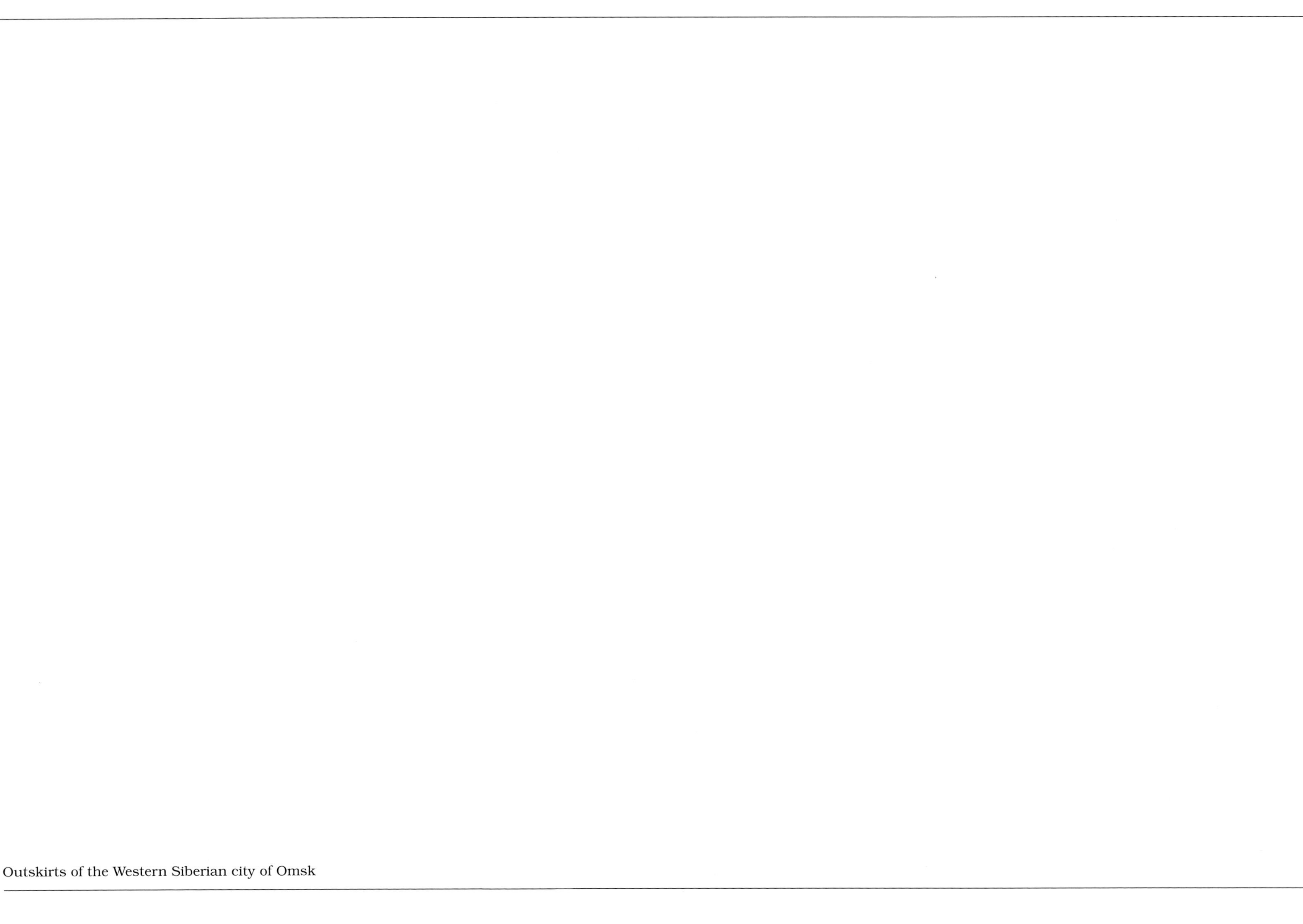

Outskirts of the Western Siberian city of Omsk

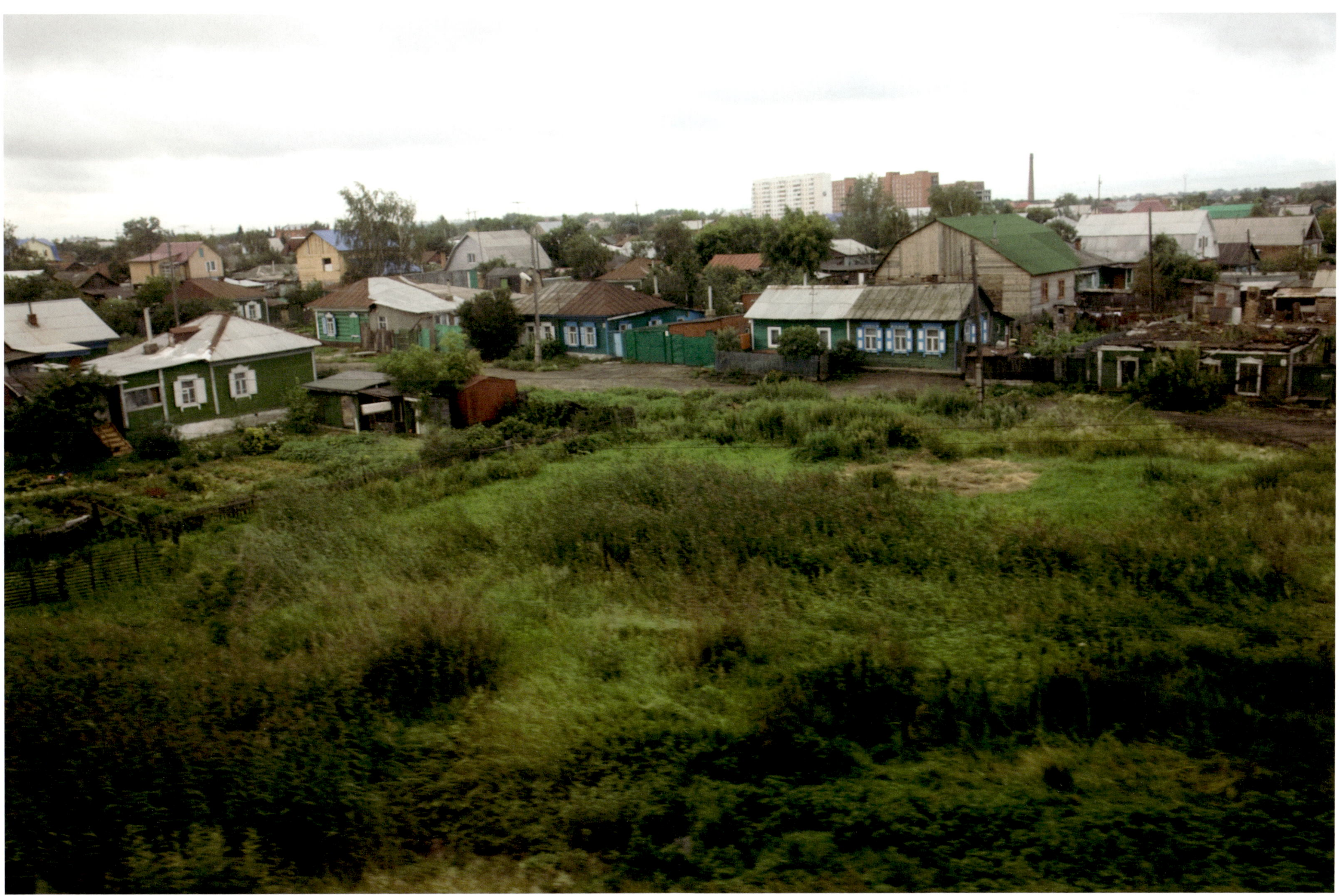

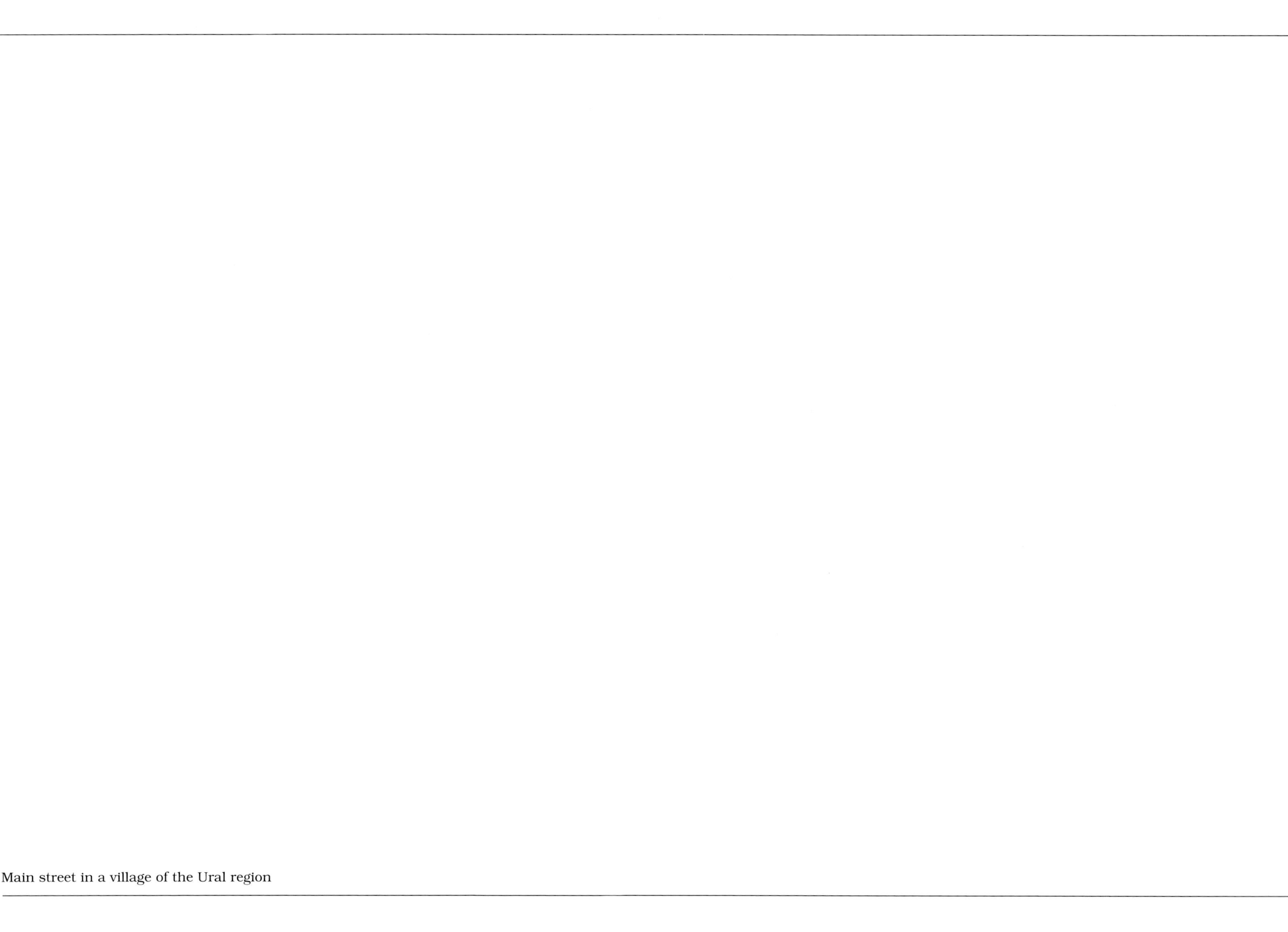

Main street in a village of the Ural region

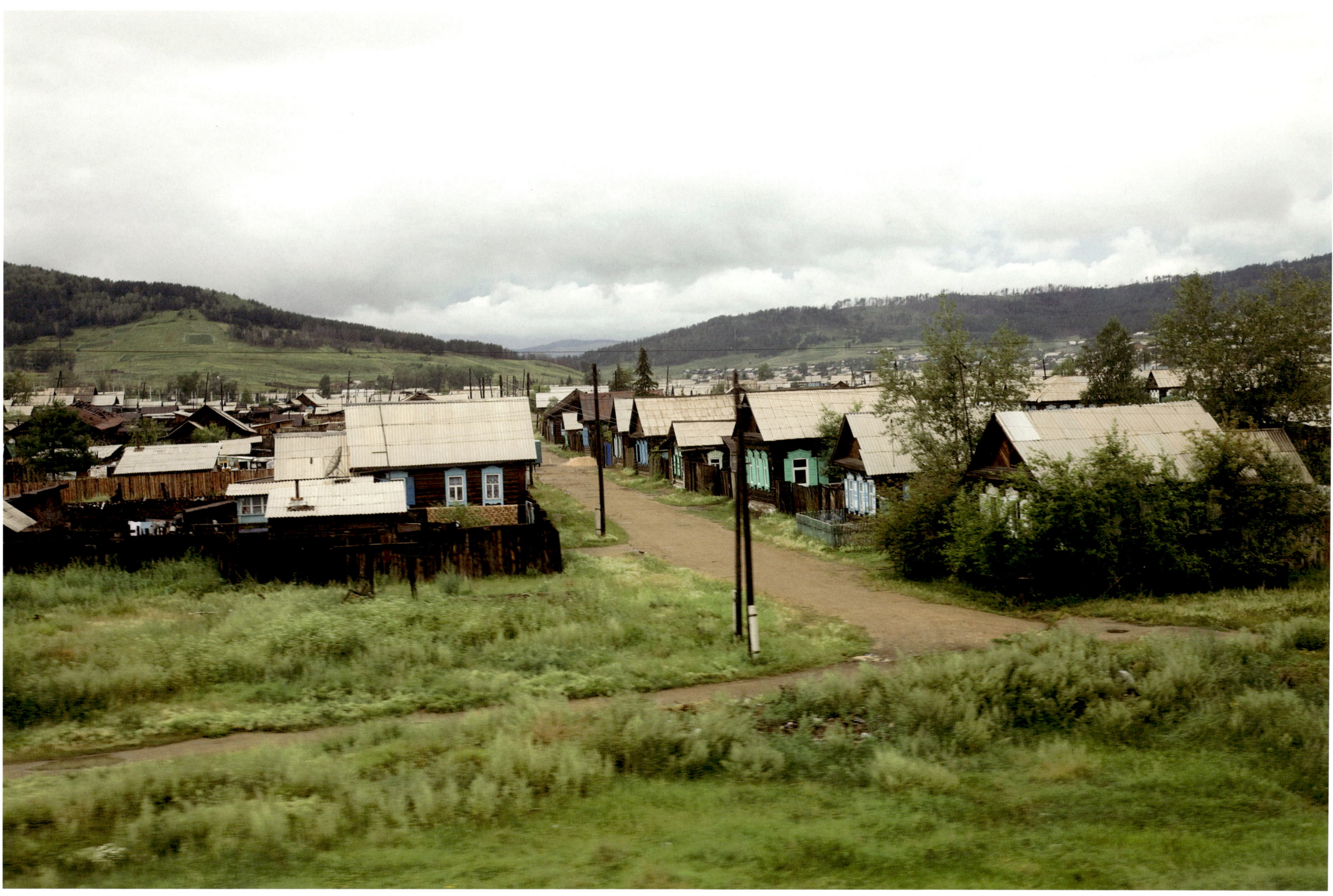

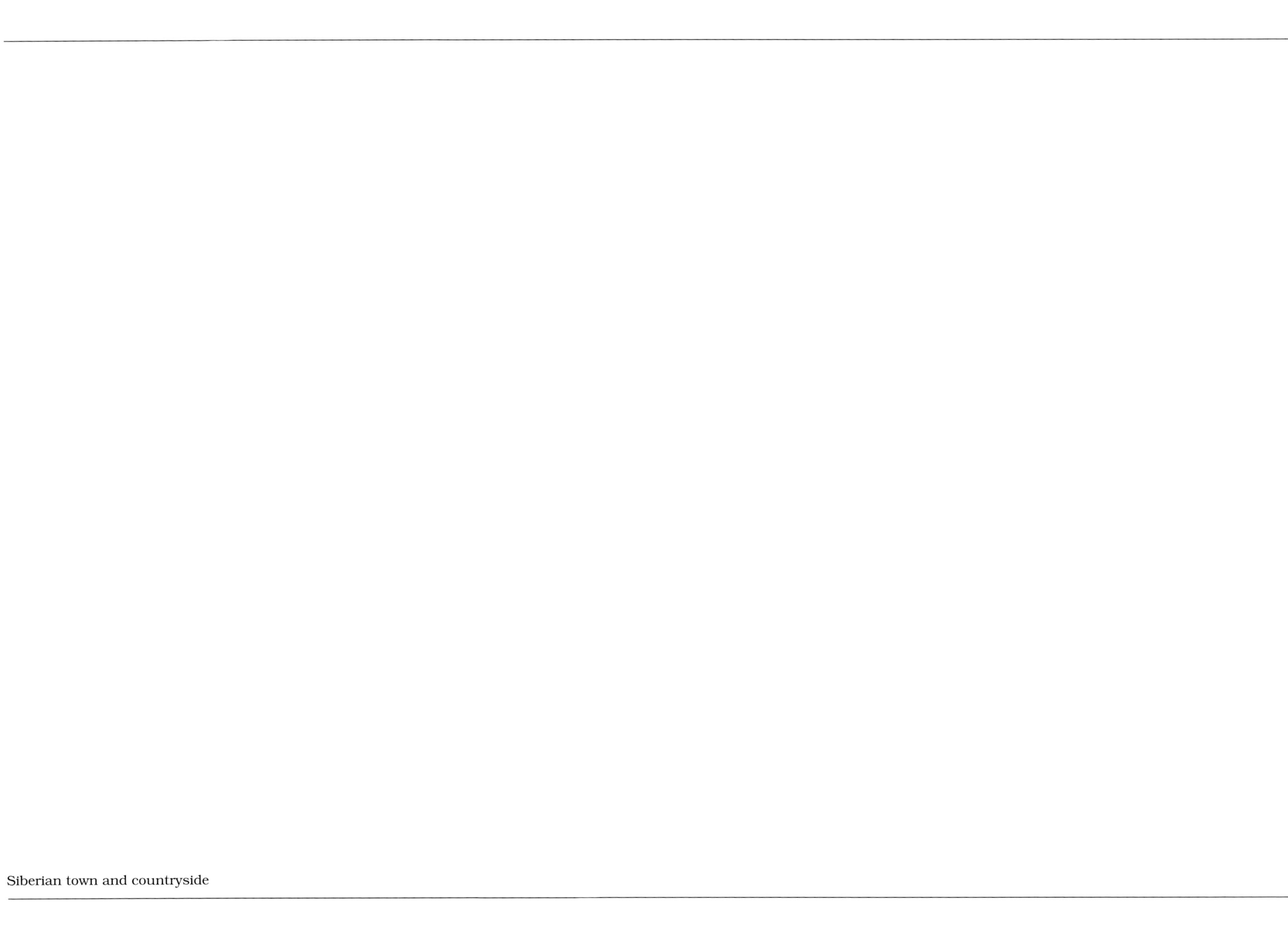

Siberian town and countryside

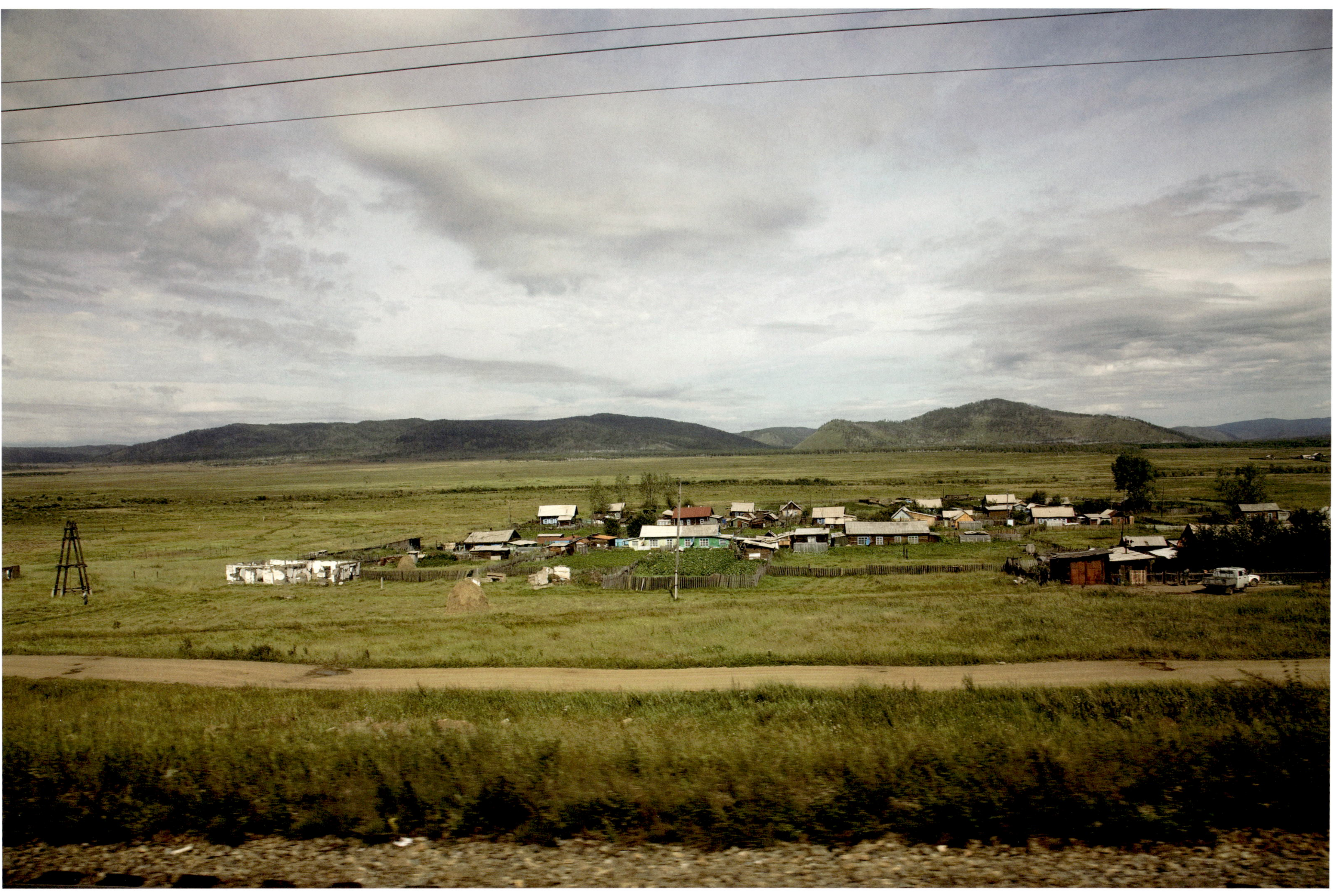

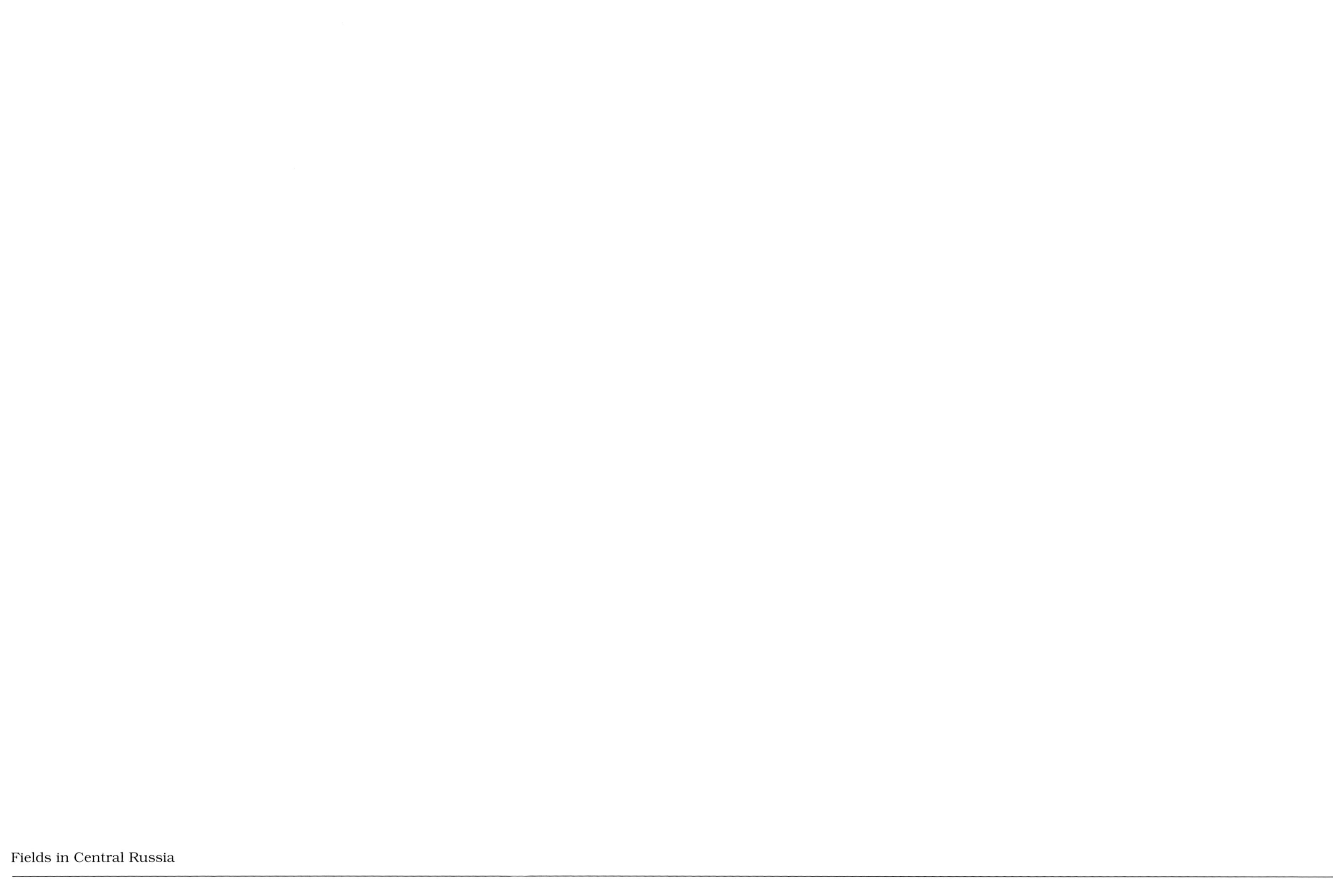

Fields in Central Russia

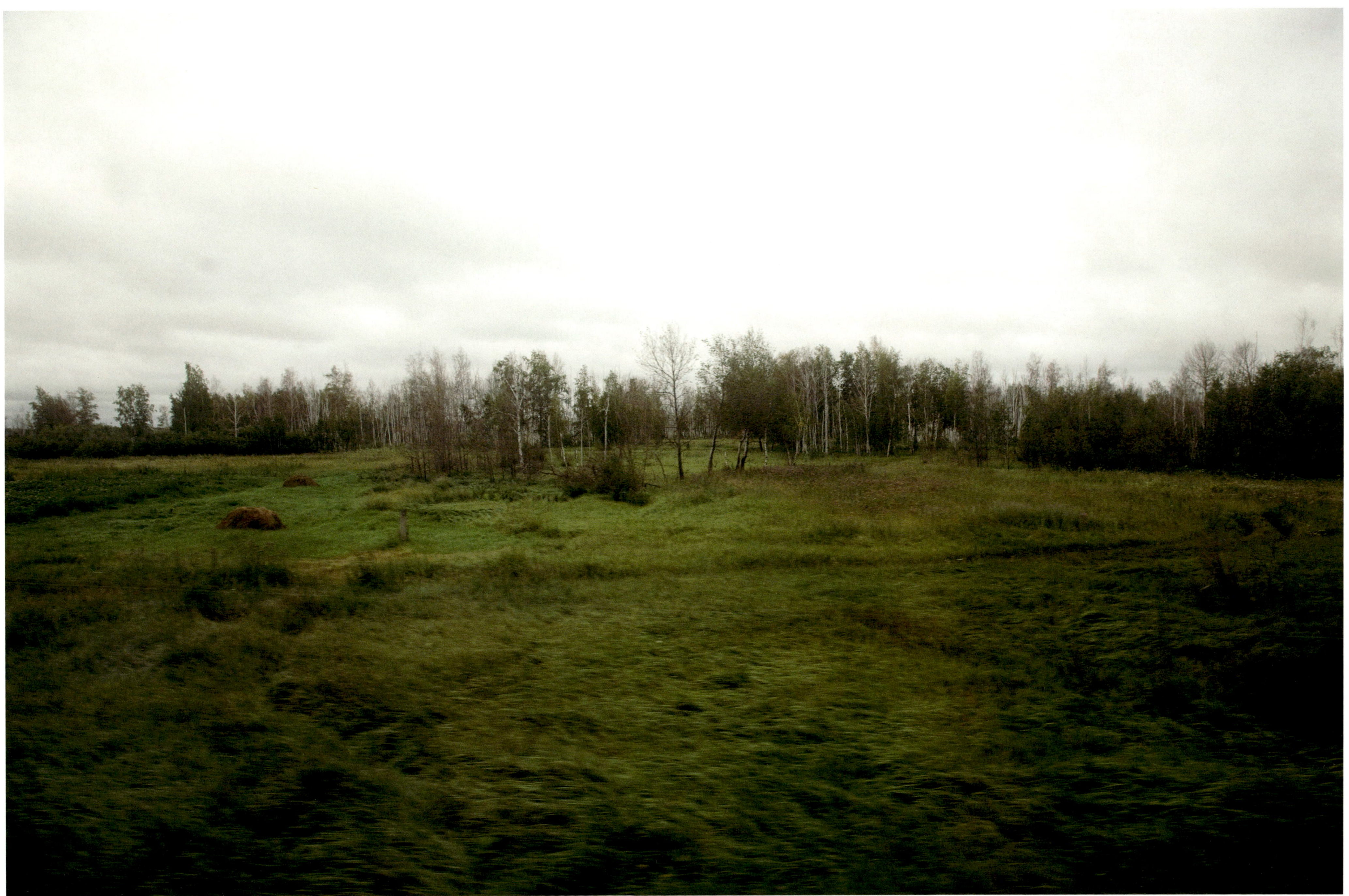

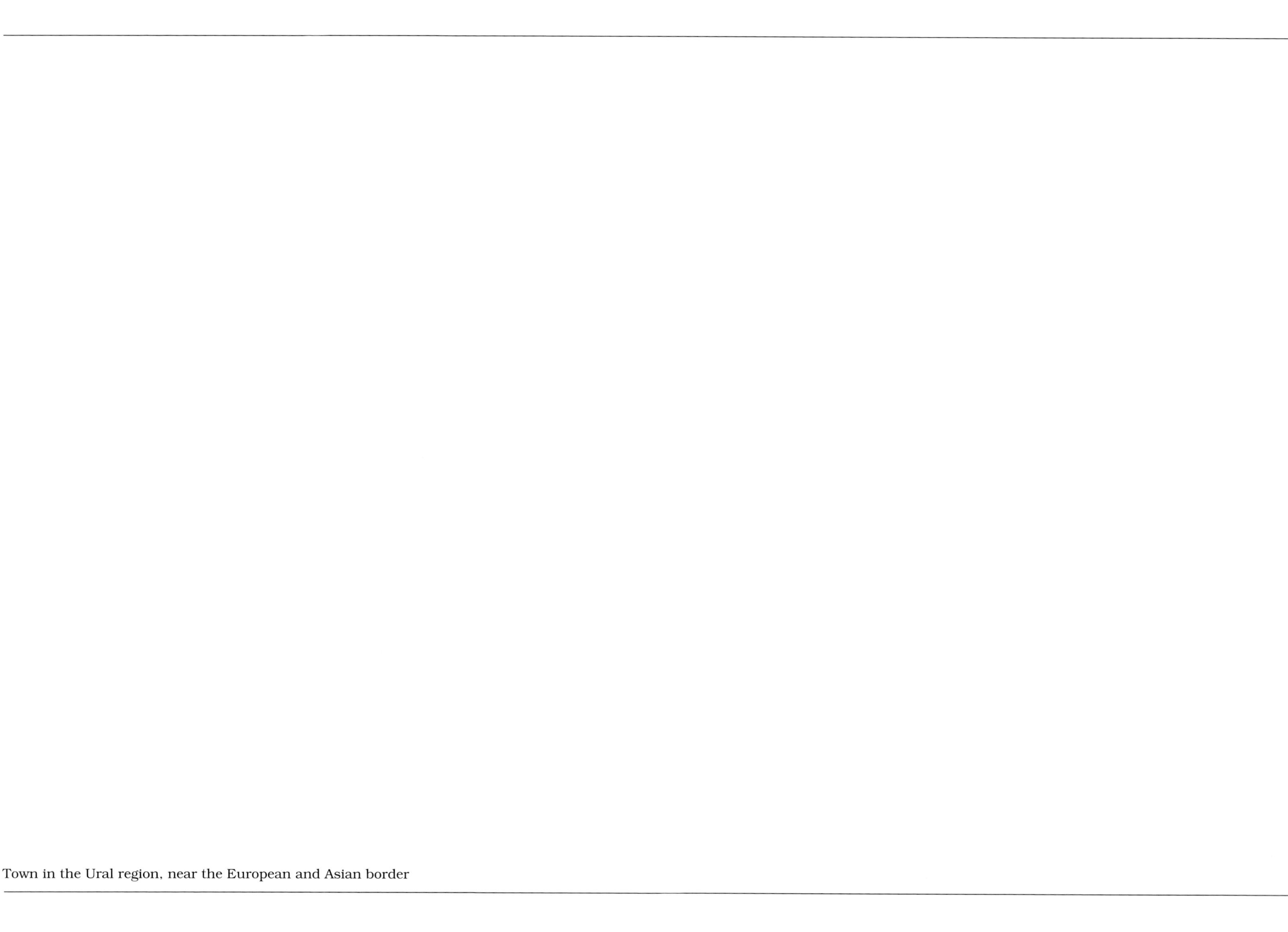

Town in the Ural region, near the European and Asian border

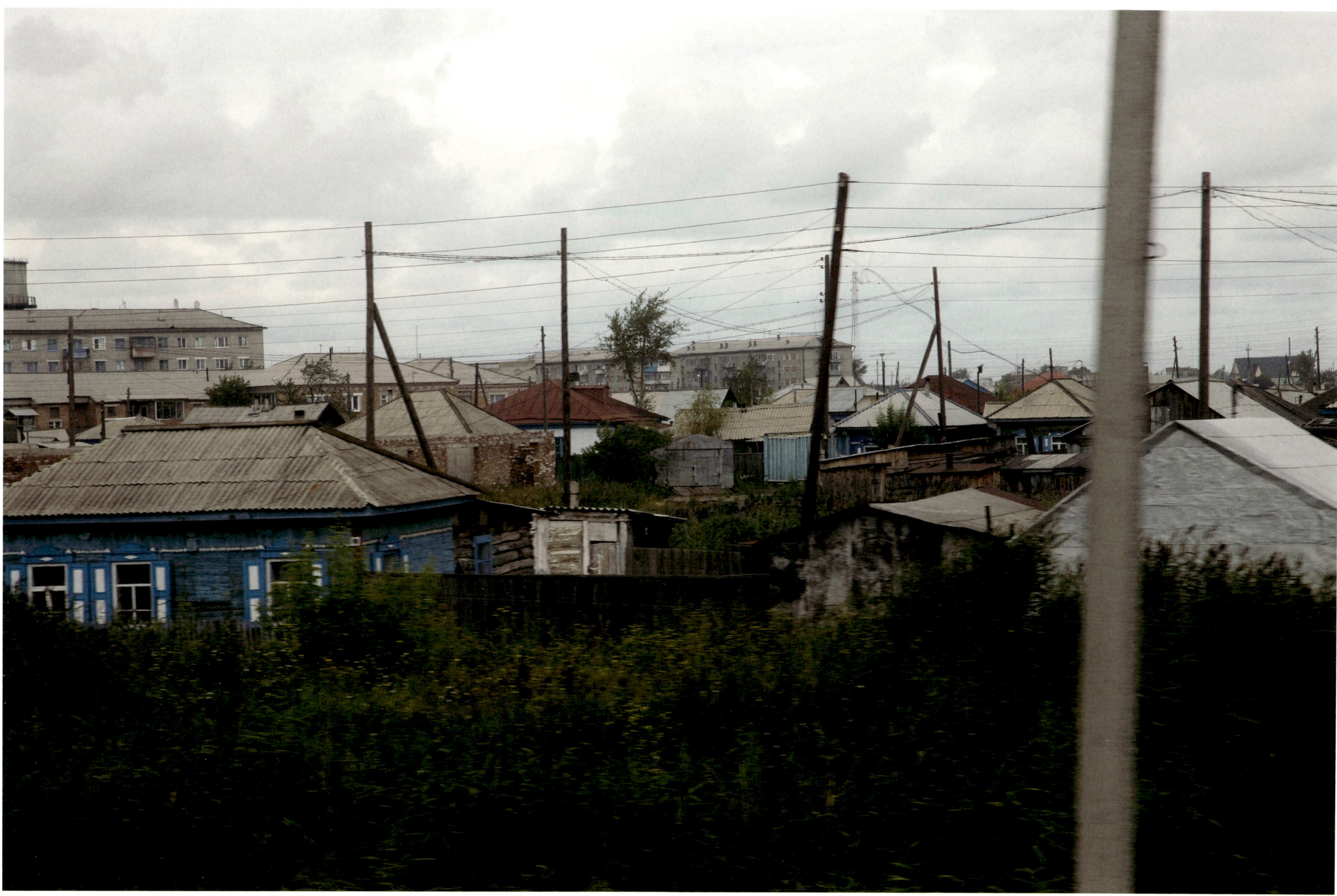

Cemetery in Eastern Siberia

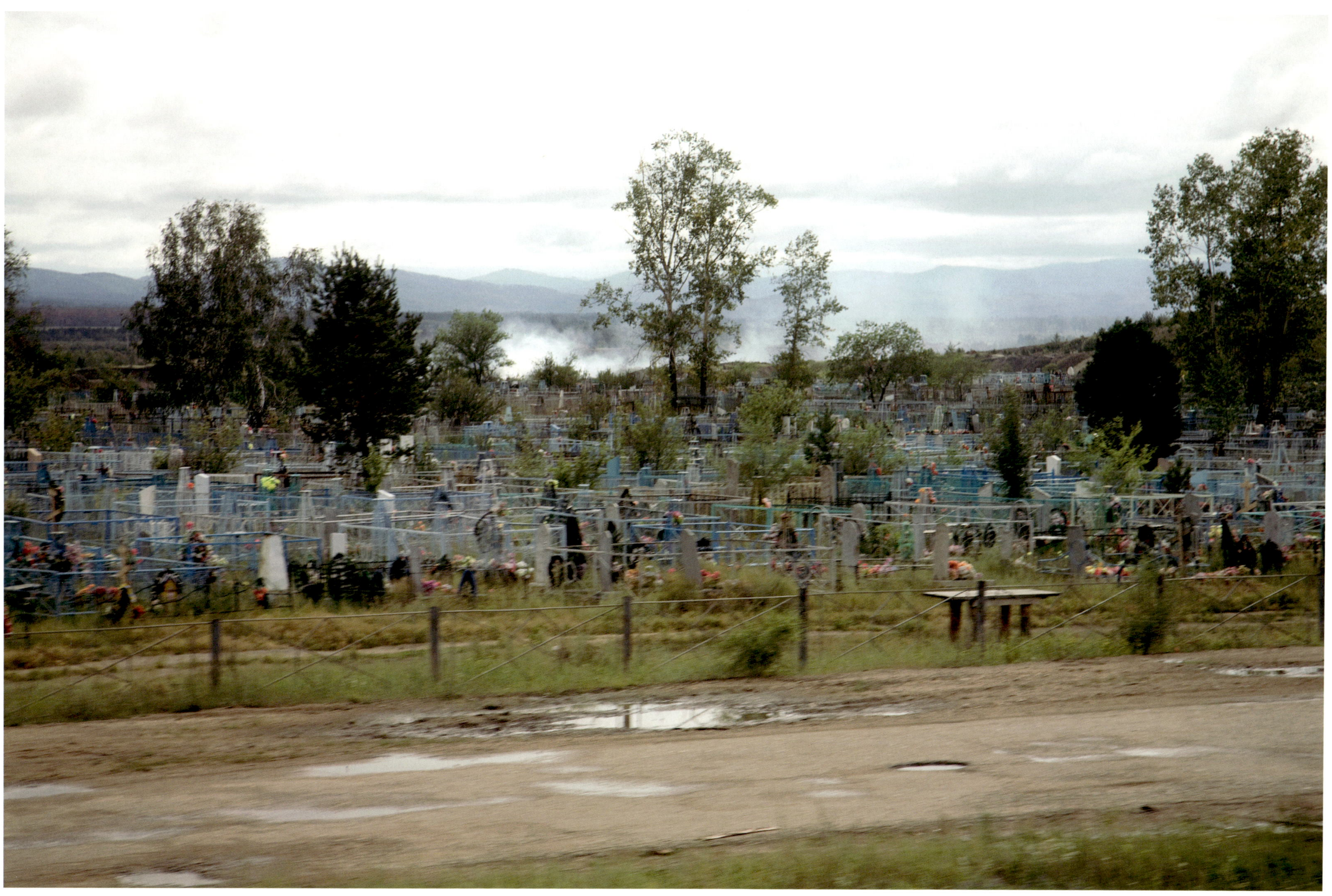

Town near Lake Baikal in Siberia

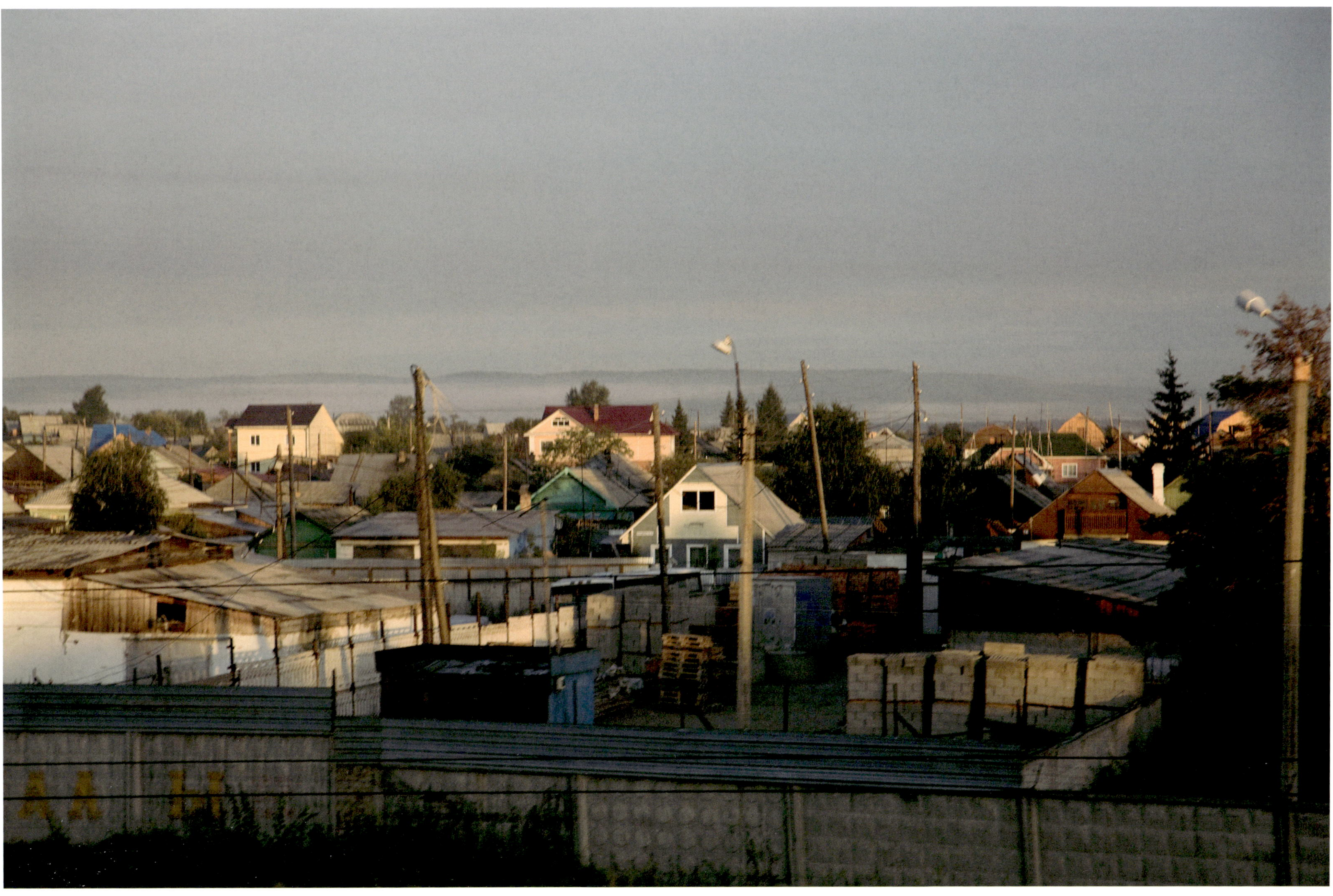

Kids playing in a village in Siberia

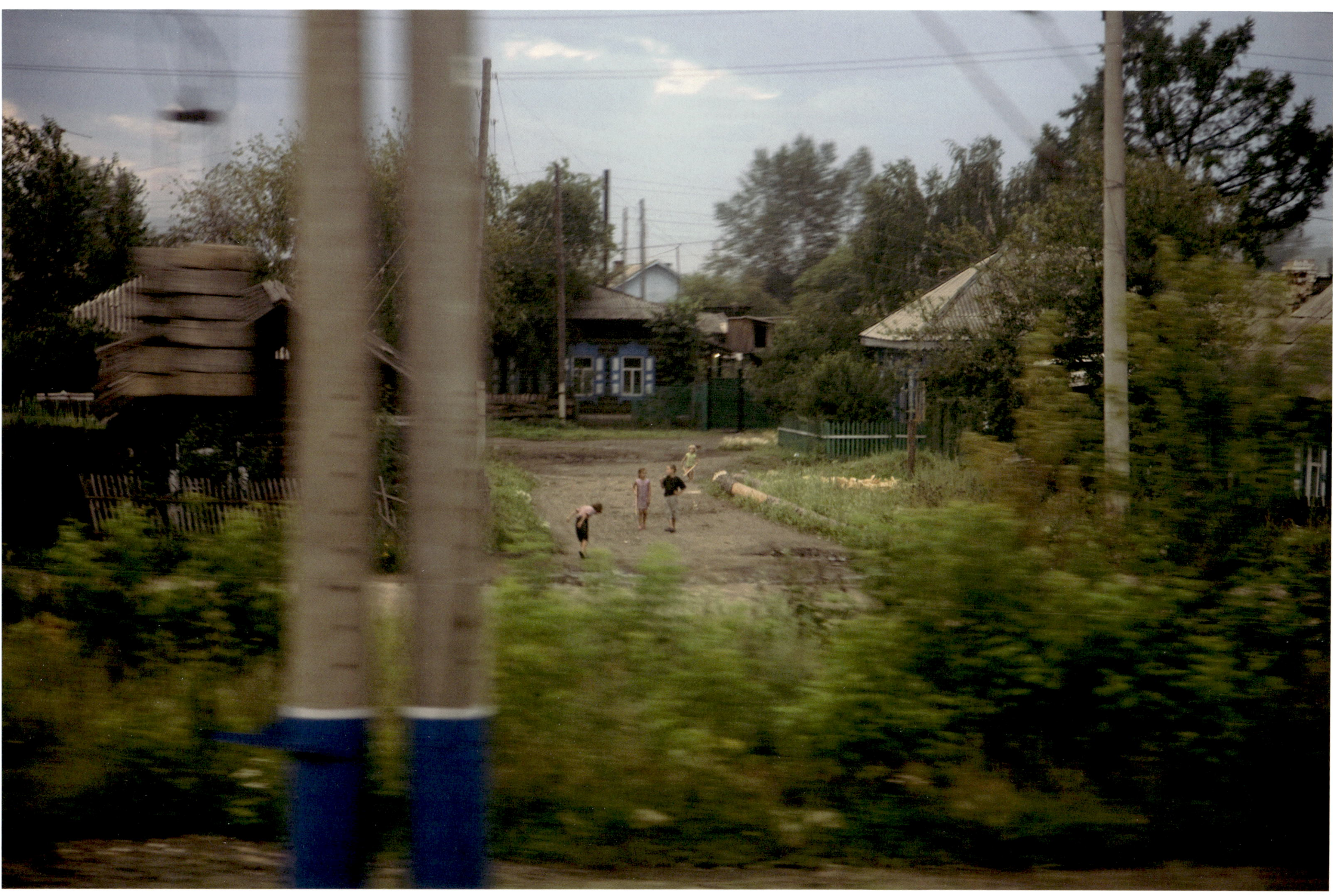

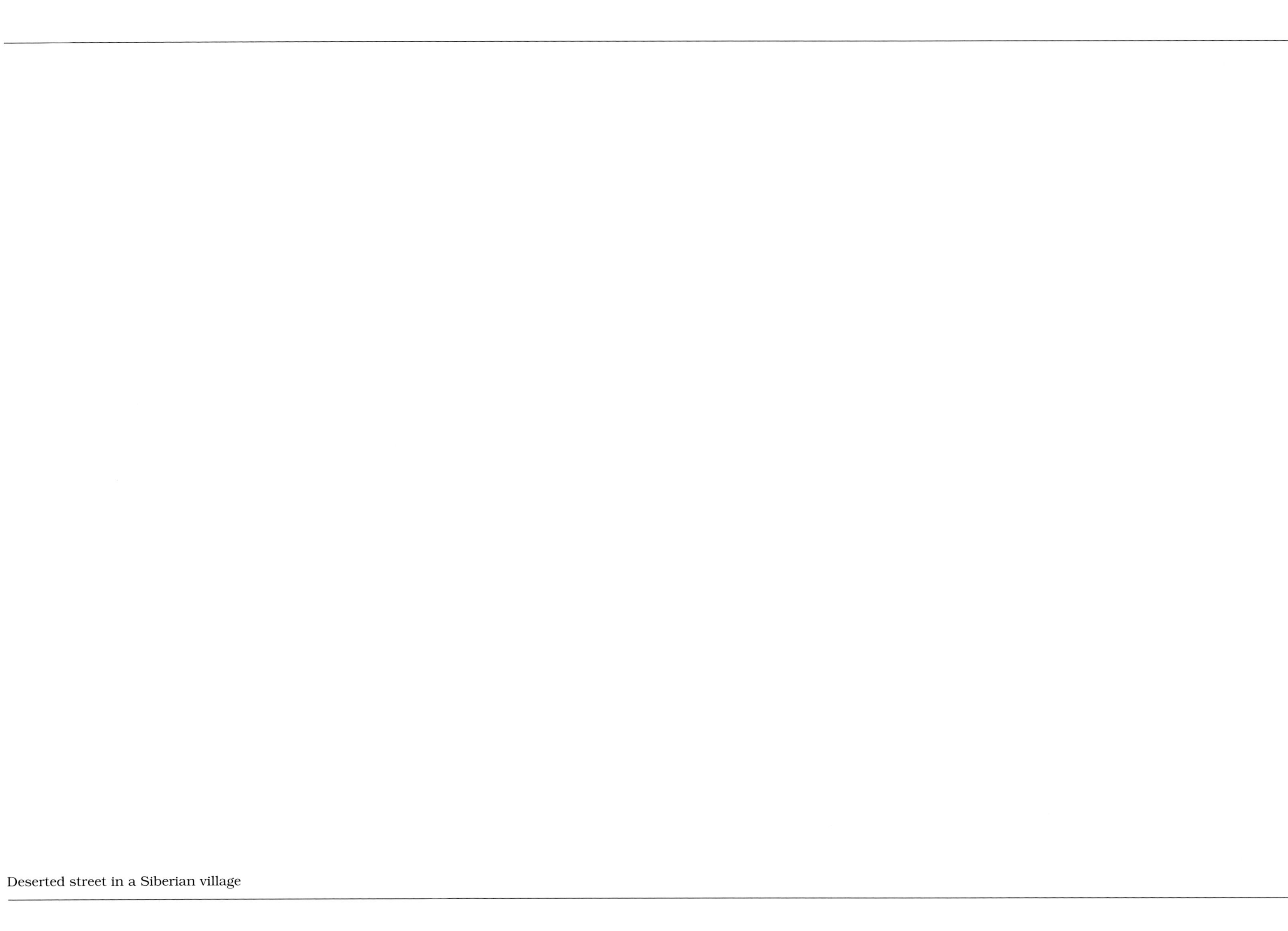

Deserted street in a Siberian village

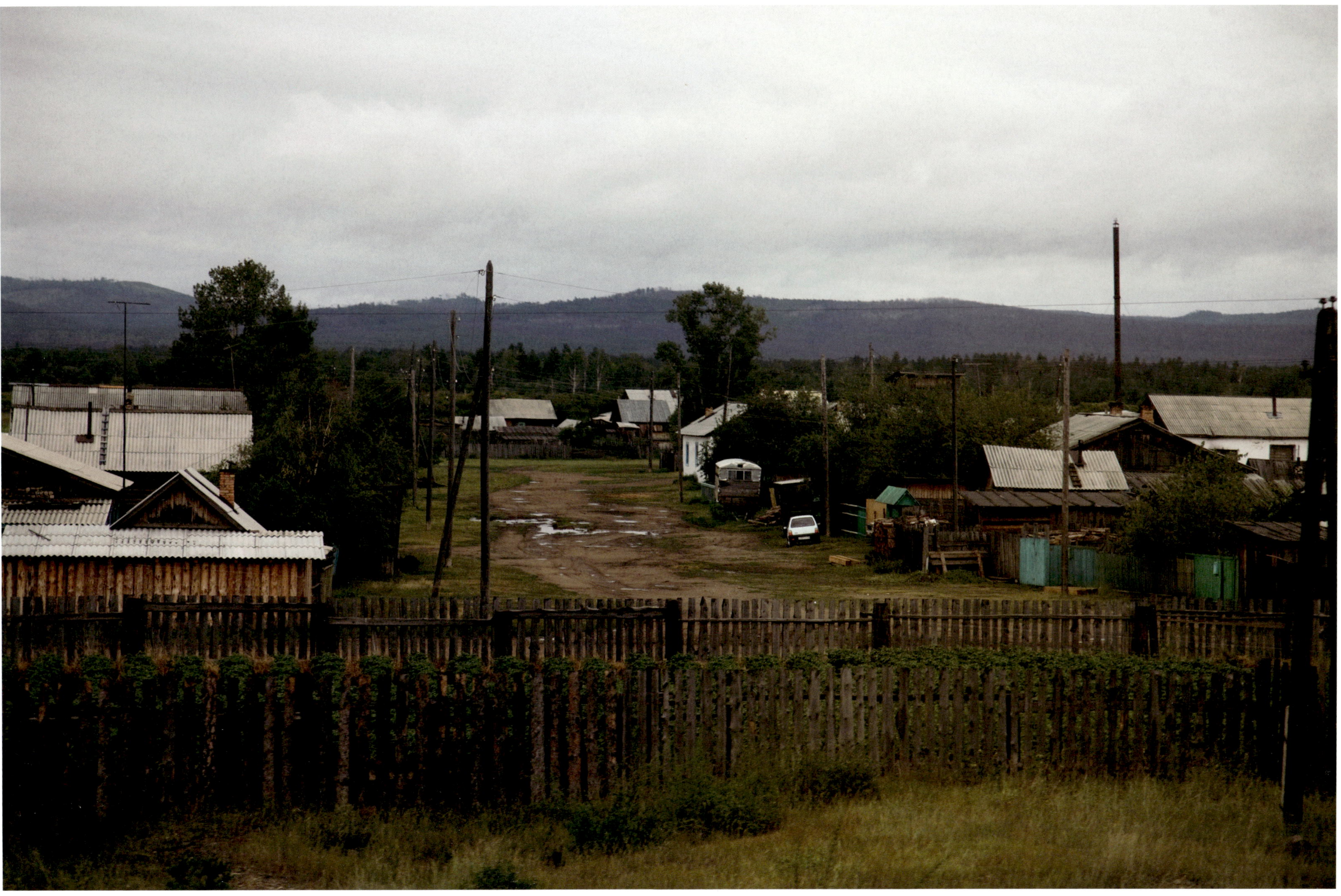

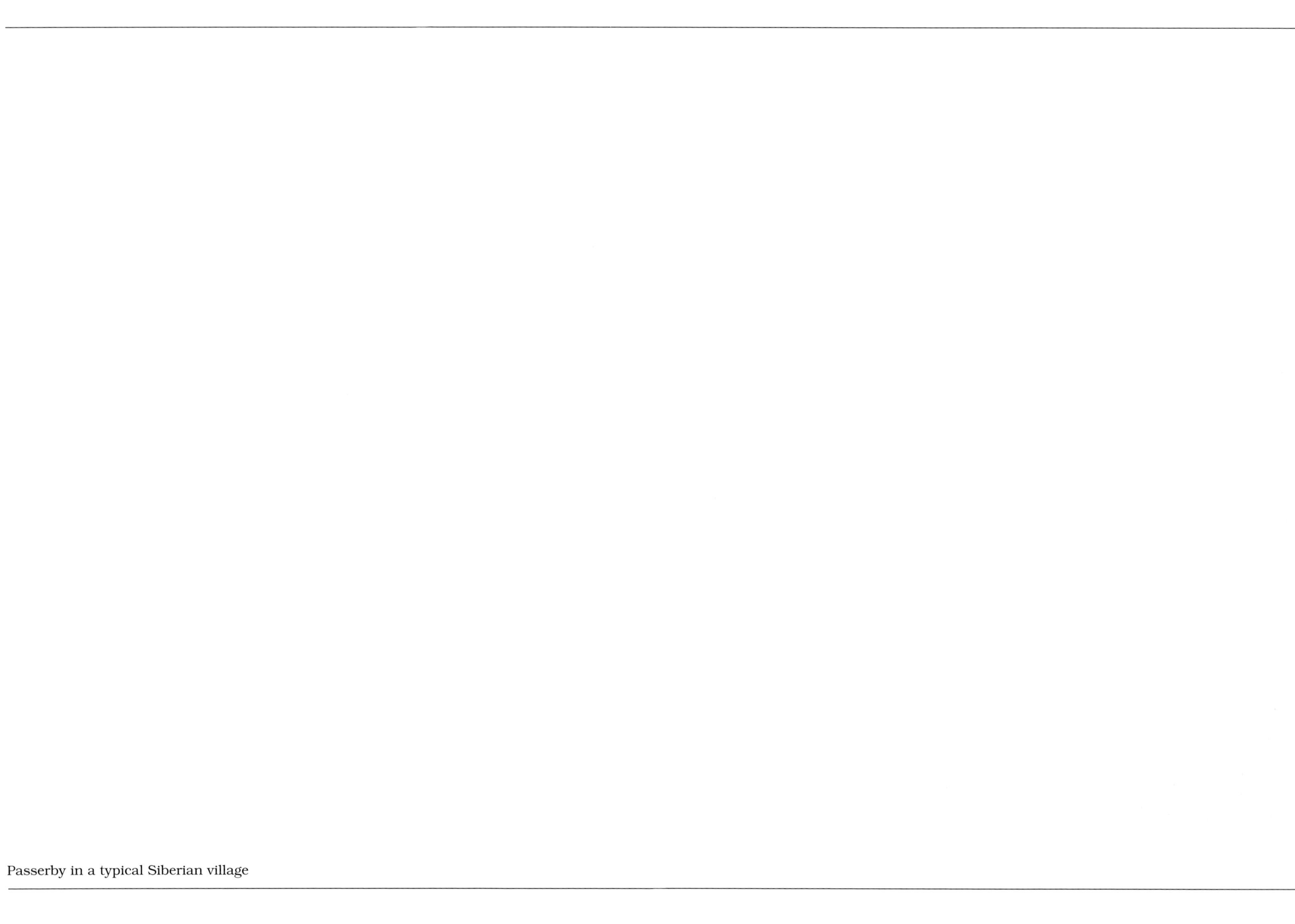

Passerby in a typical Siberian village

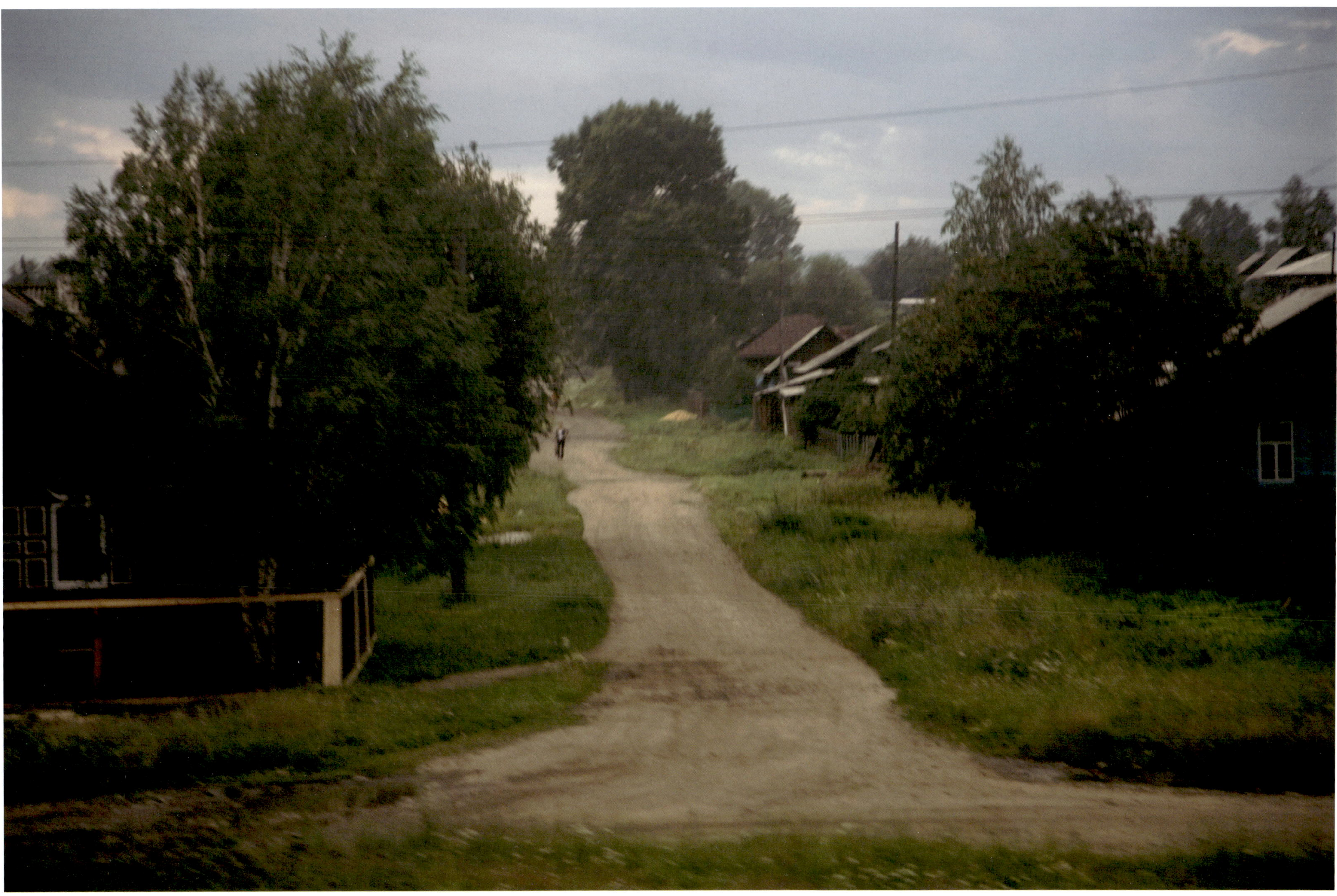

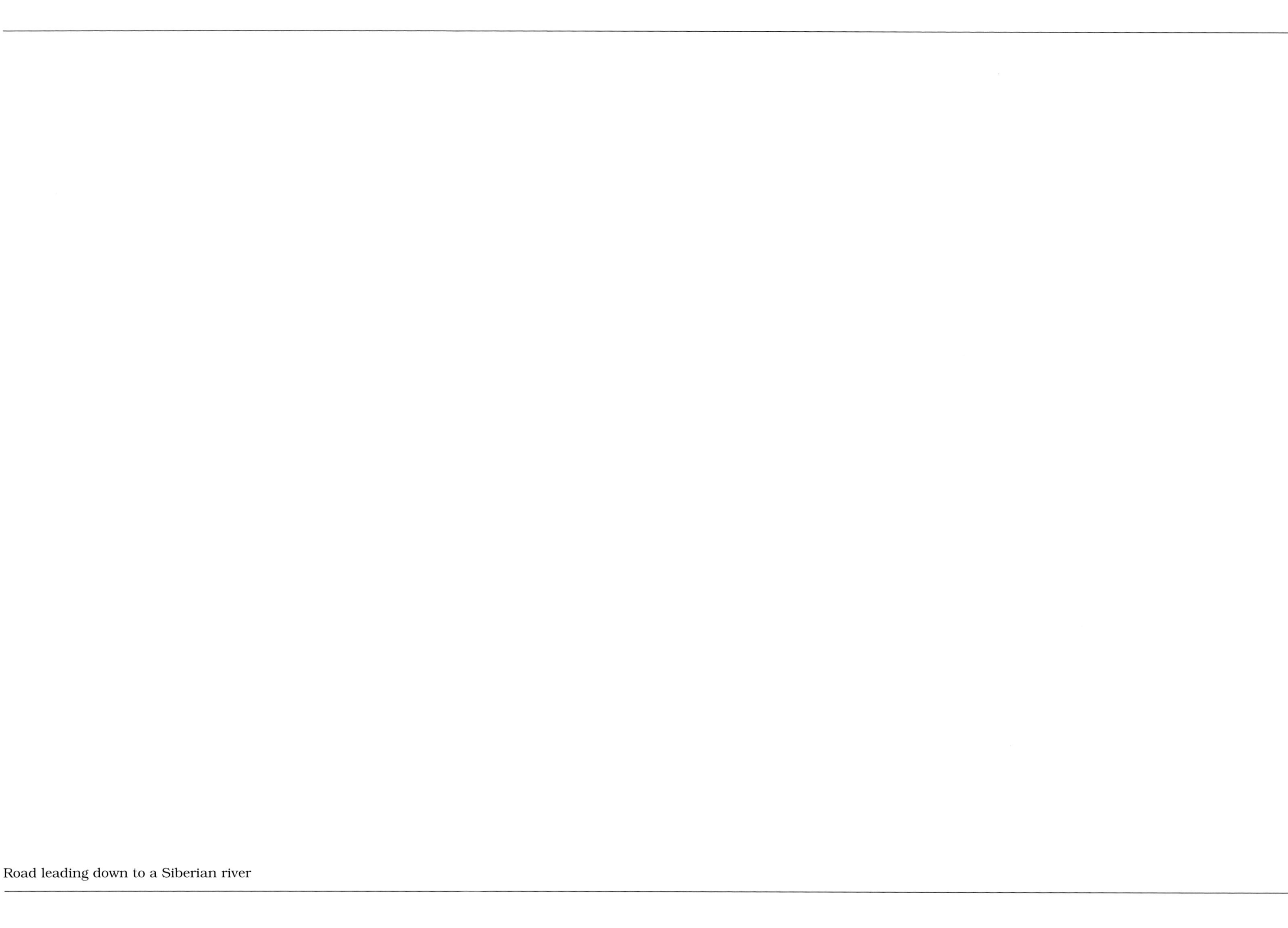

Road leading down to a Siberian river

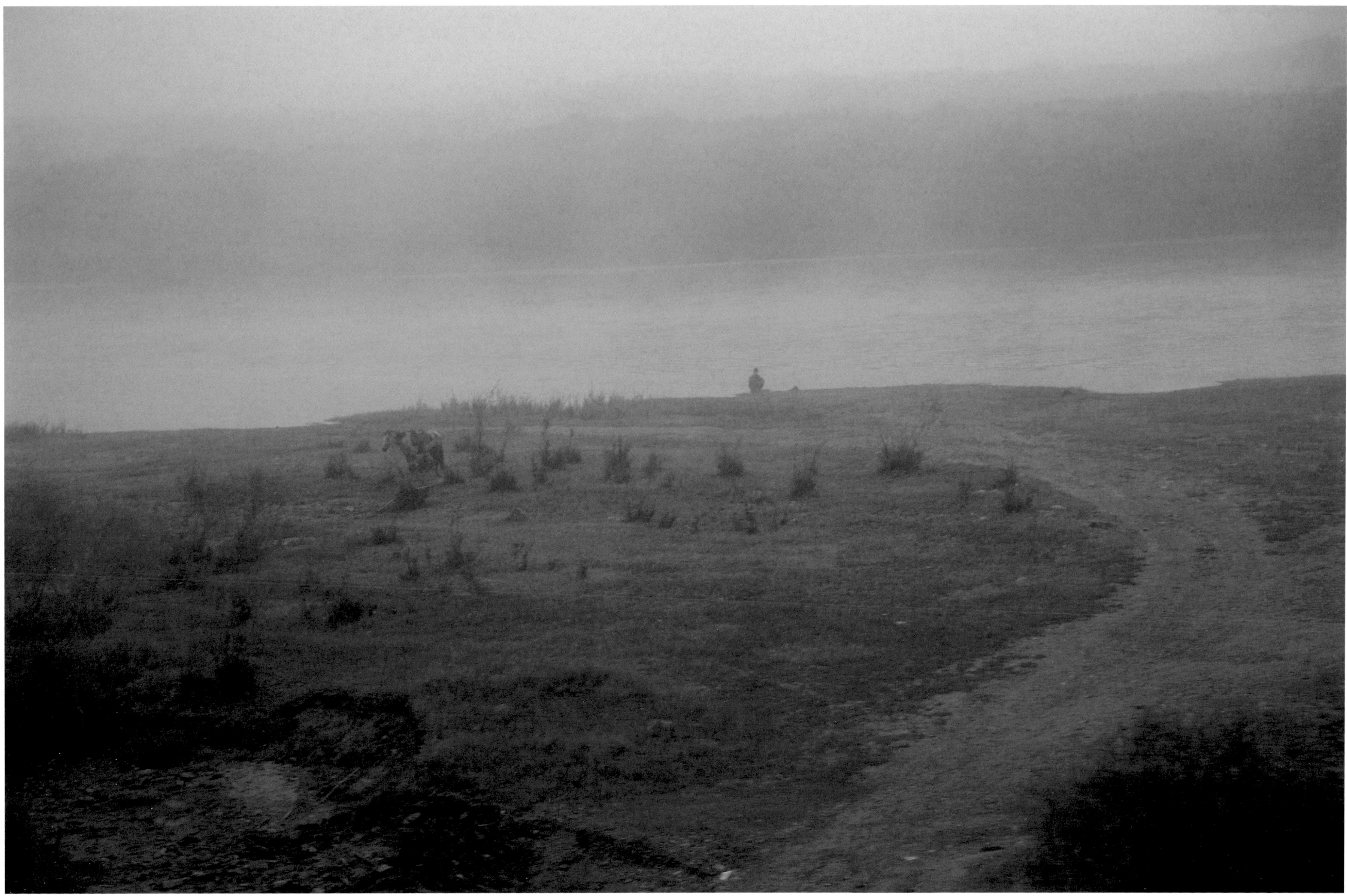

Large winding river in Siberia

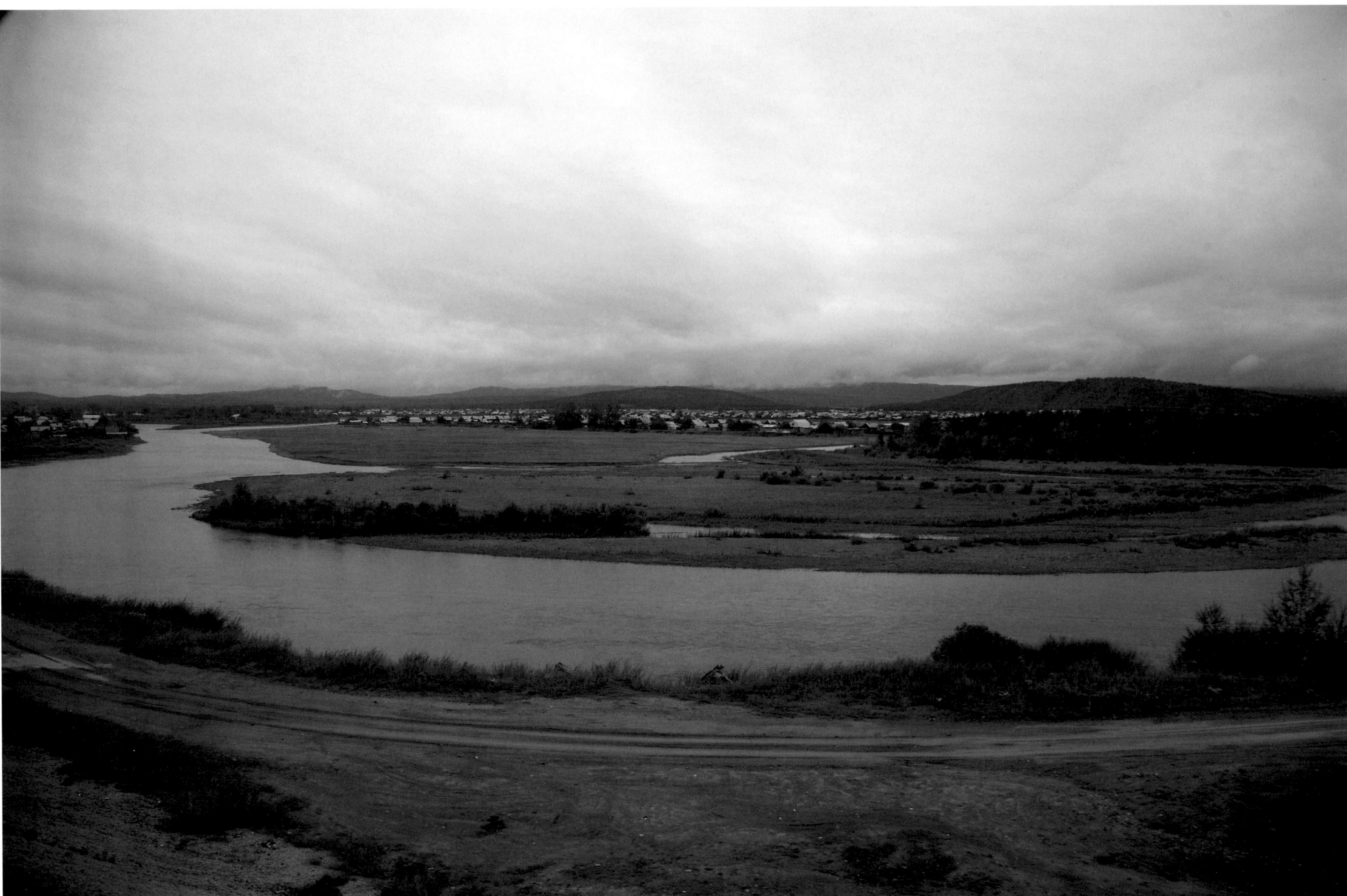

Siberian river at twilight

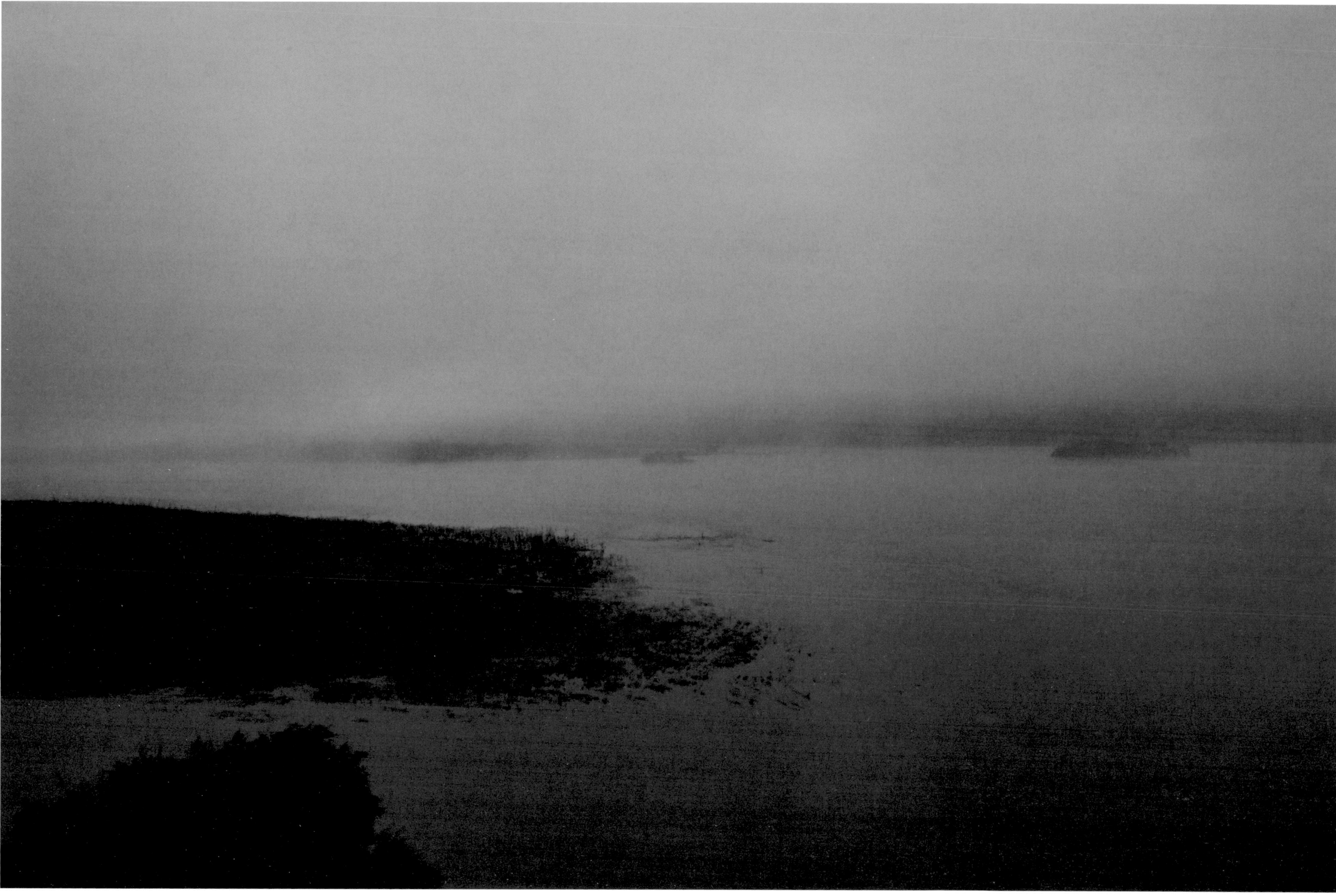

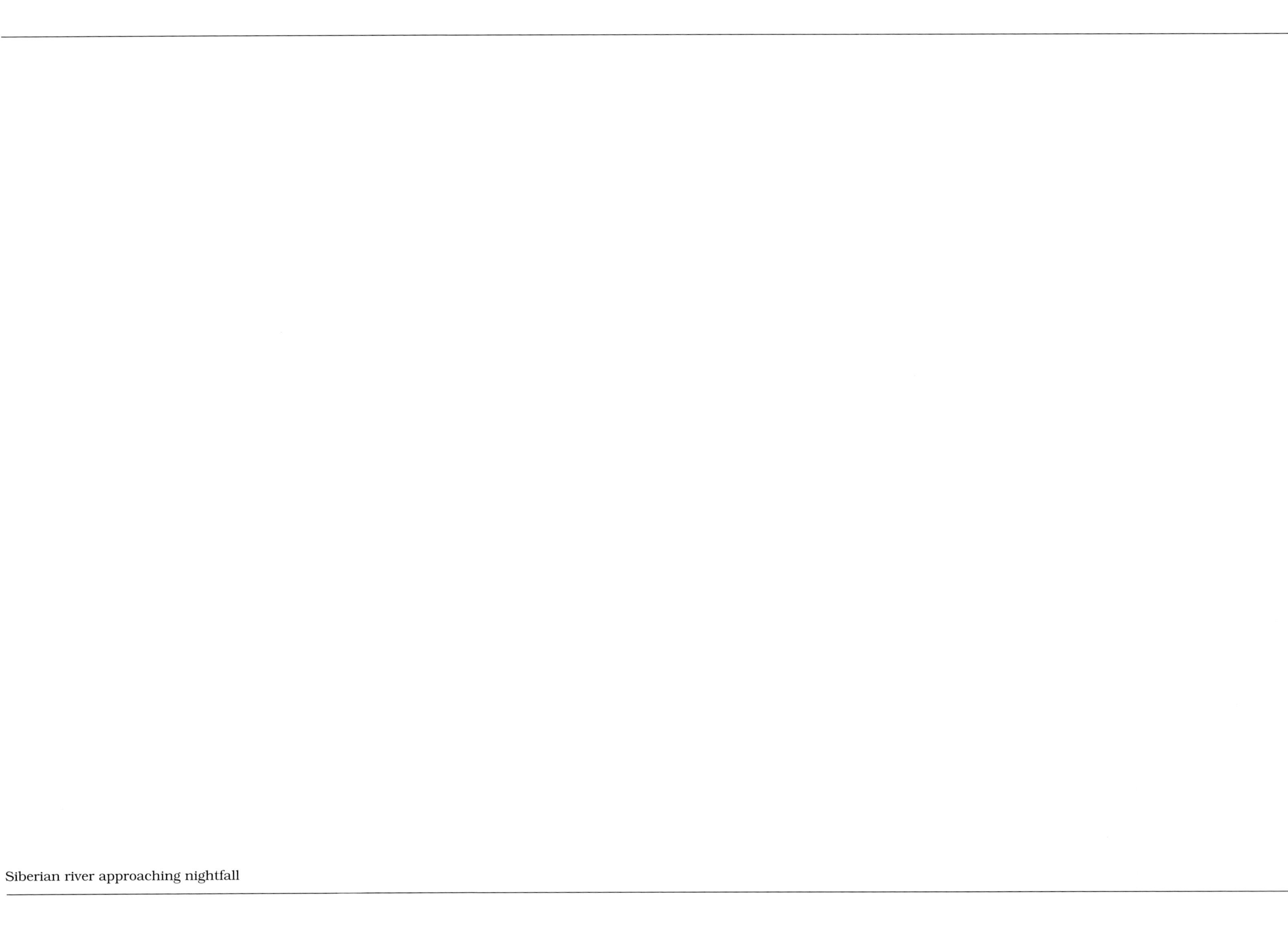

Siberian river approaching nightfall

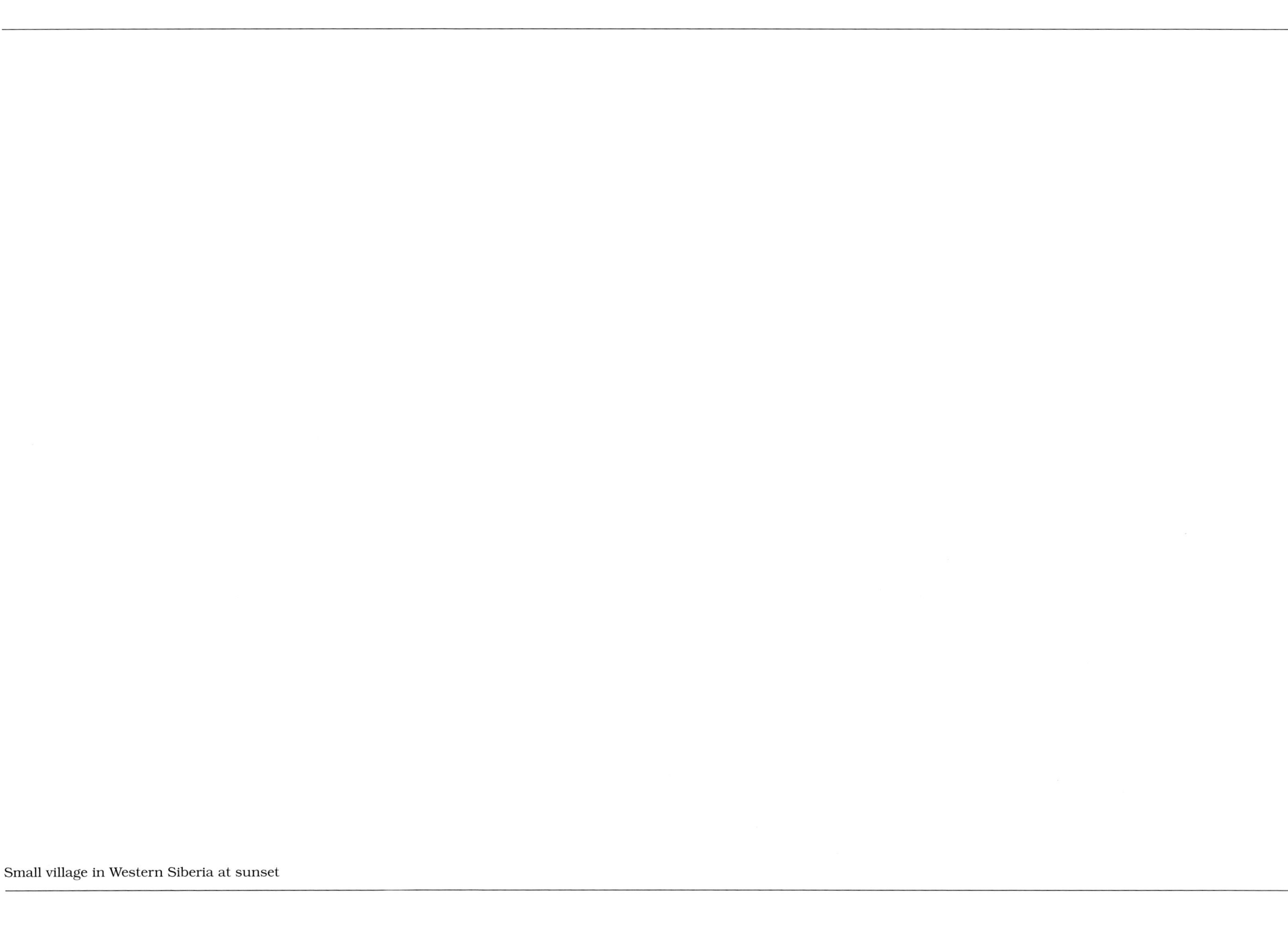

Small village in Western Siberia at sunset

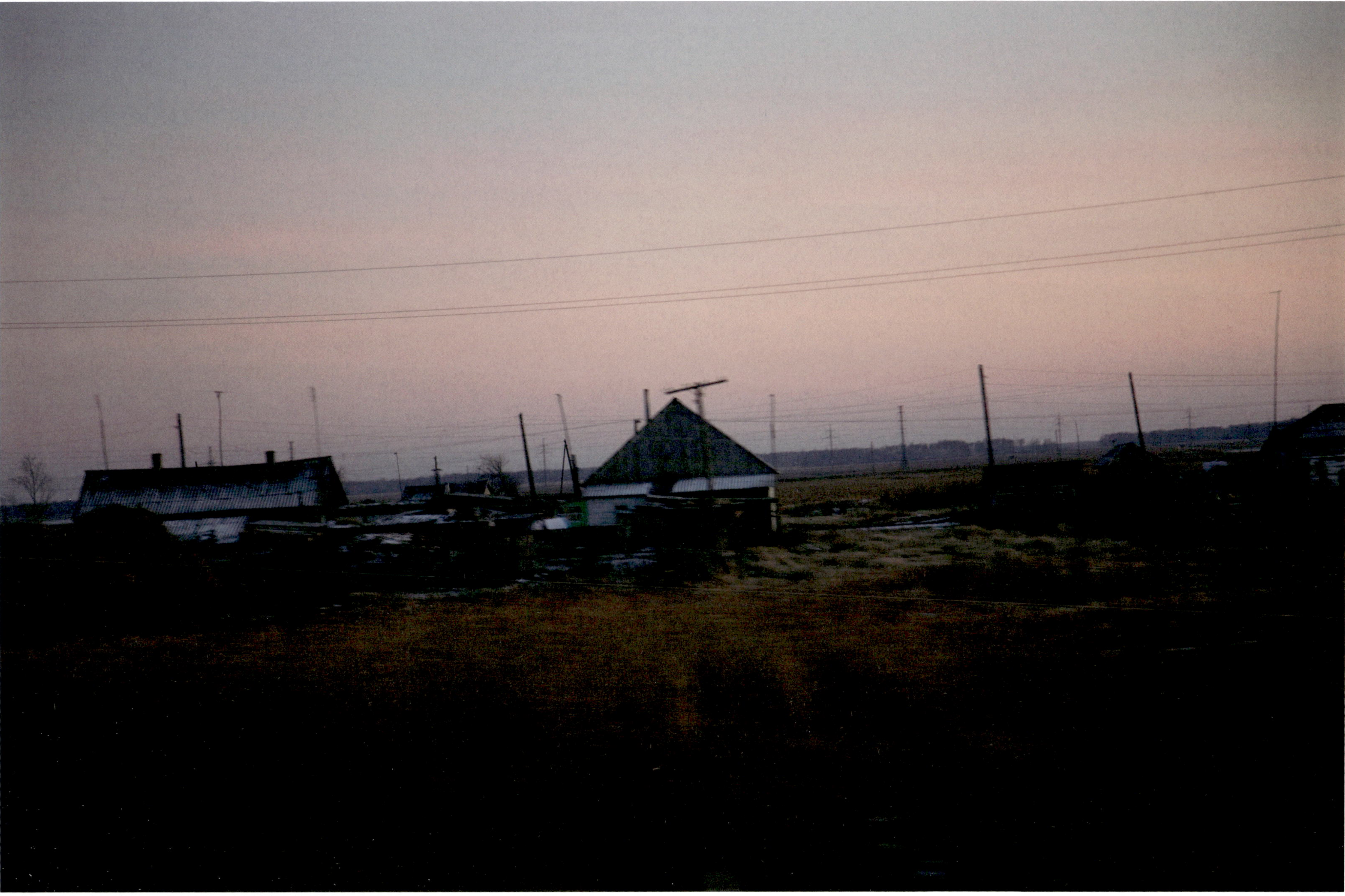

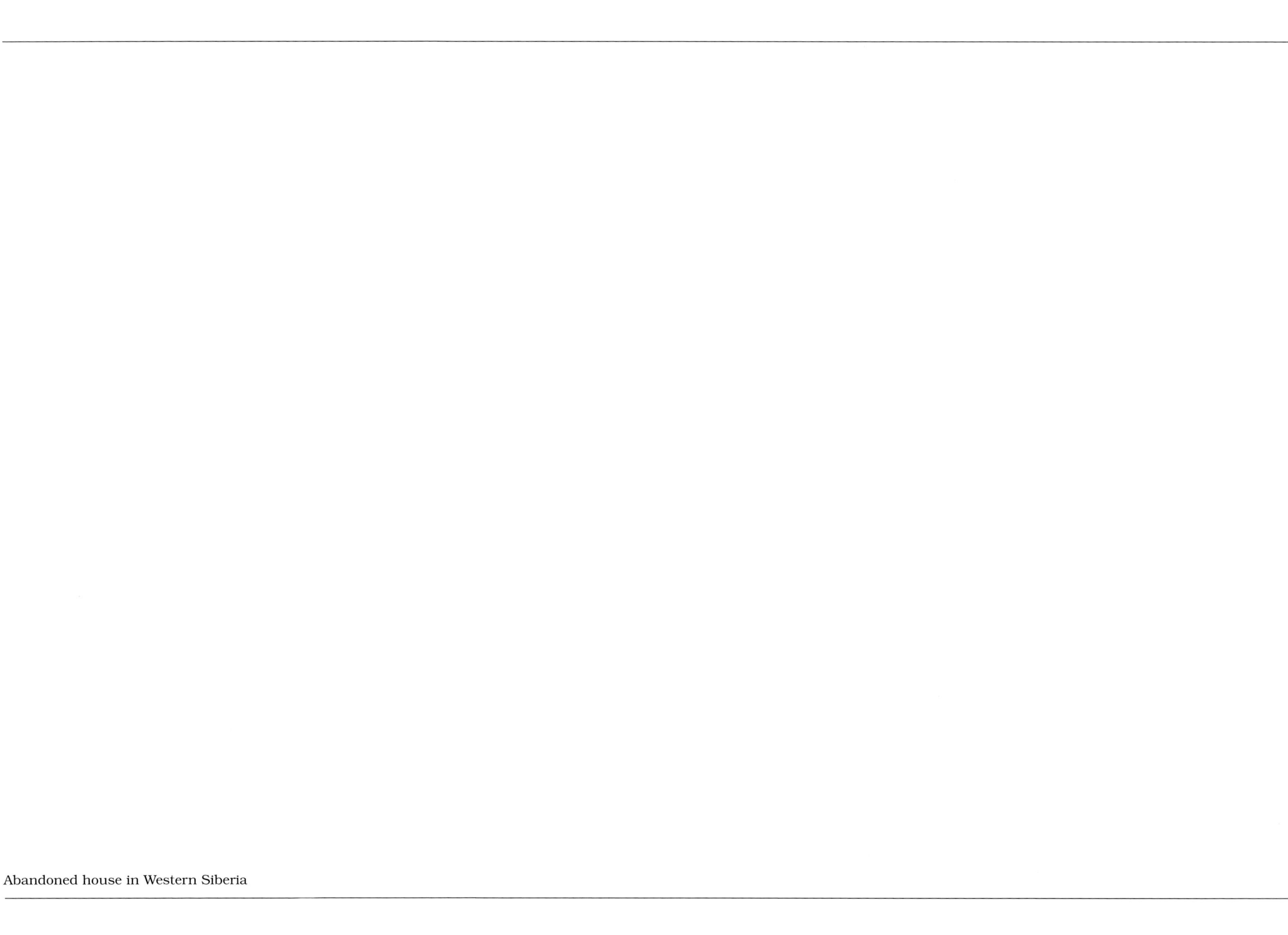

Abandoned house in Western Siberia

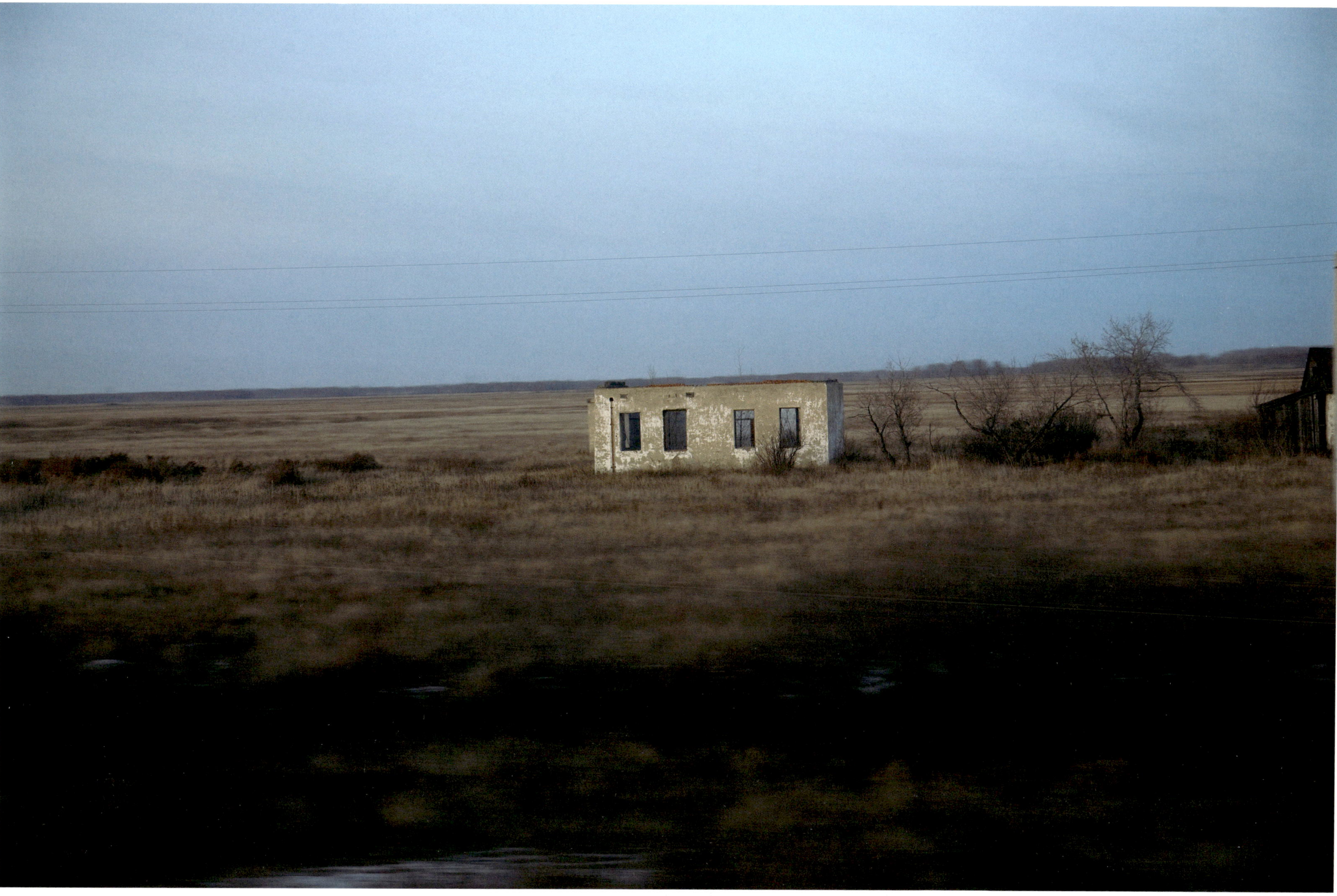

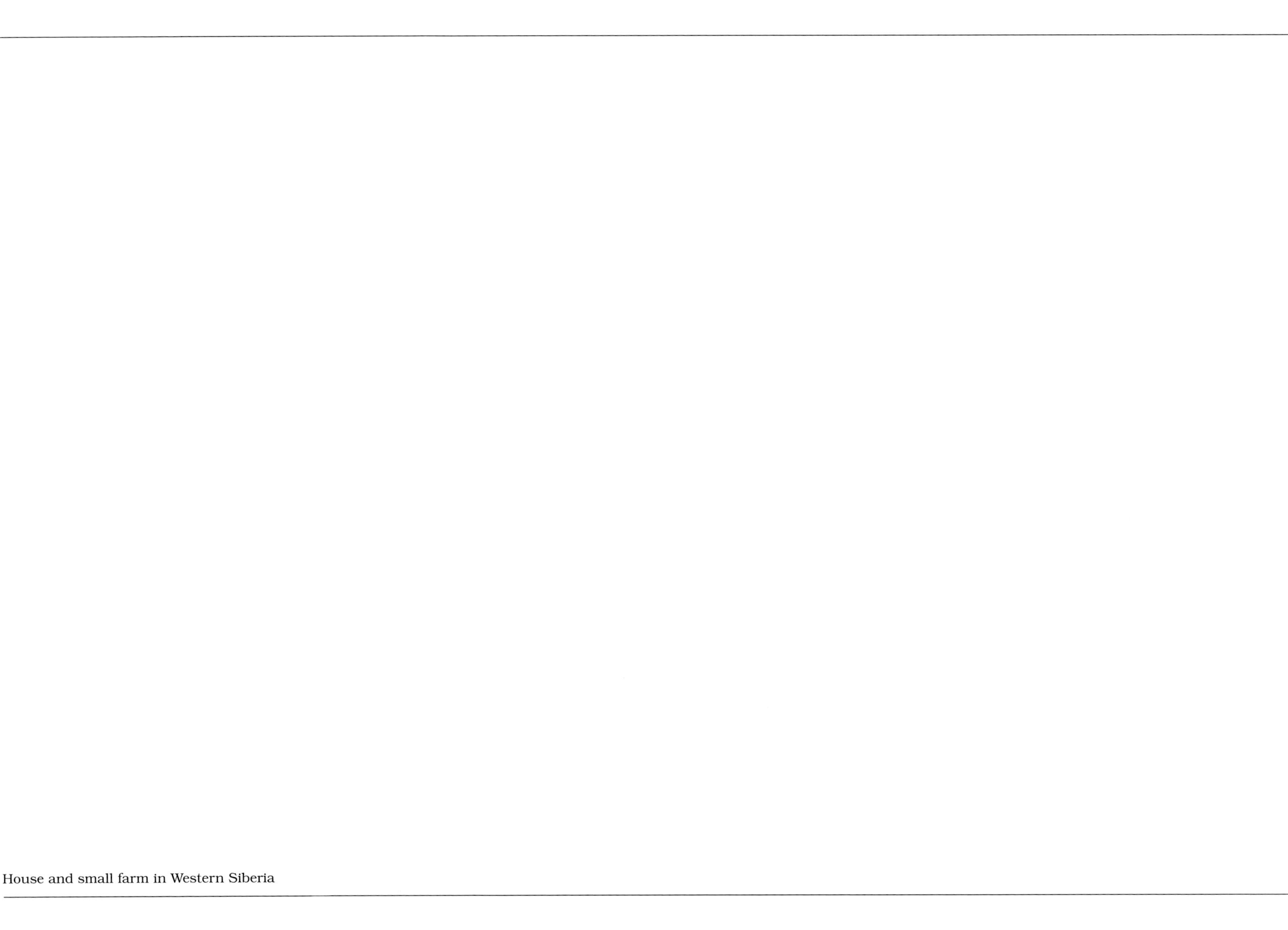

House and small farm in Western Siberia

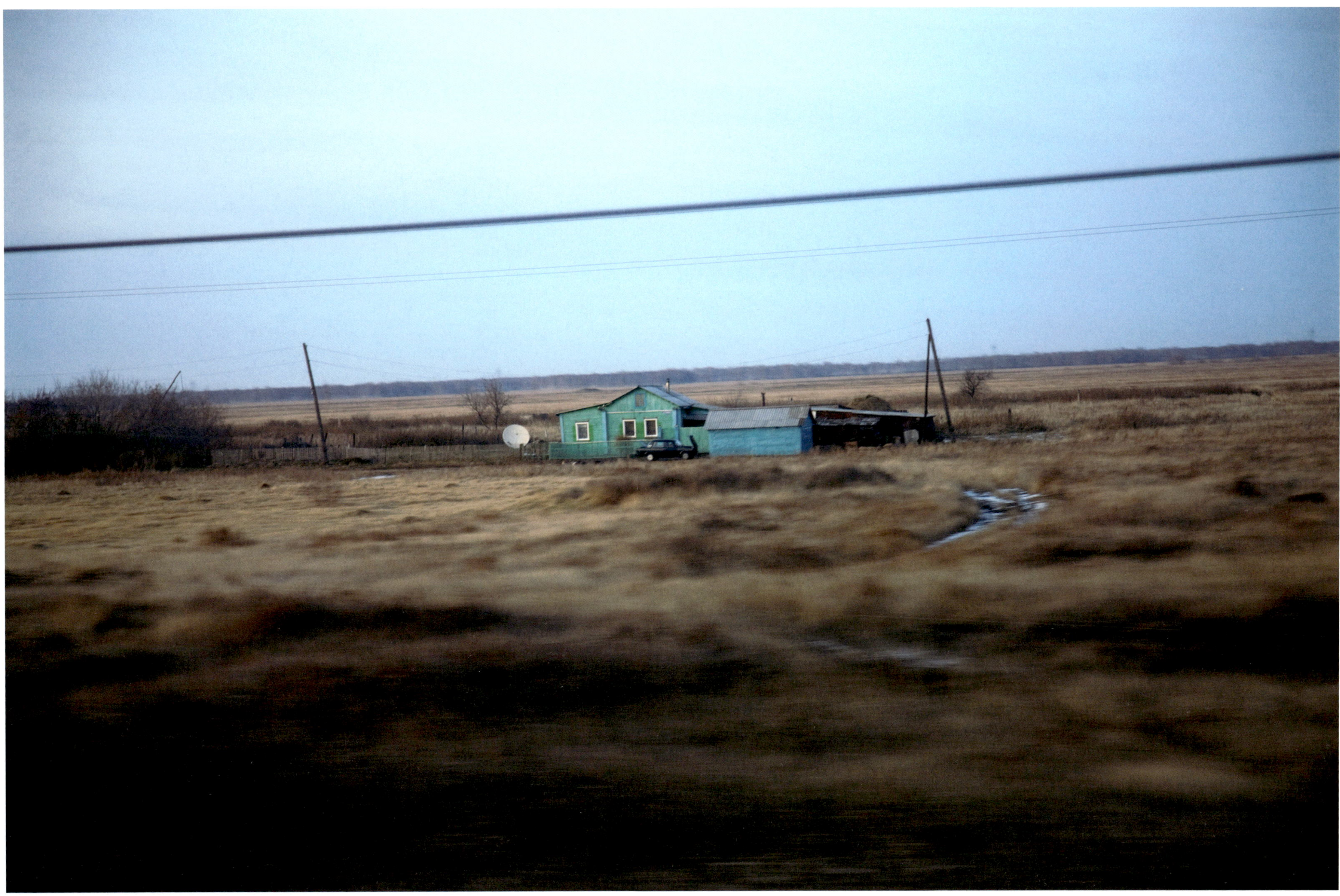

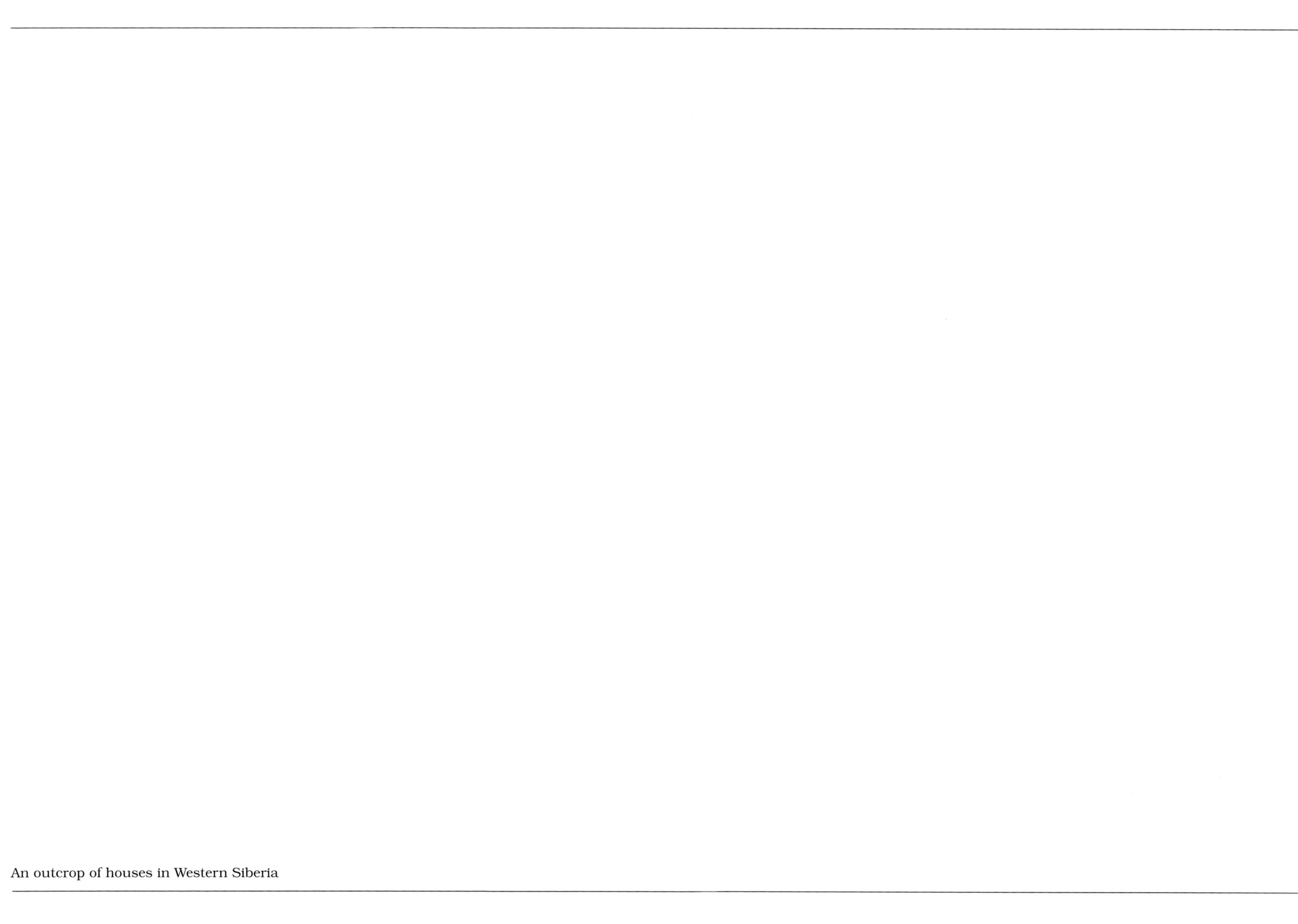

An outcrop of houses in Western Siberia

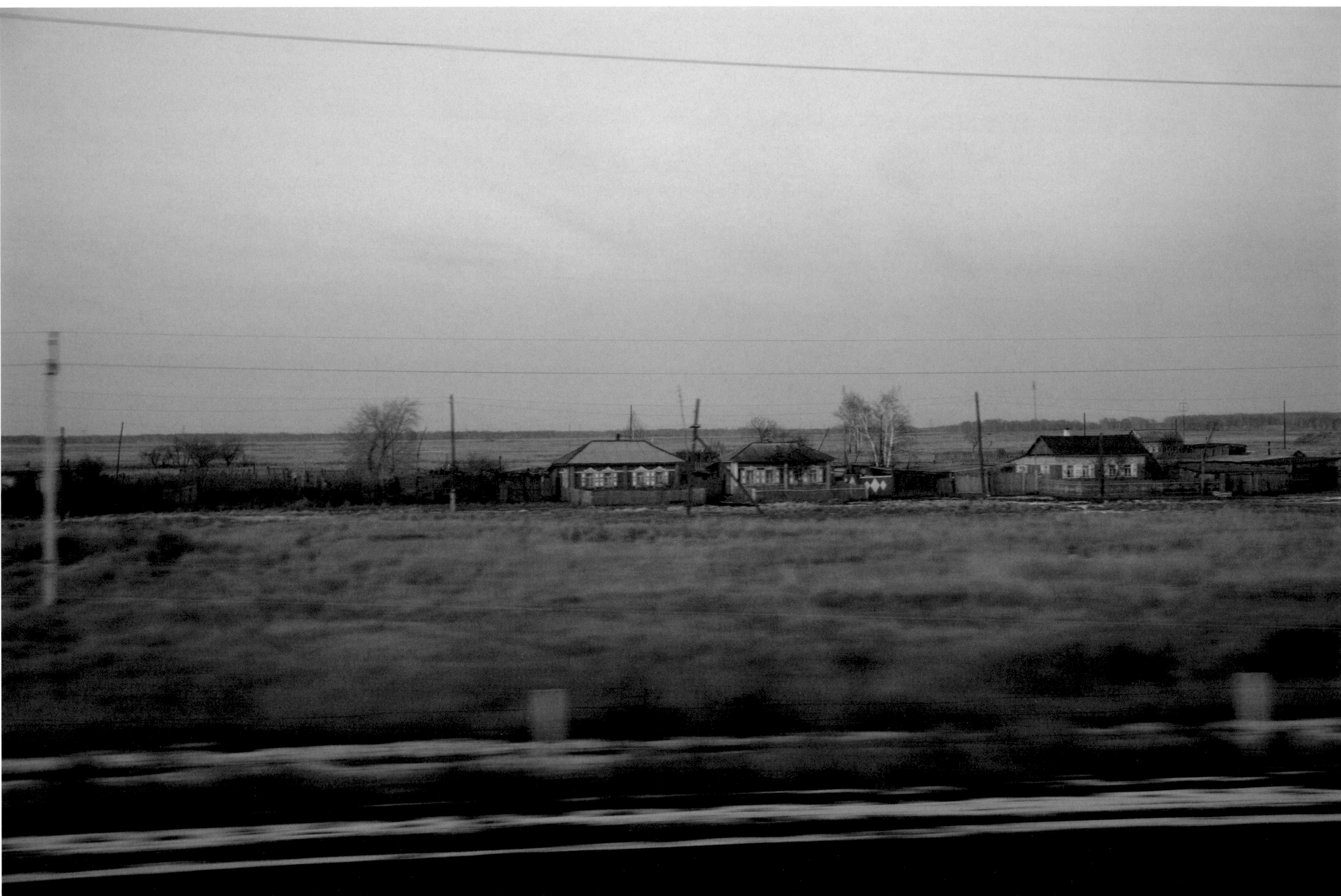

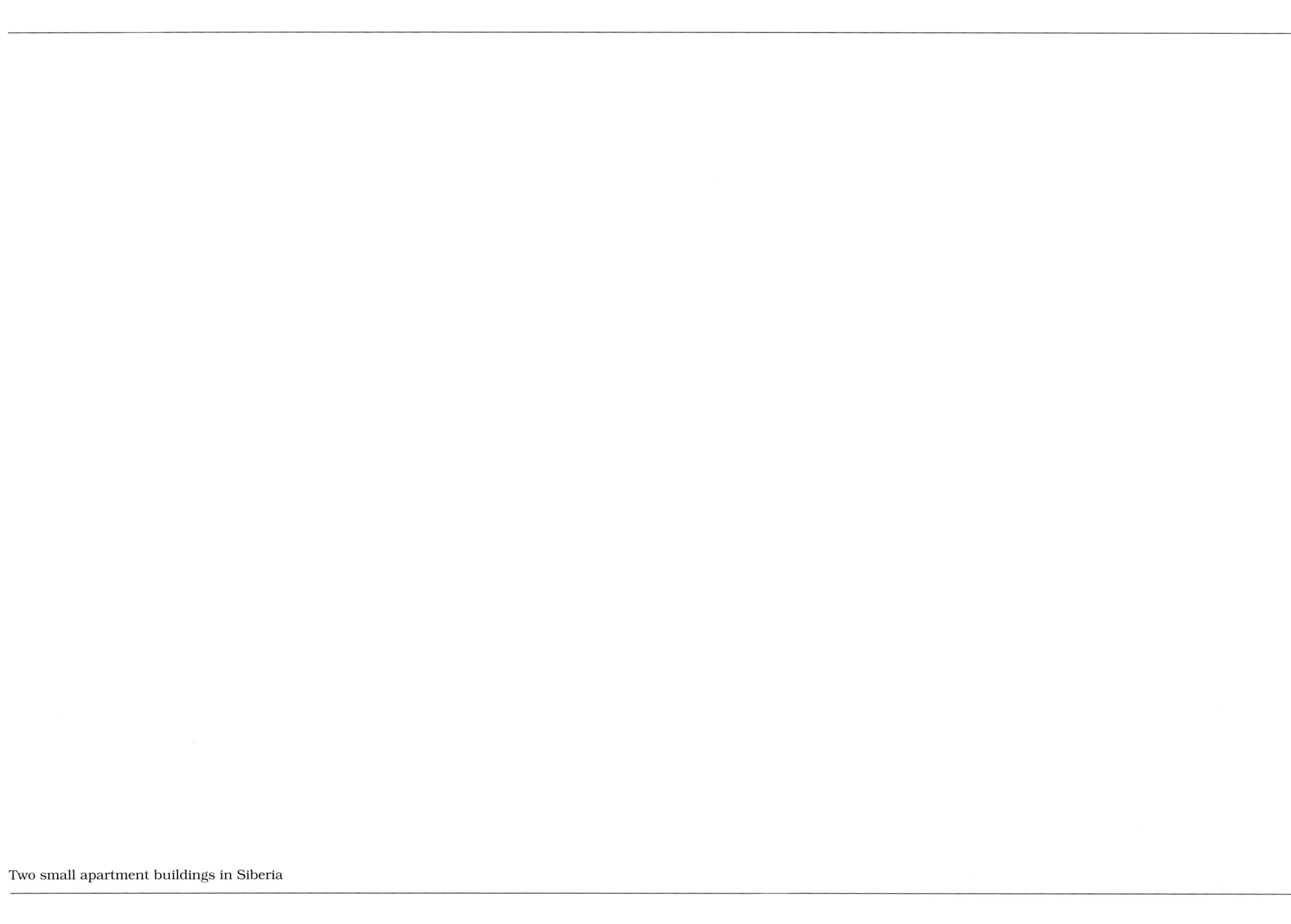

Two small apartment buildings in Siberia

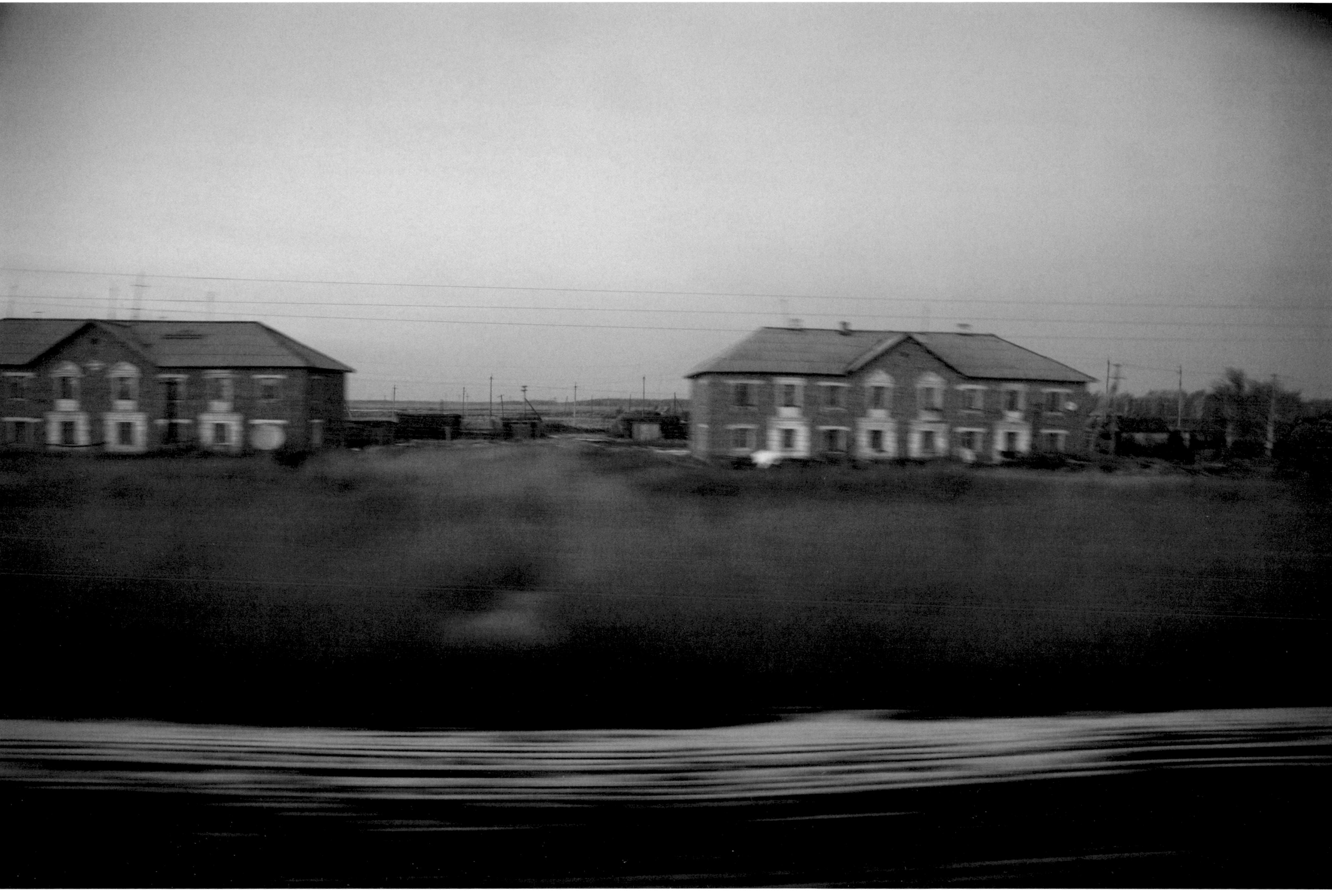

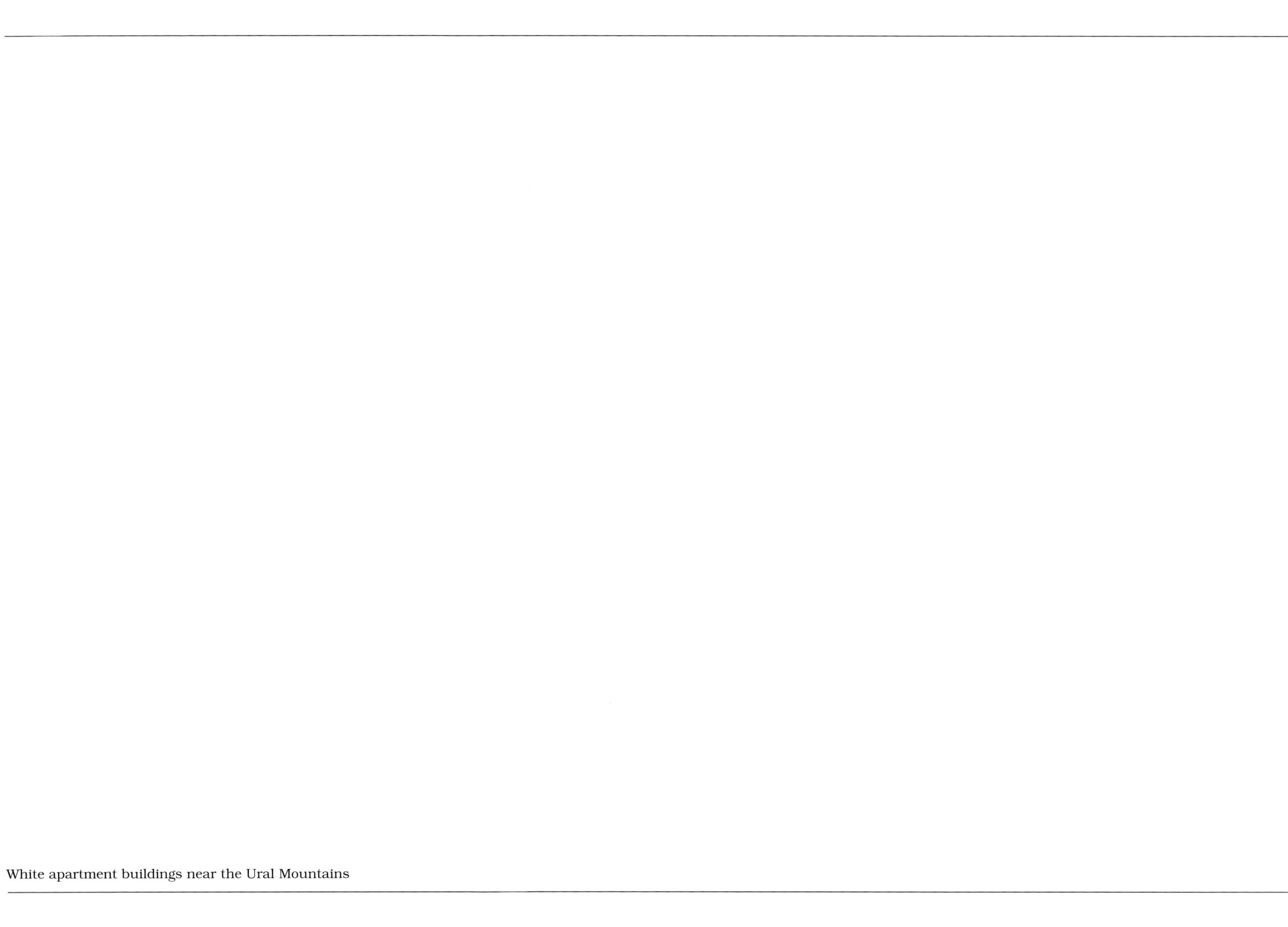

White apartment buildings near the Ural Mountains

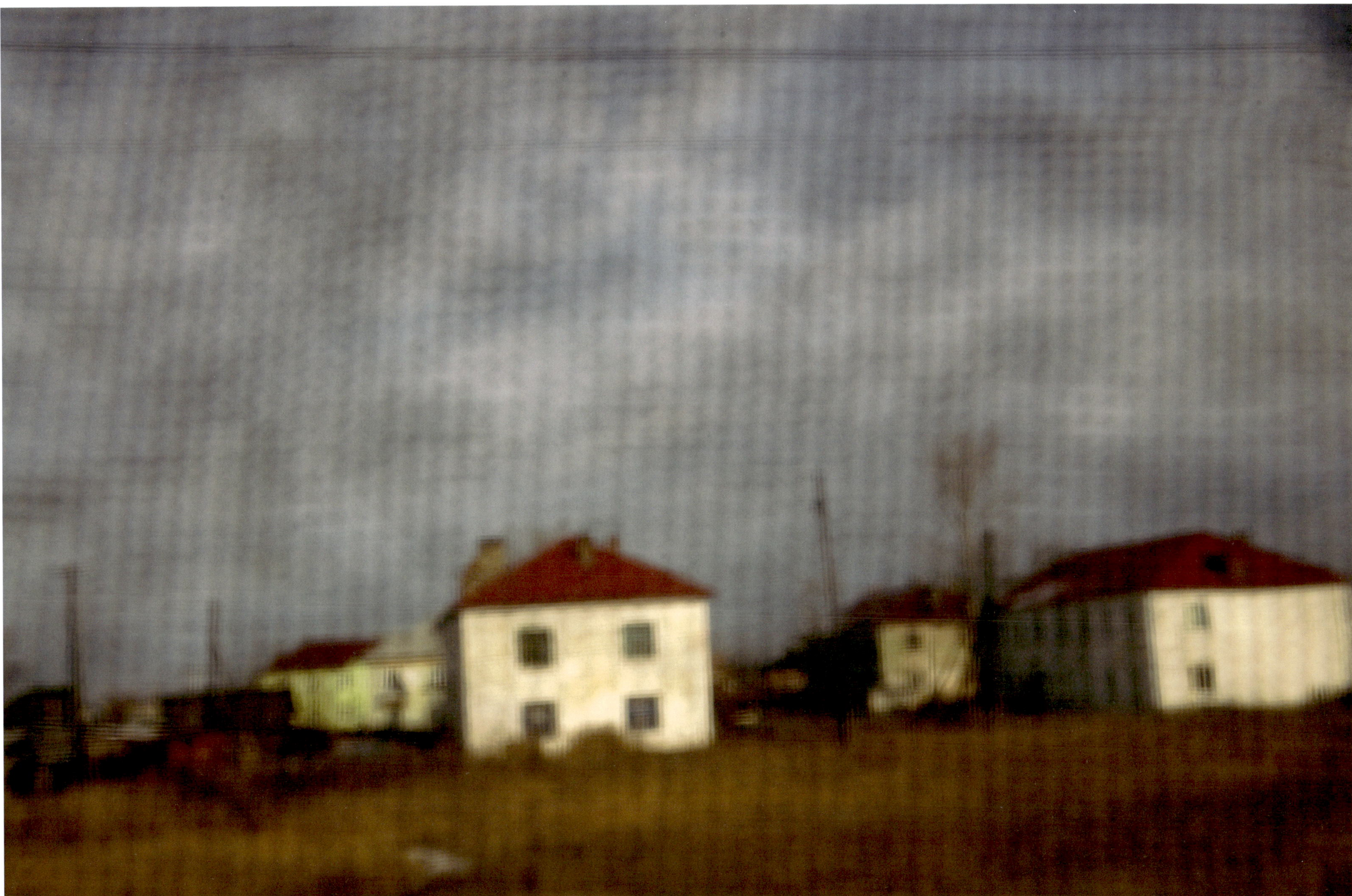

Factory near the Urals

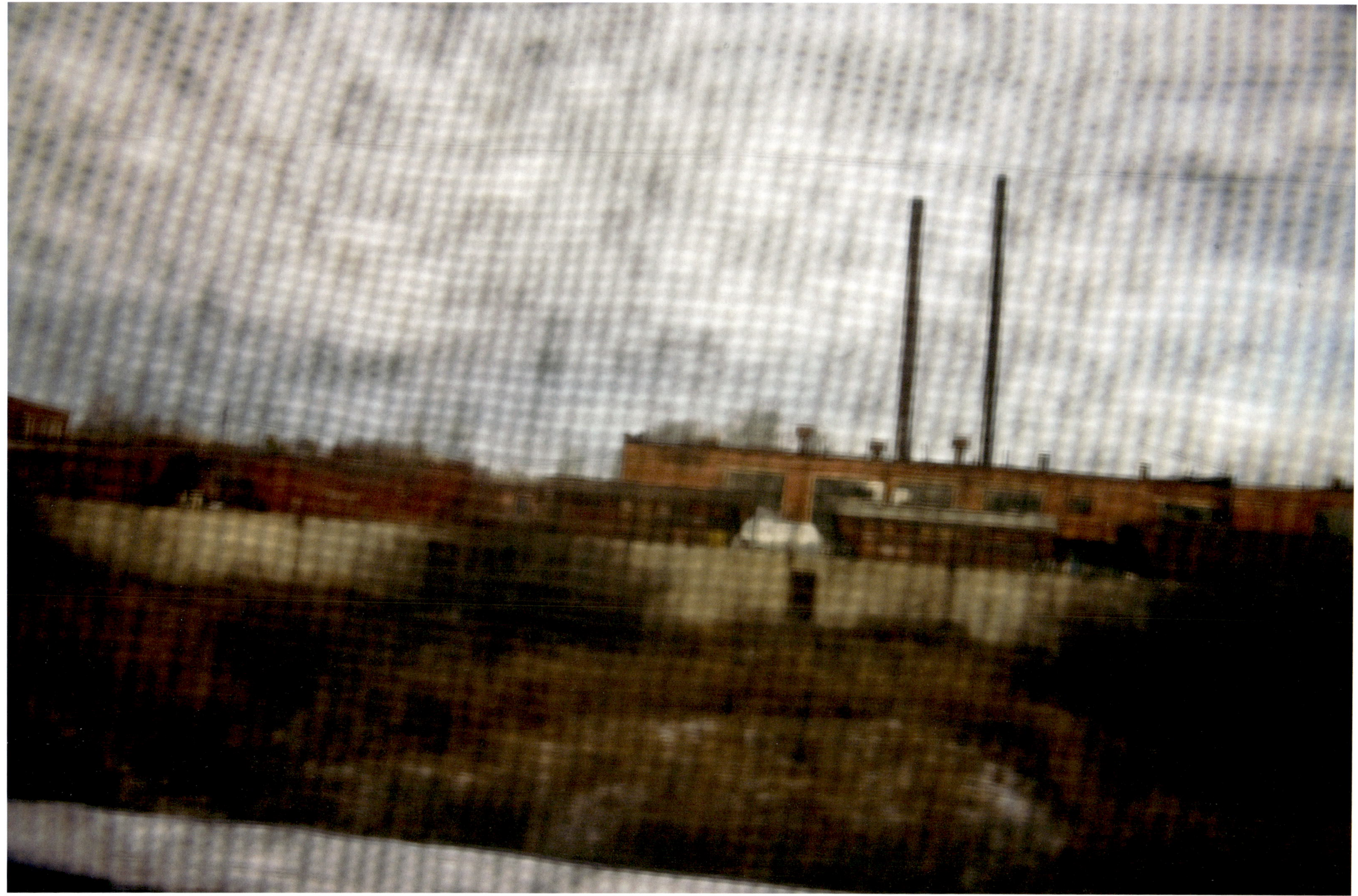

Small city near the Urals

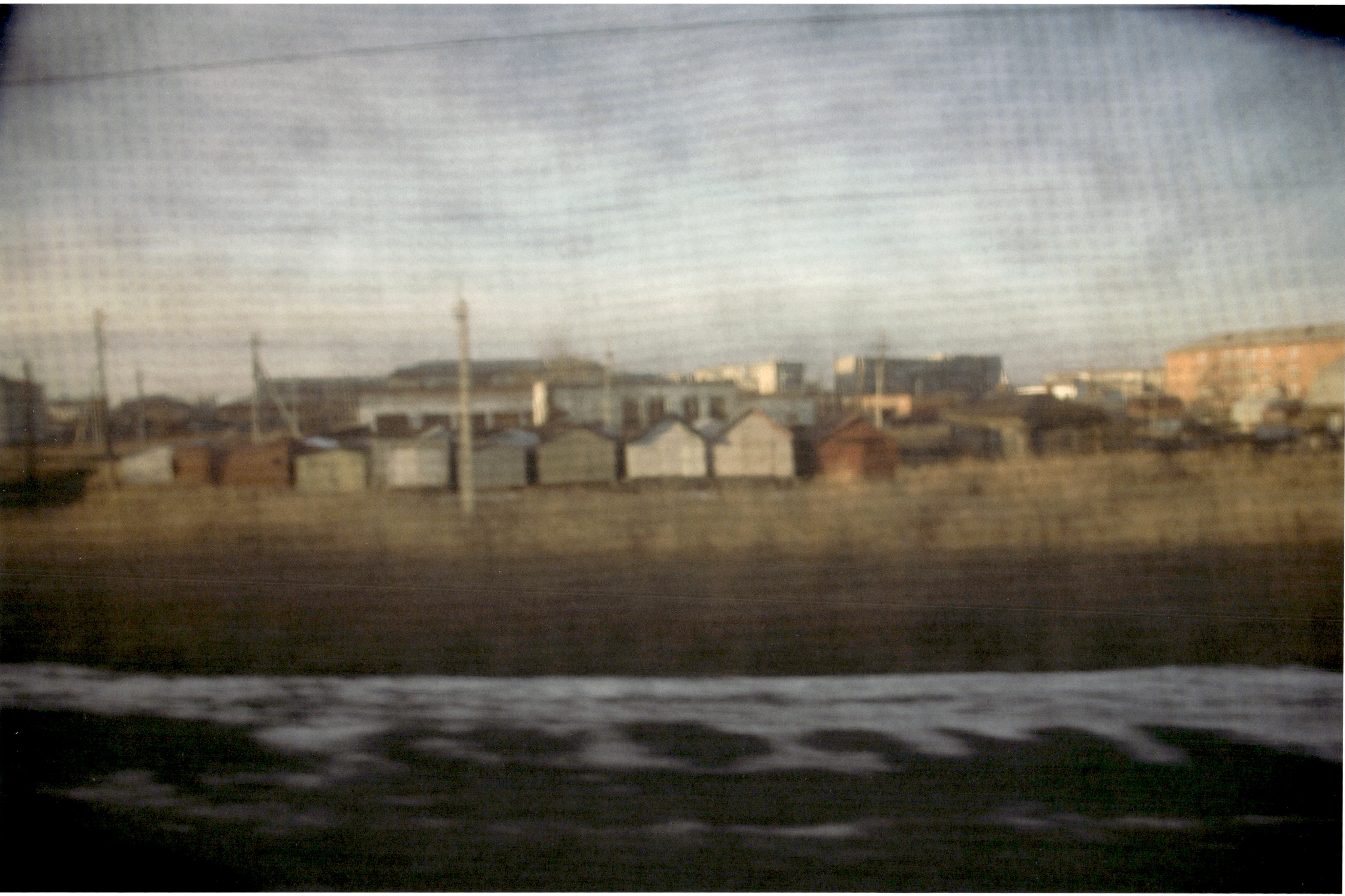

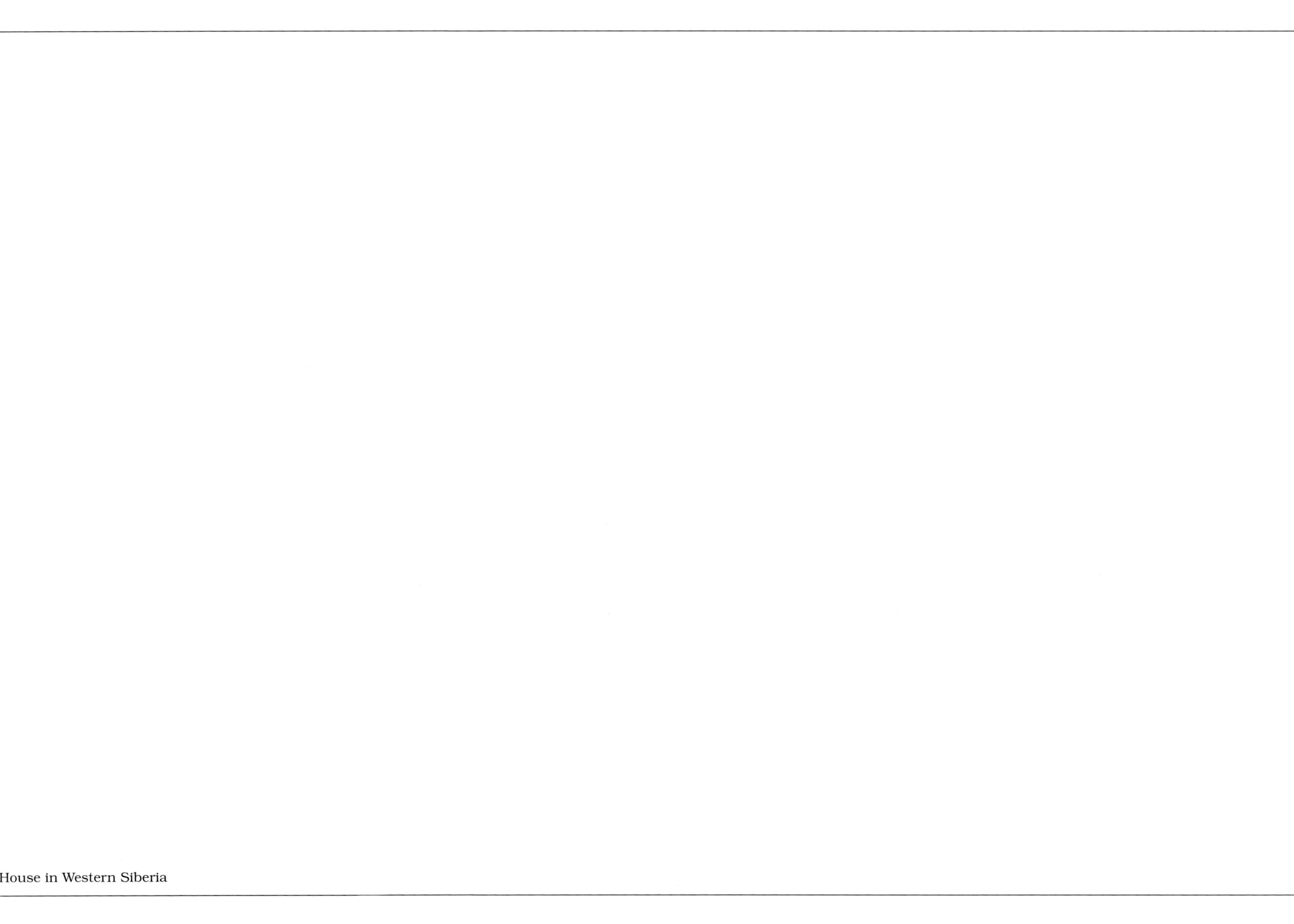

House in Western Siberia

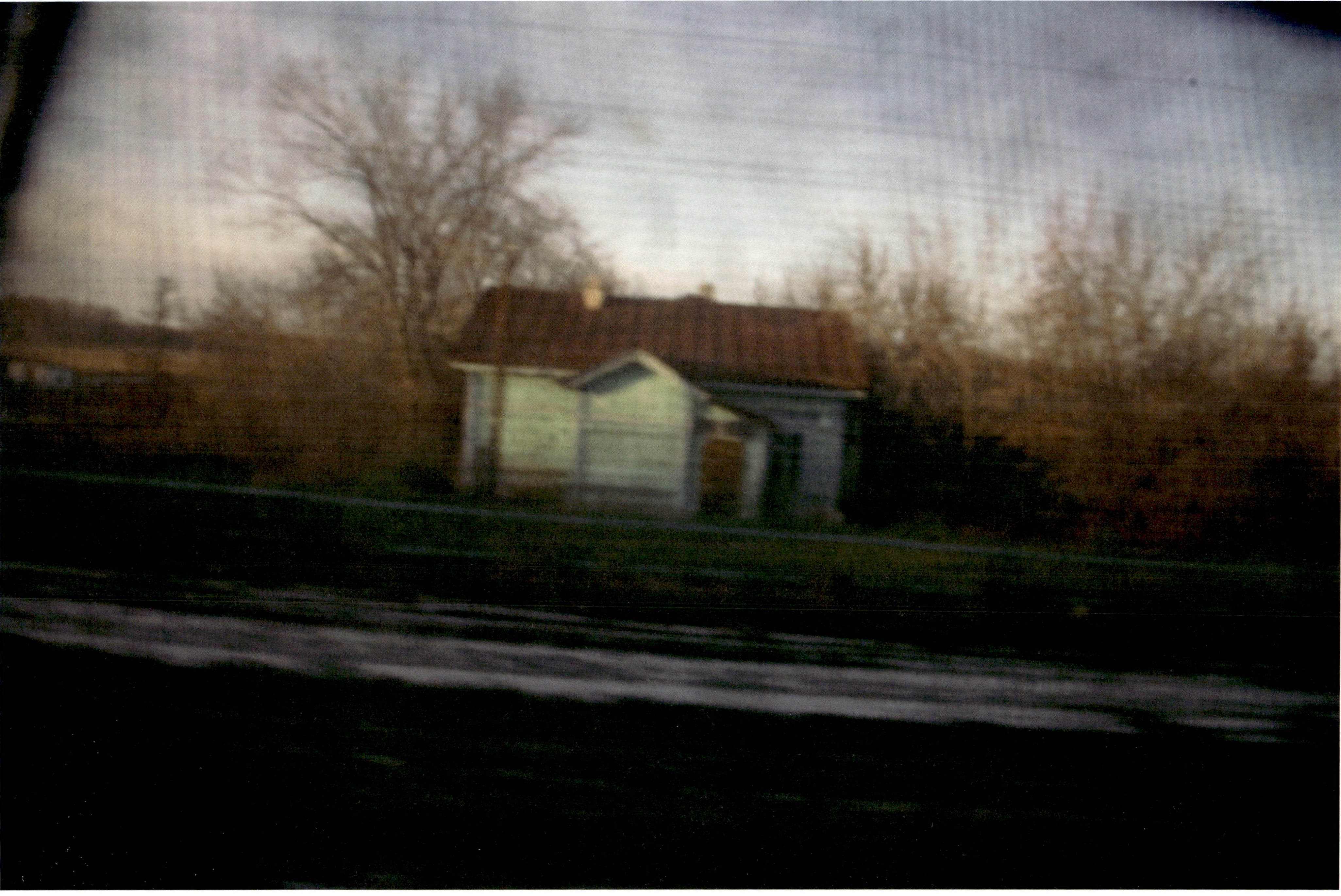

Snowy street corner in Siberia

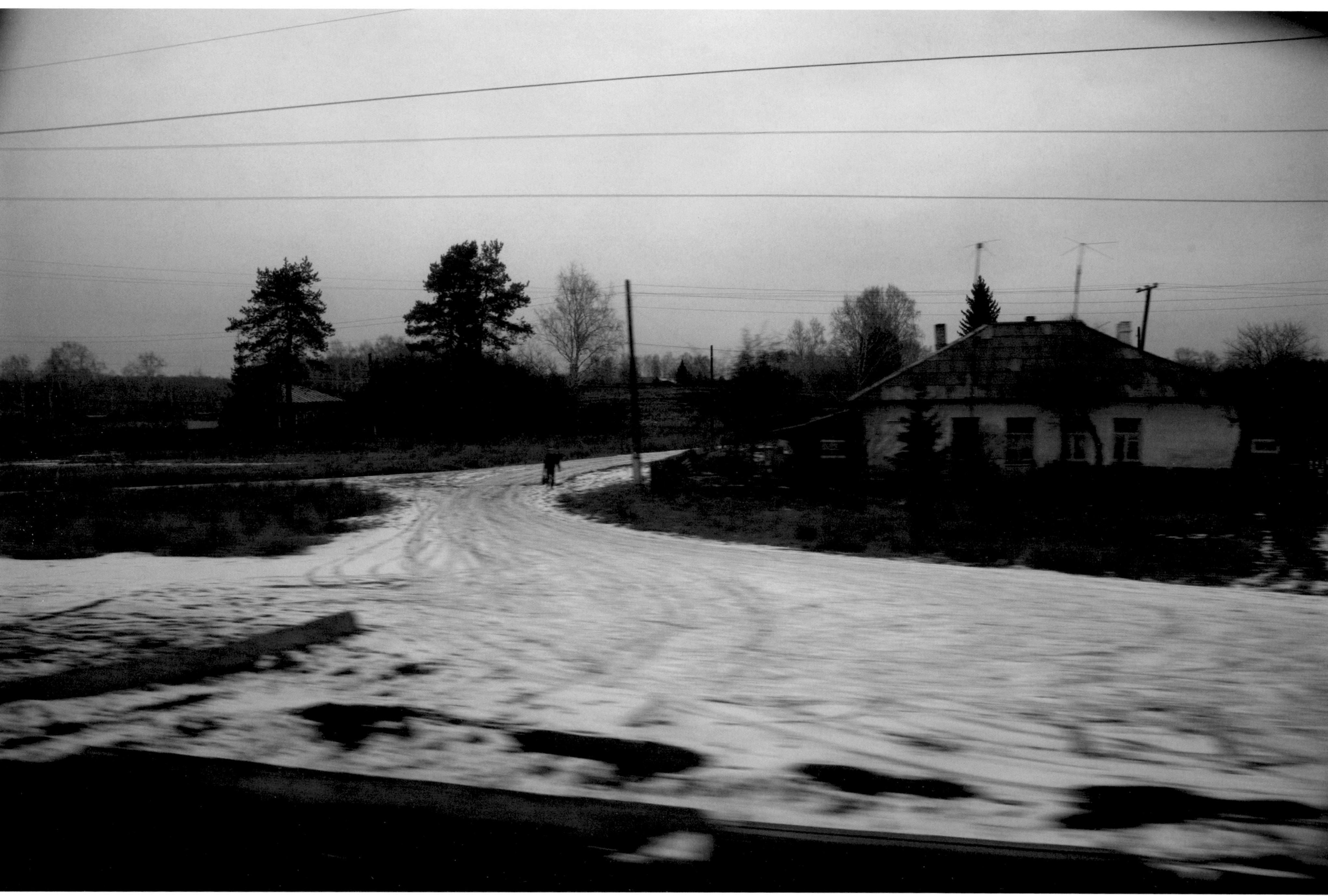

Lone house in Central Russia

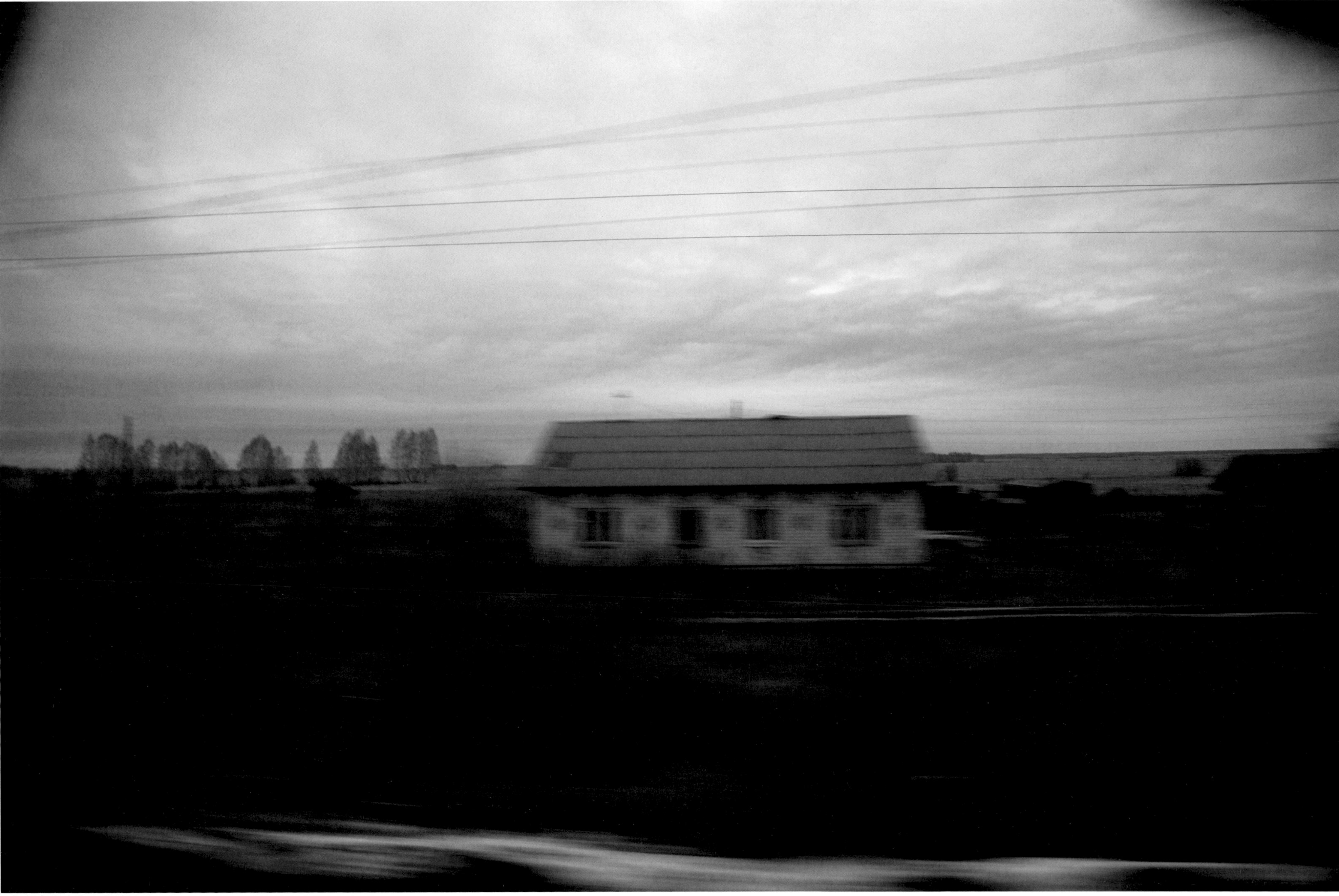

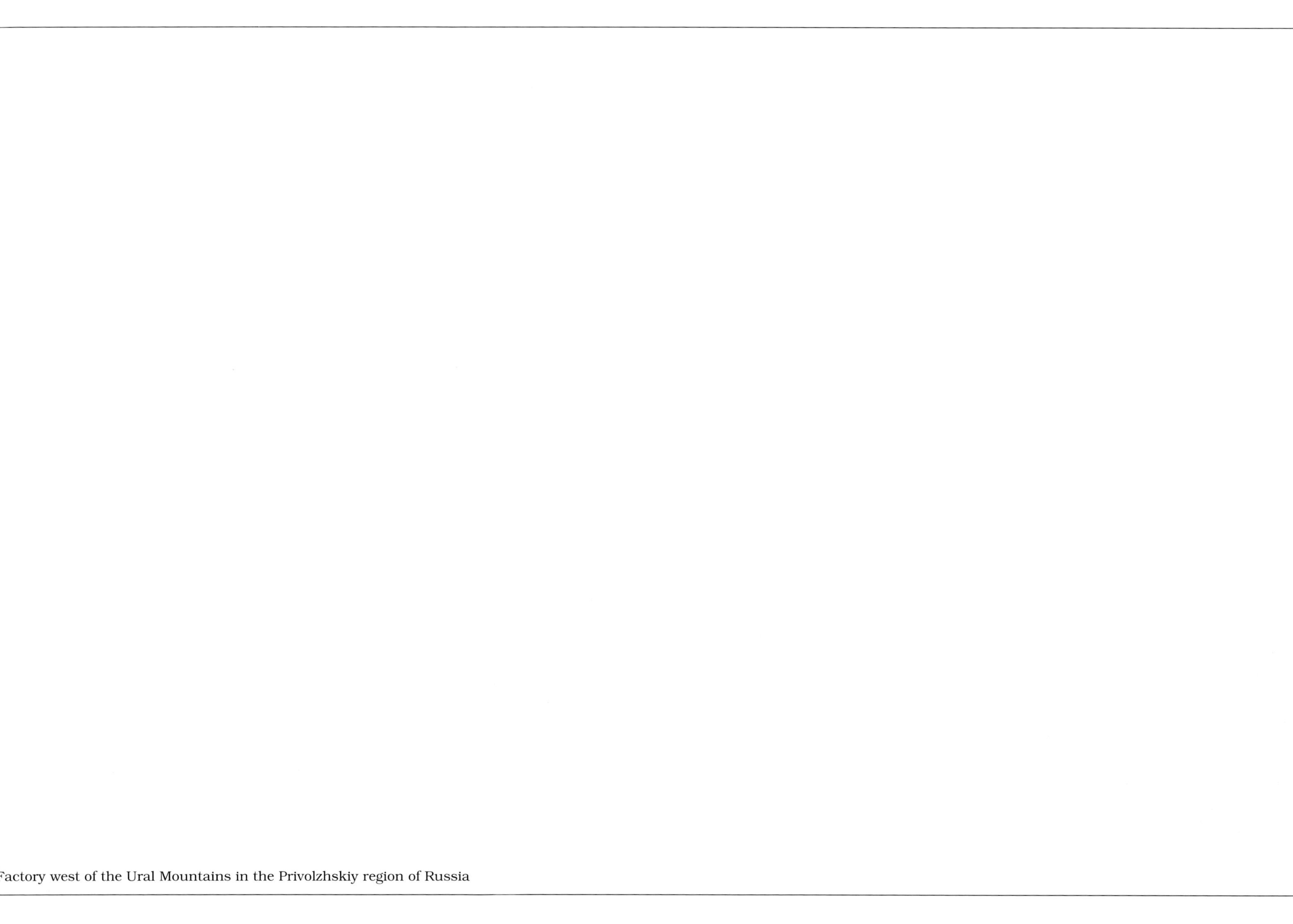

Factory west of the Ural Mountains in the Privolzhskiy region of Russia

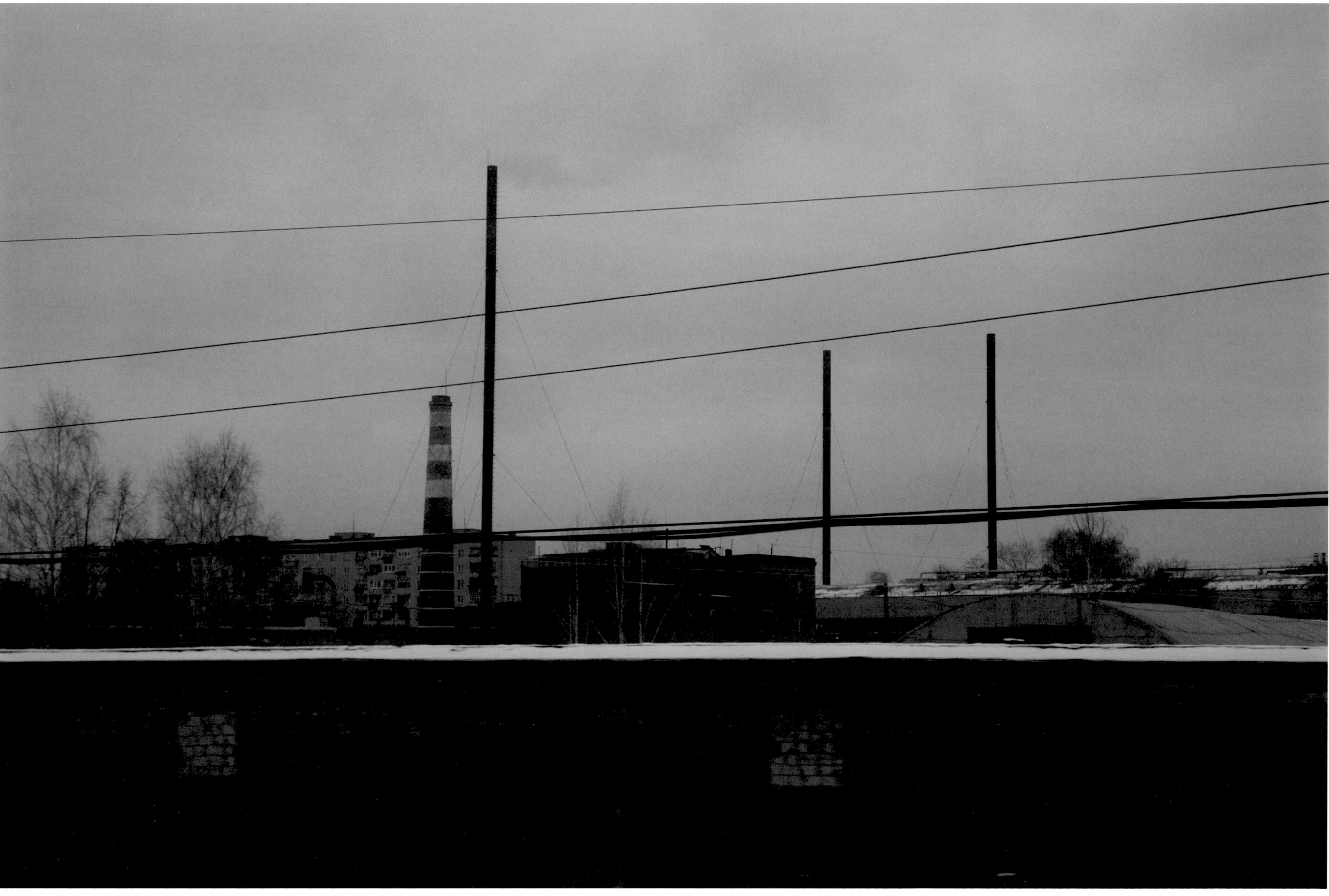

Factory ruins in Central Russia

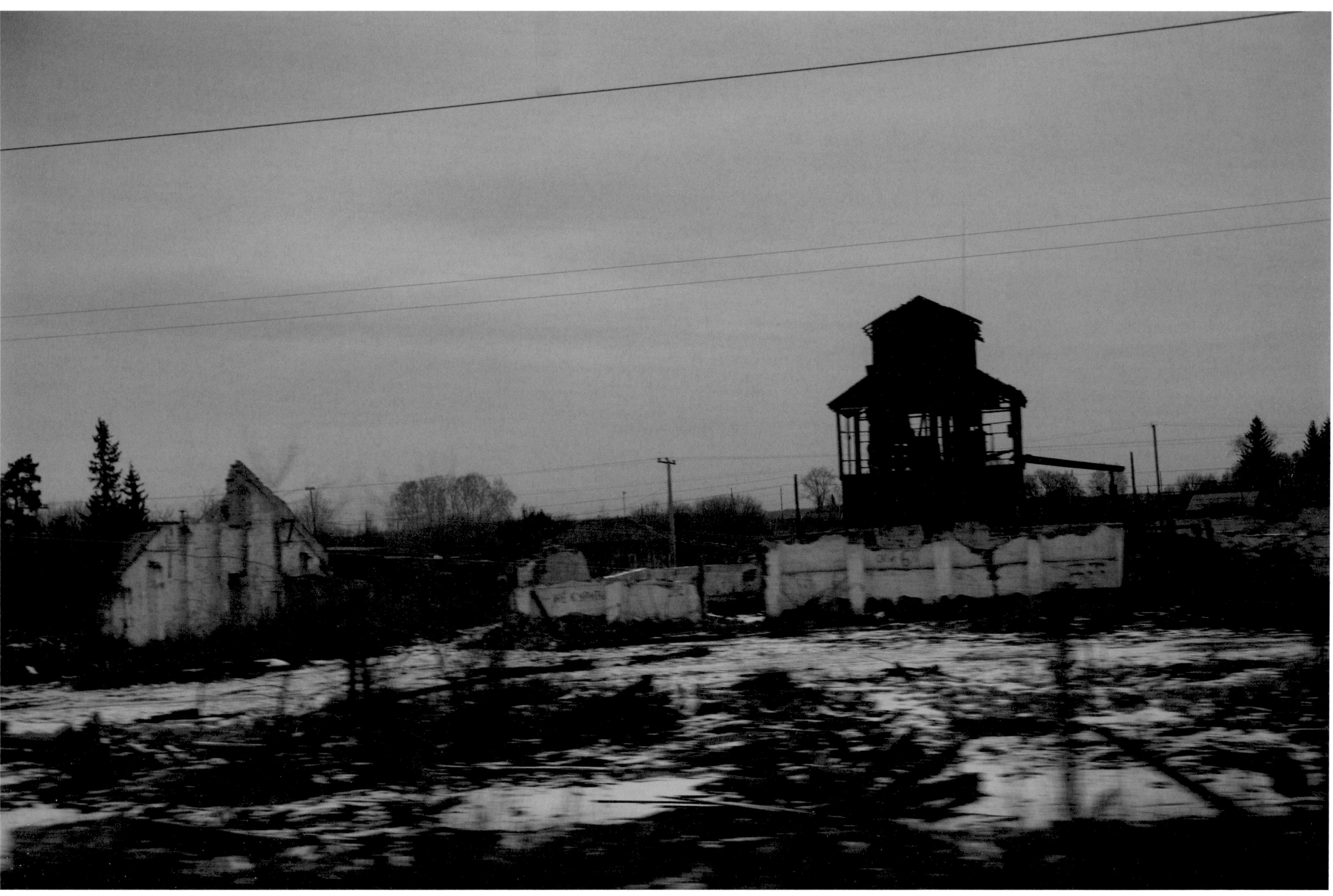

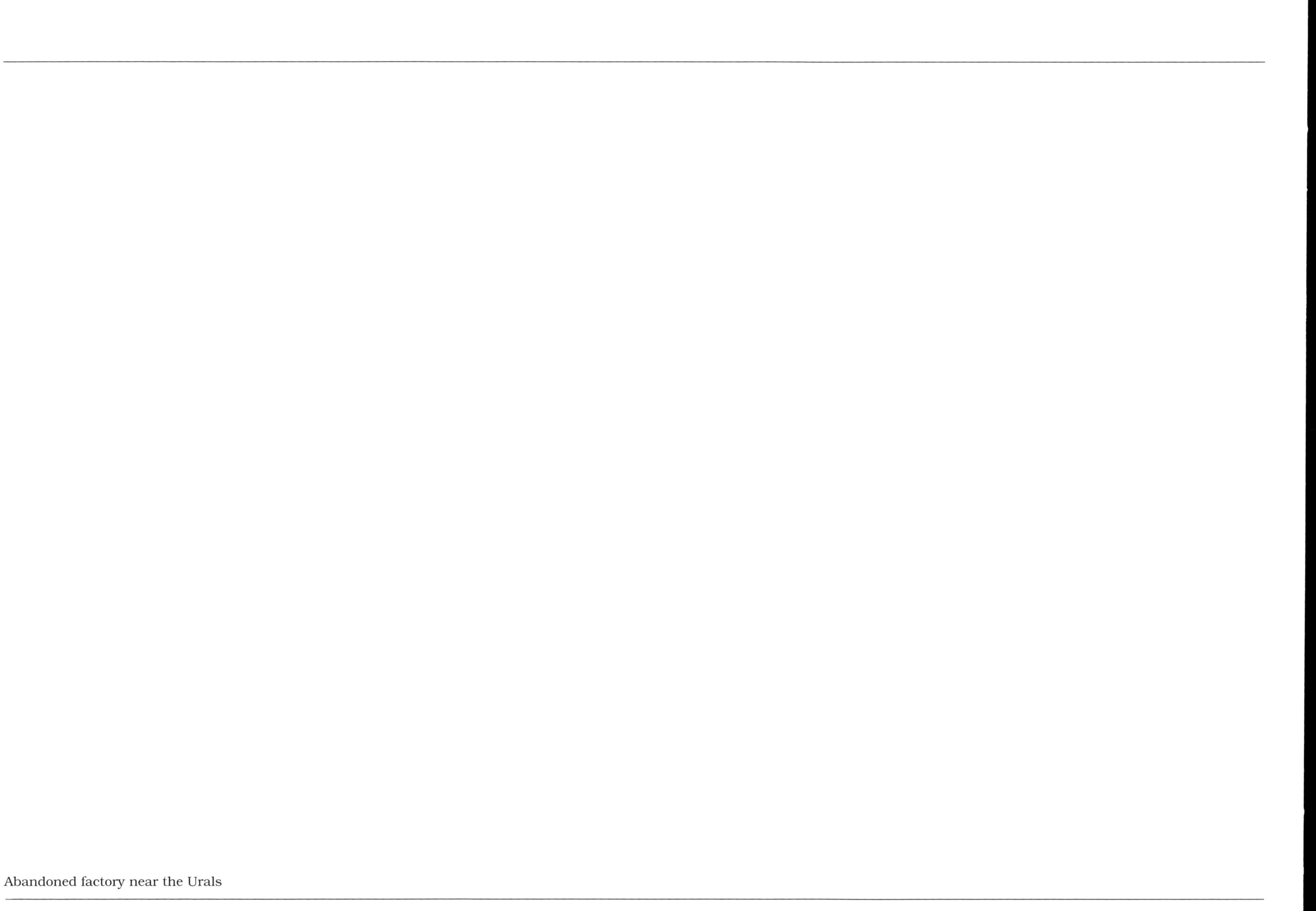

Abandoned factory near the Urals

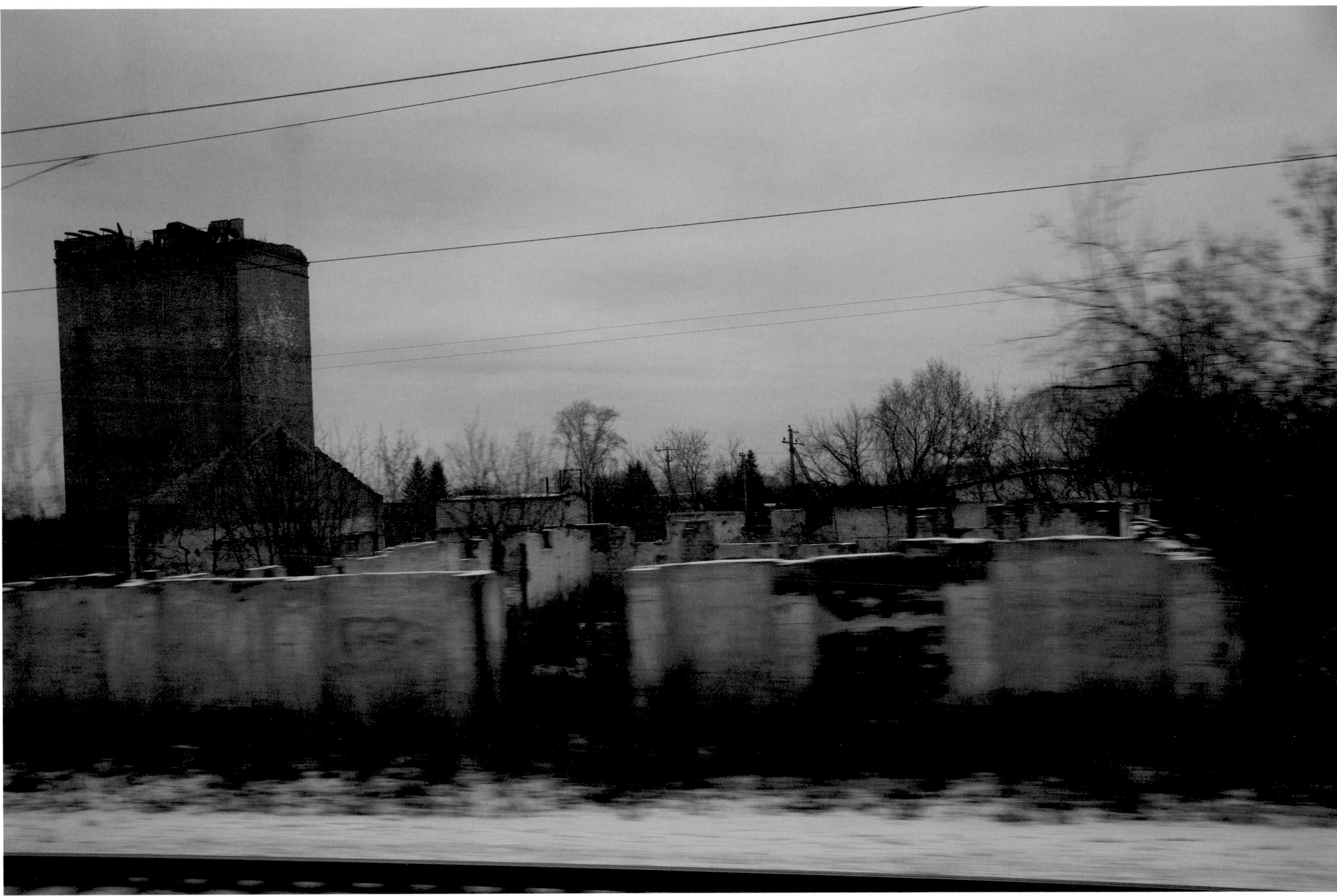

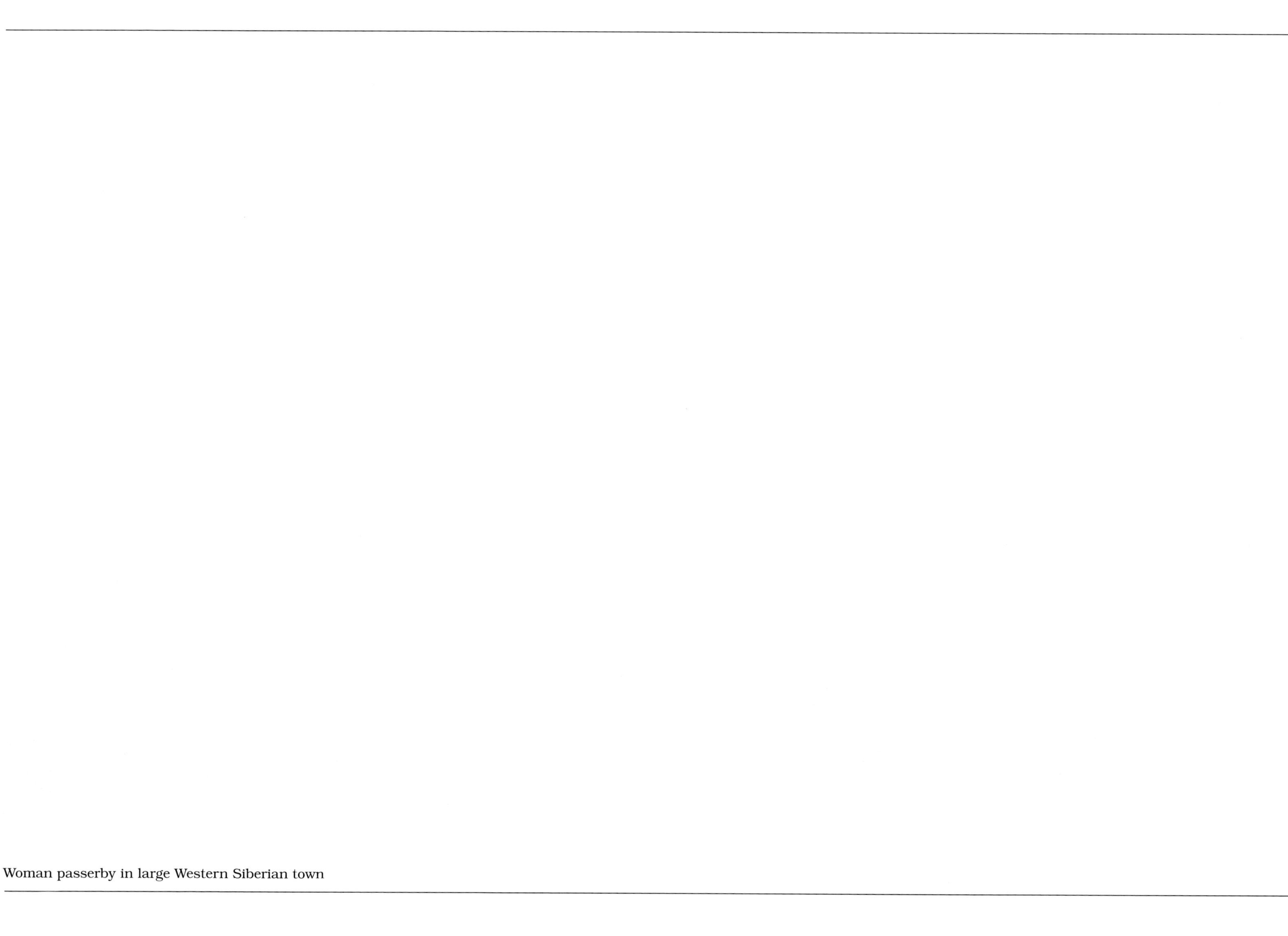

Woman passerby in large Western Siberian town

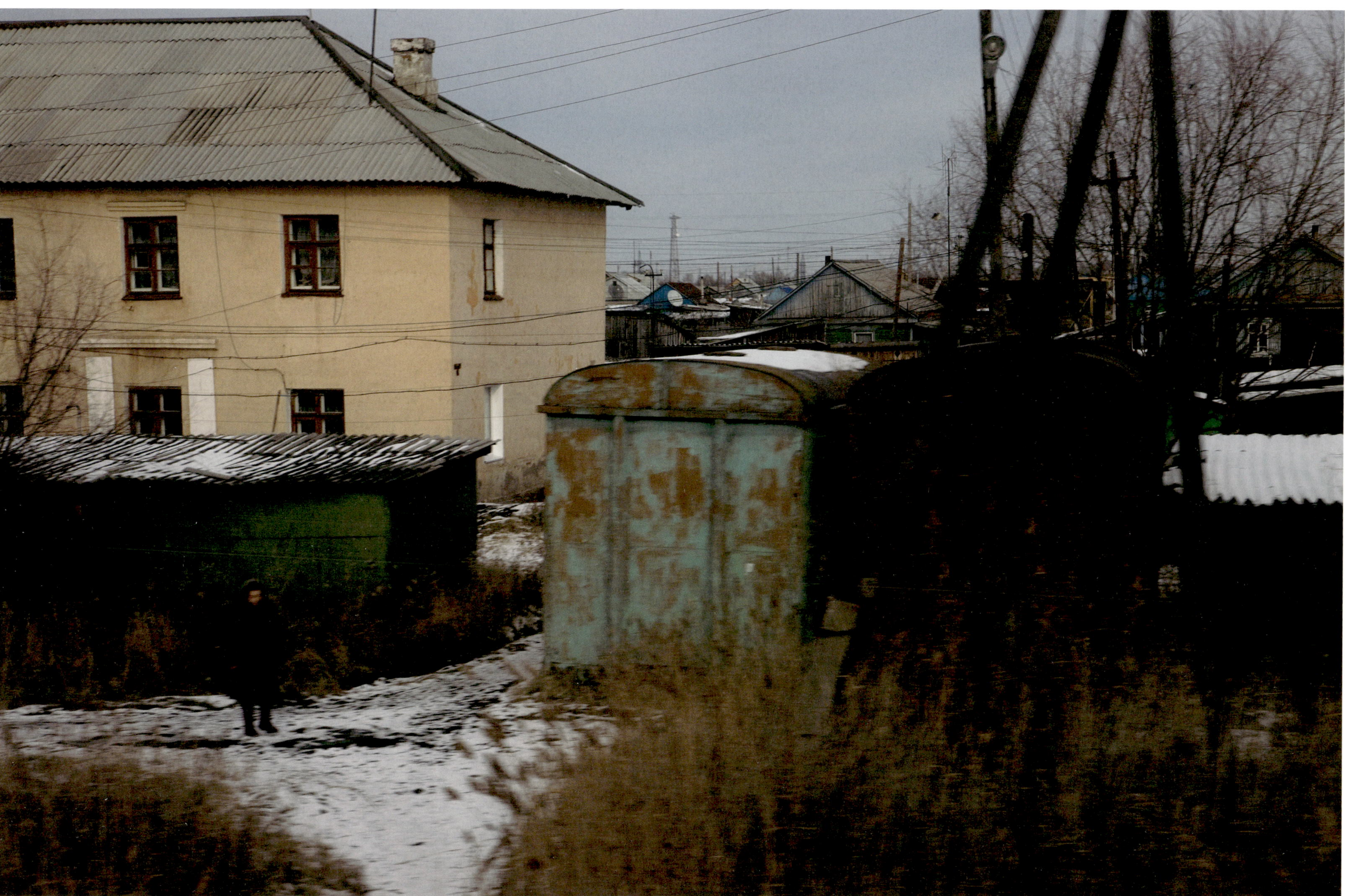

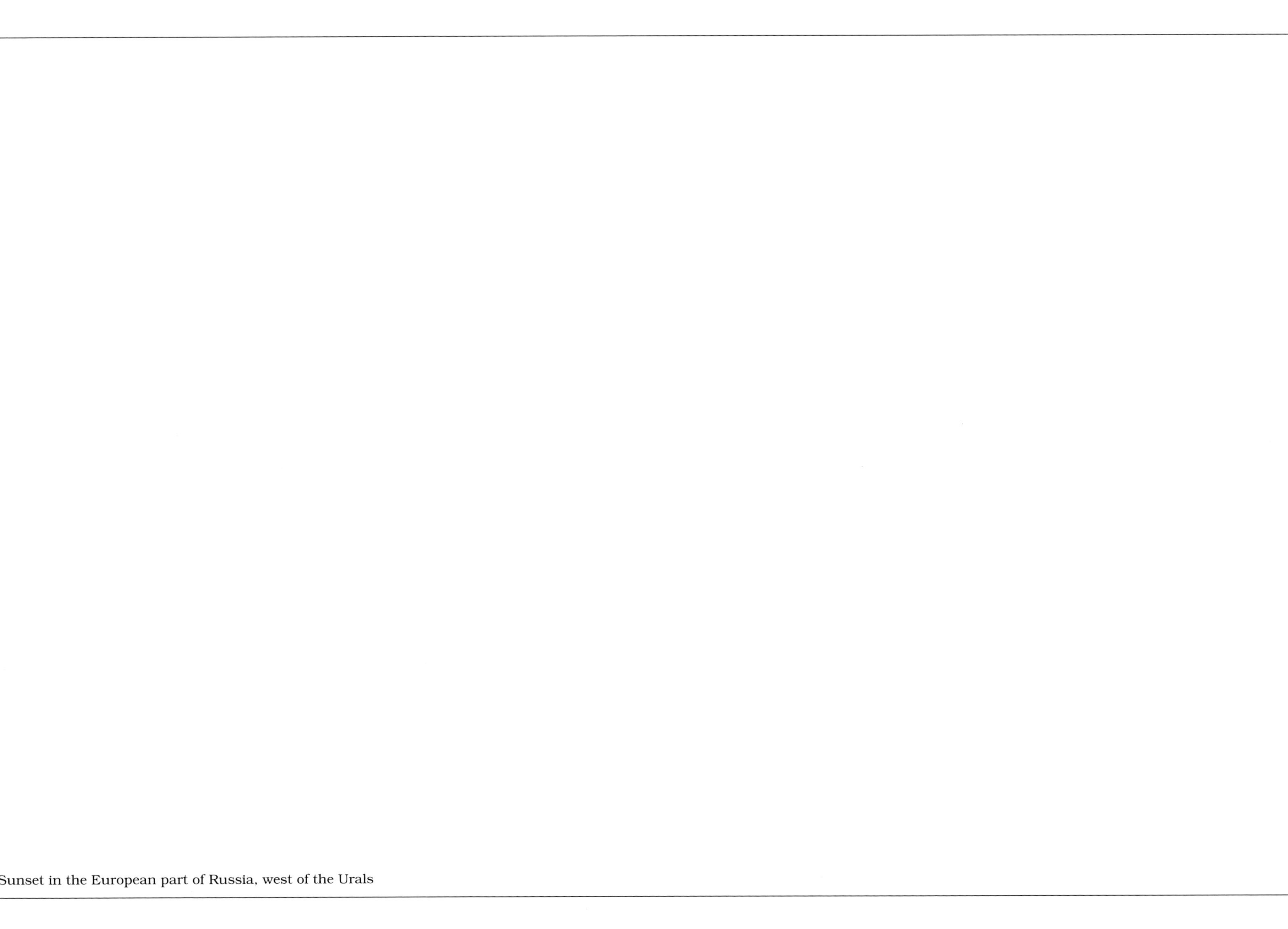

Sunset in the European part of Russia, west of the Urals

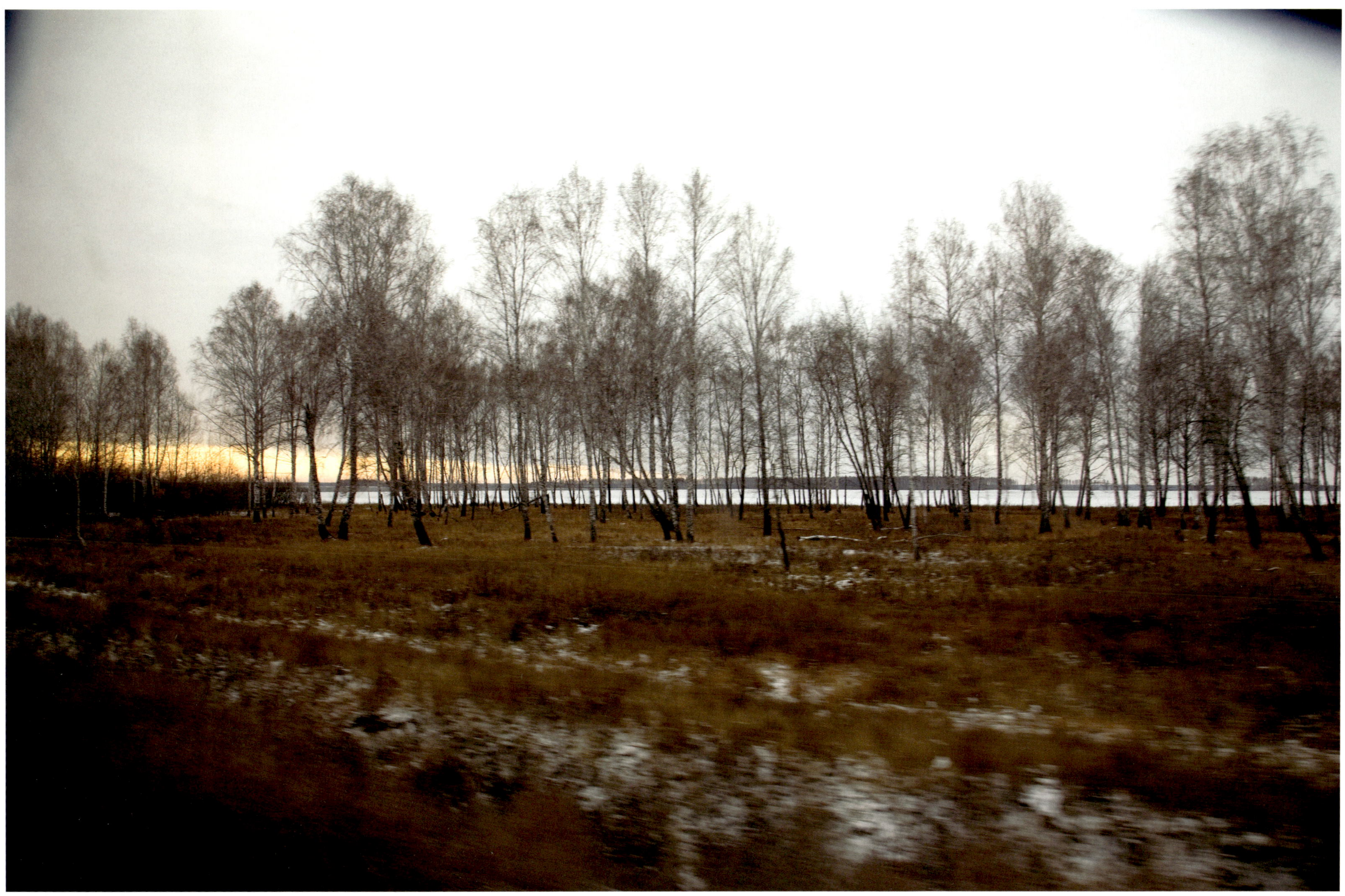

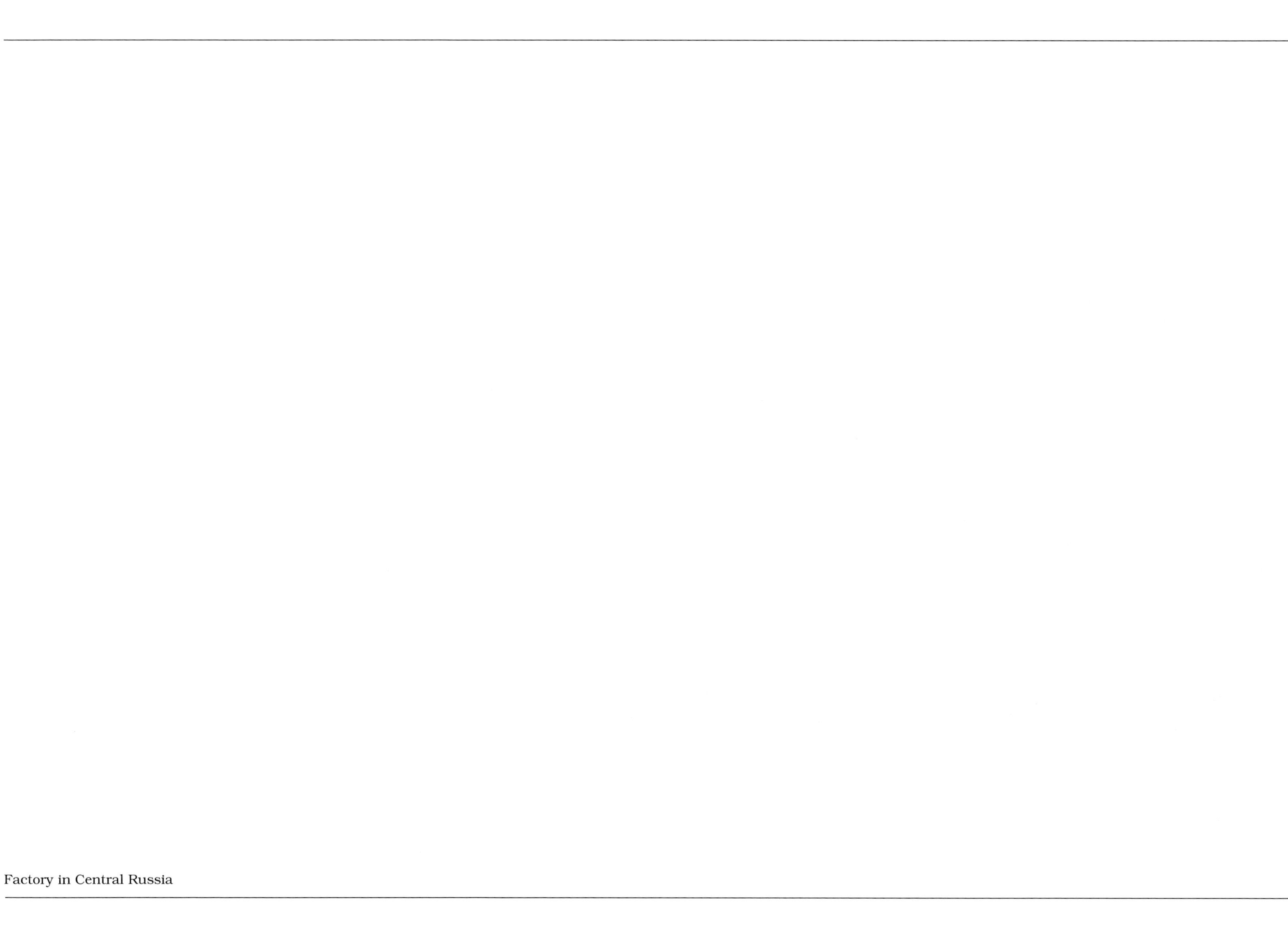

Factory in Central Russia

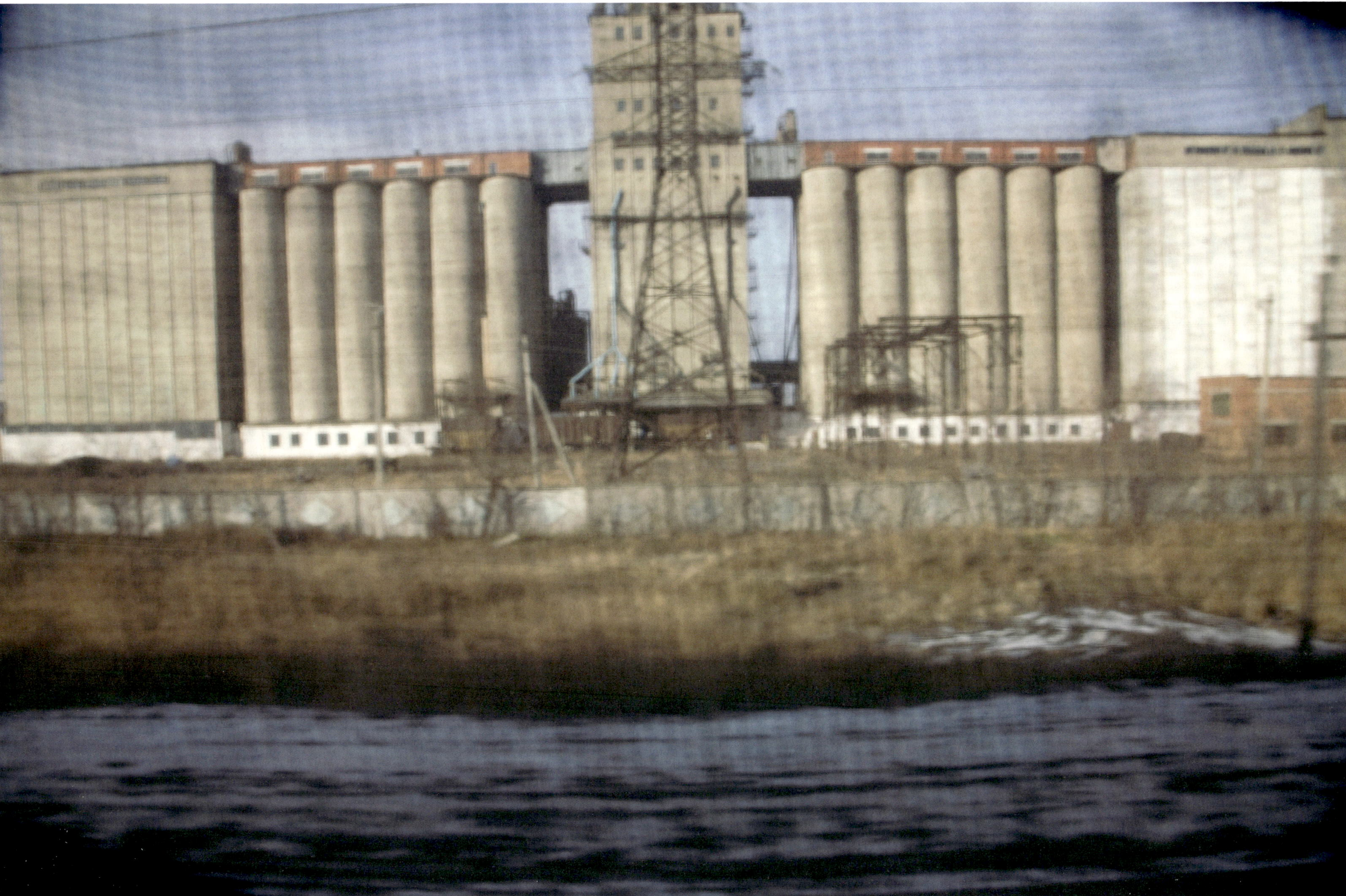

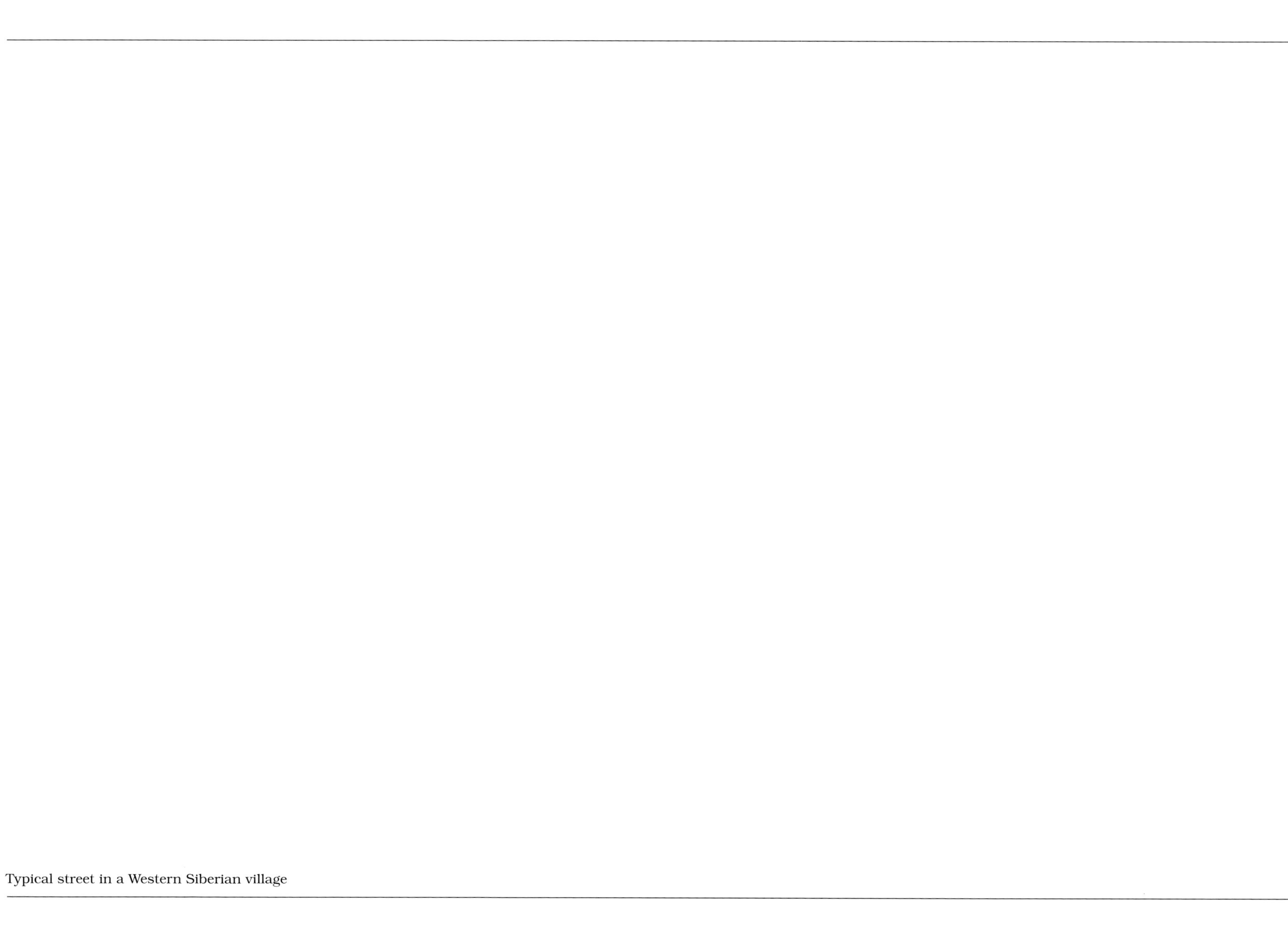

Typical street in a Western Siberian village

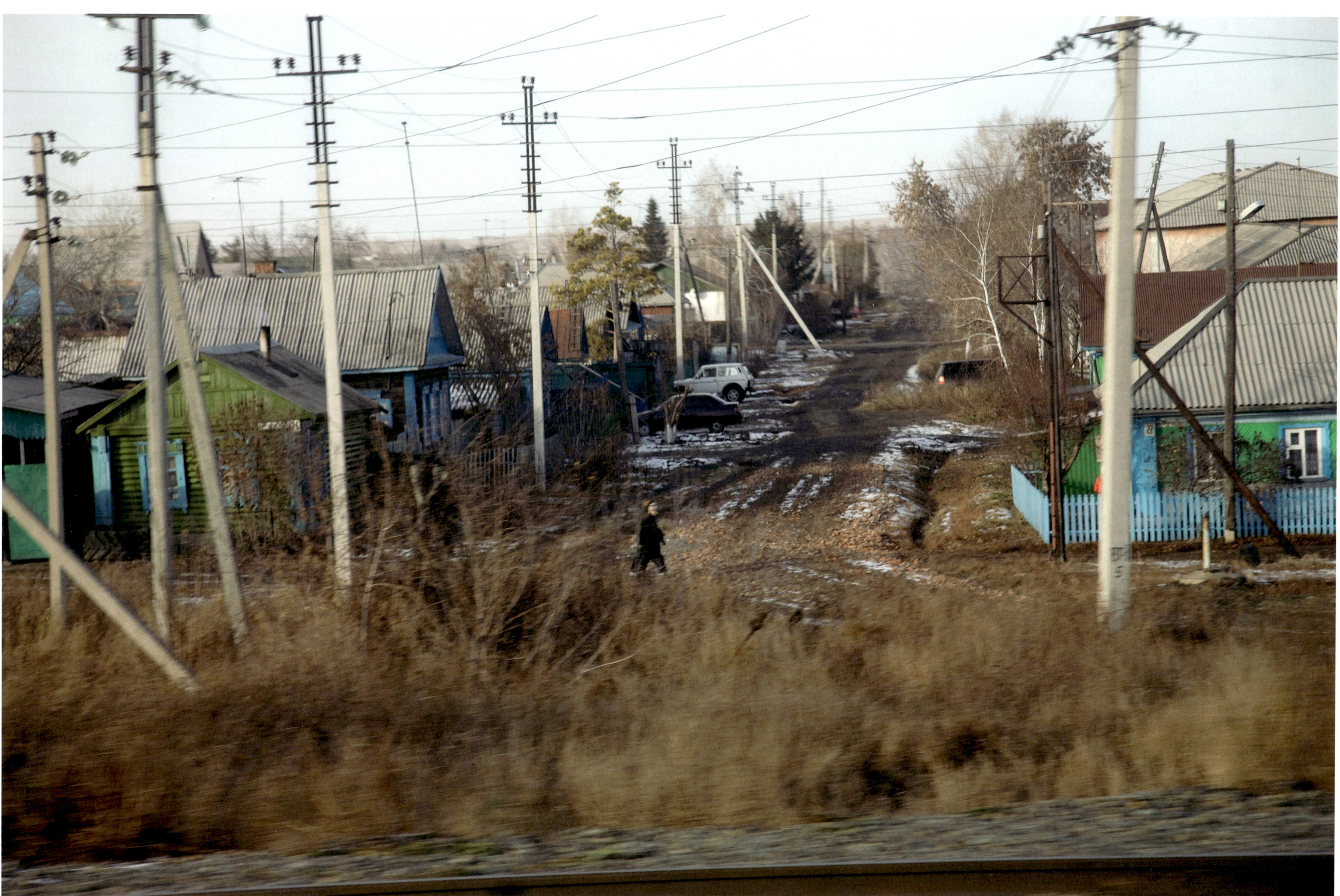

Town east of the Urals

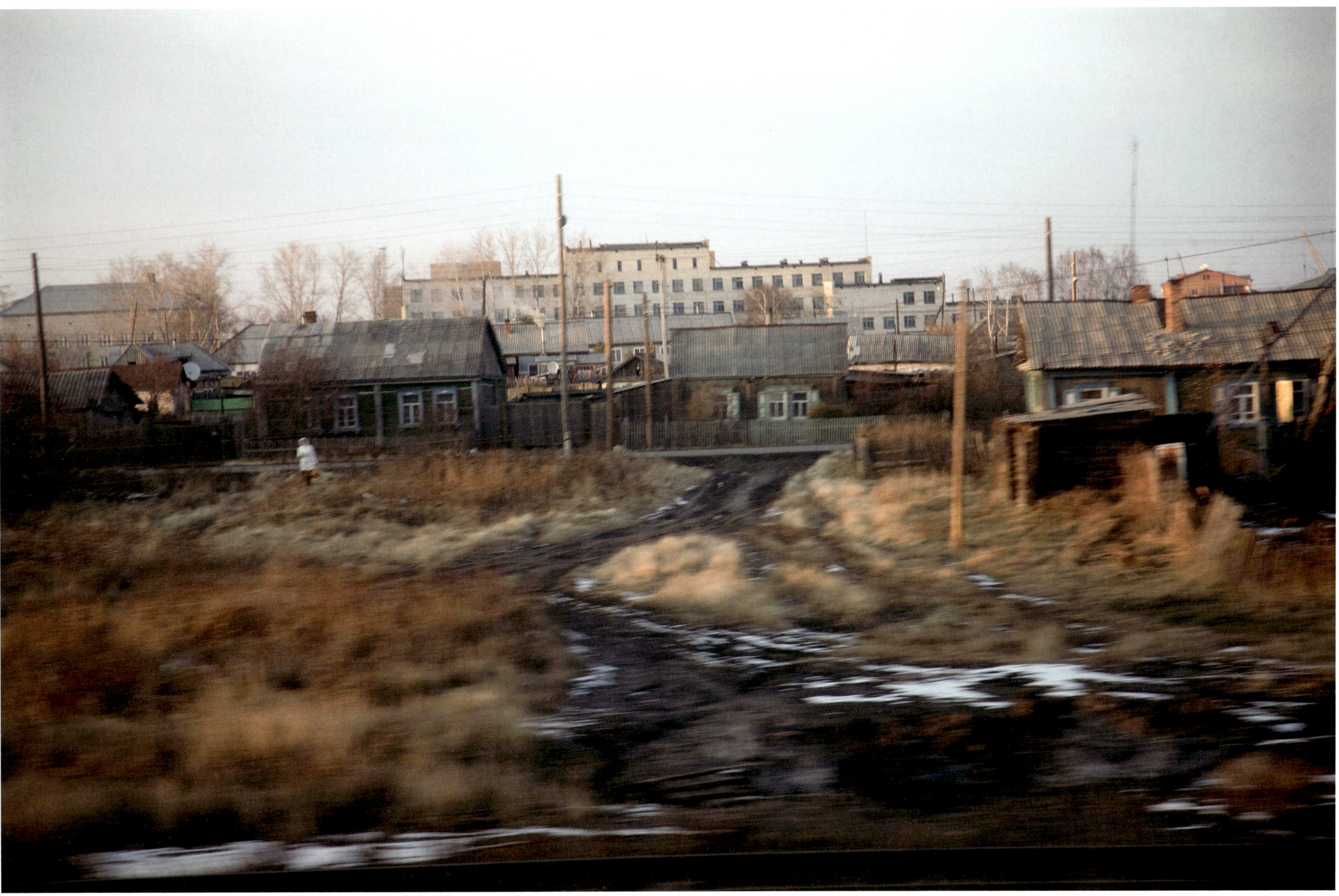

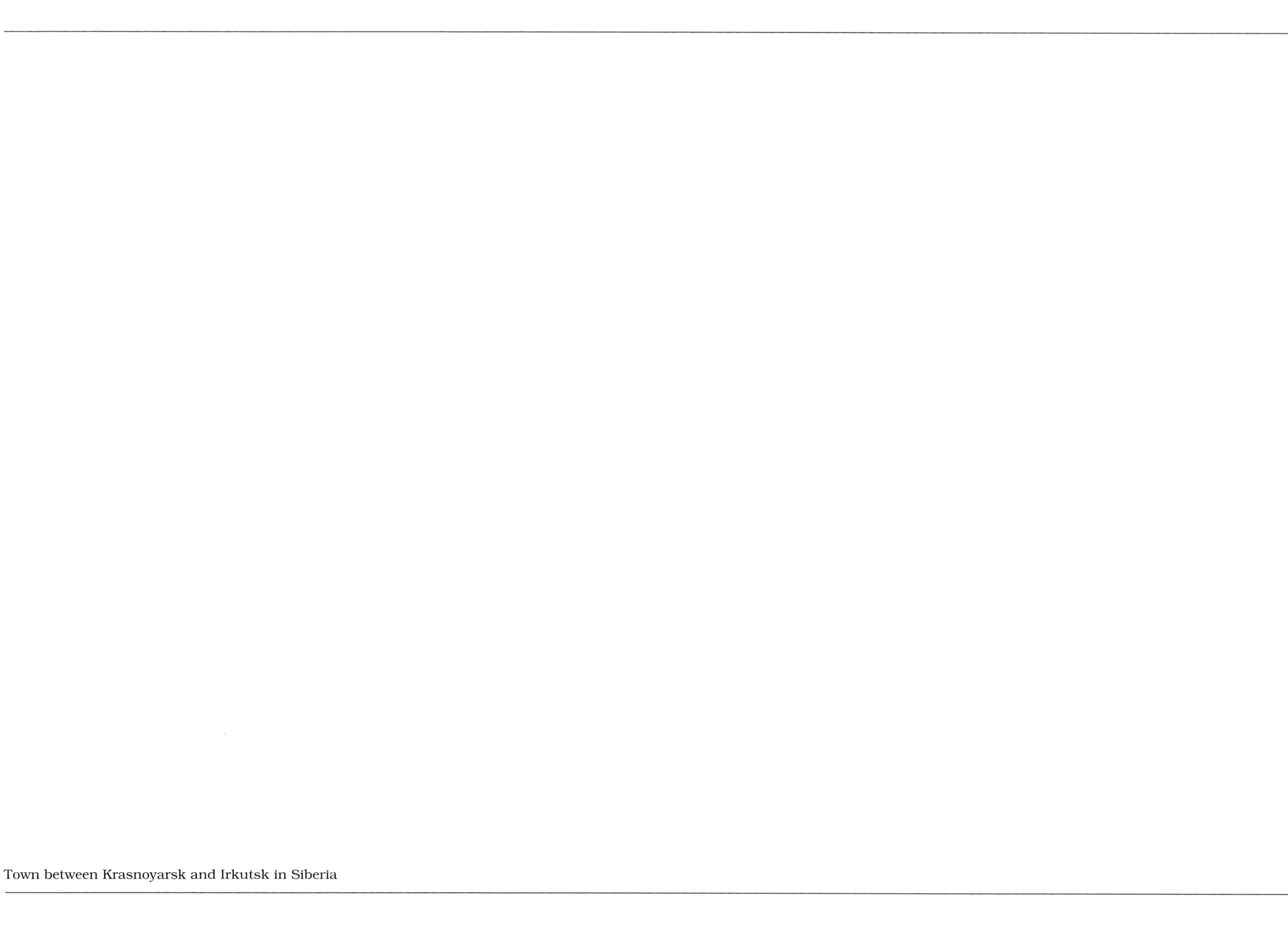

Town between Krasnoyarsk and Irkutsk in Siberia

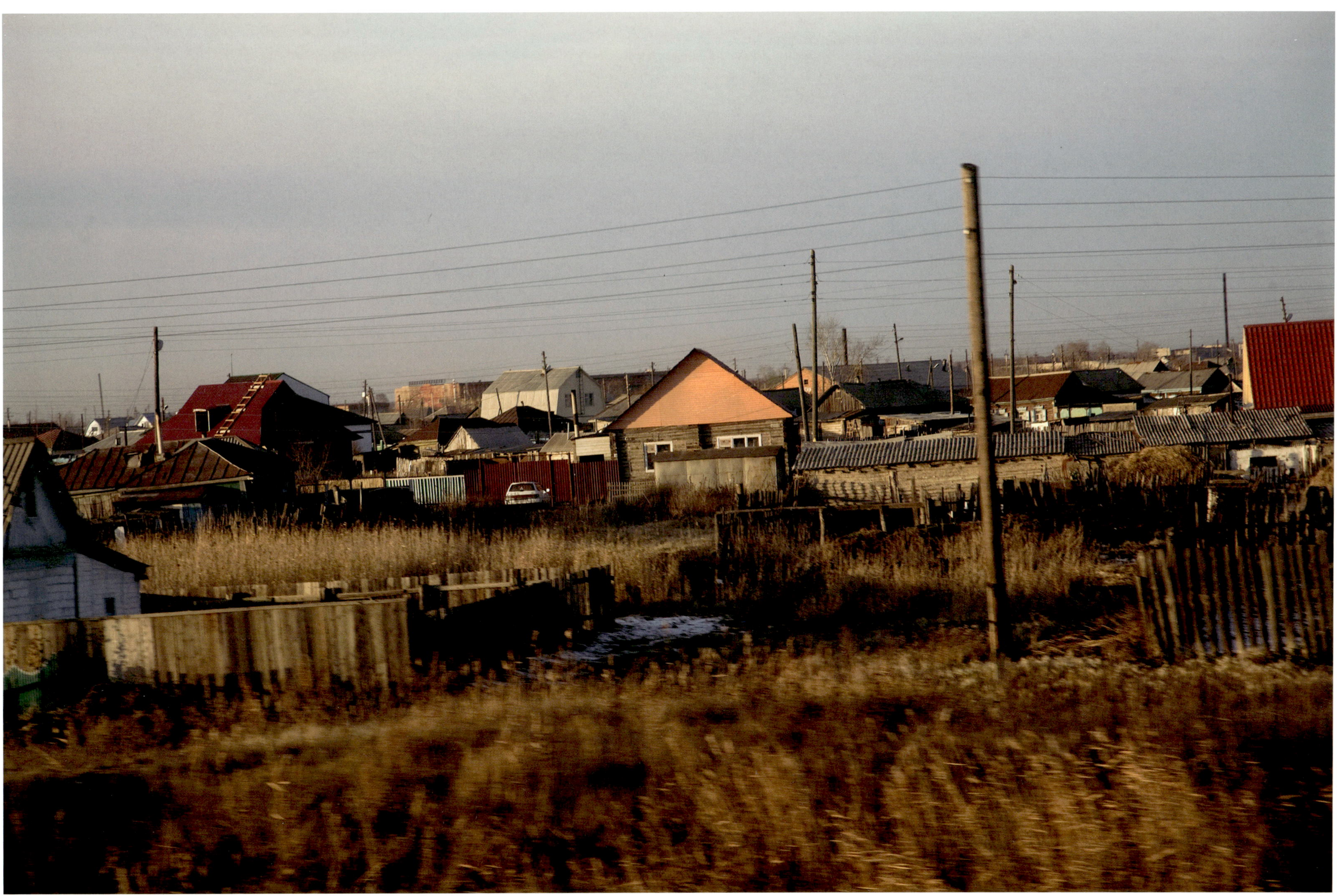

Church in Siberian town

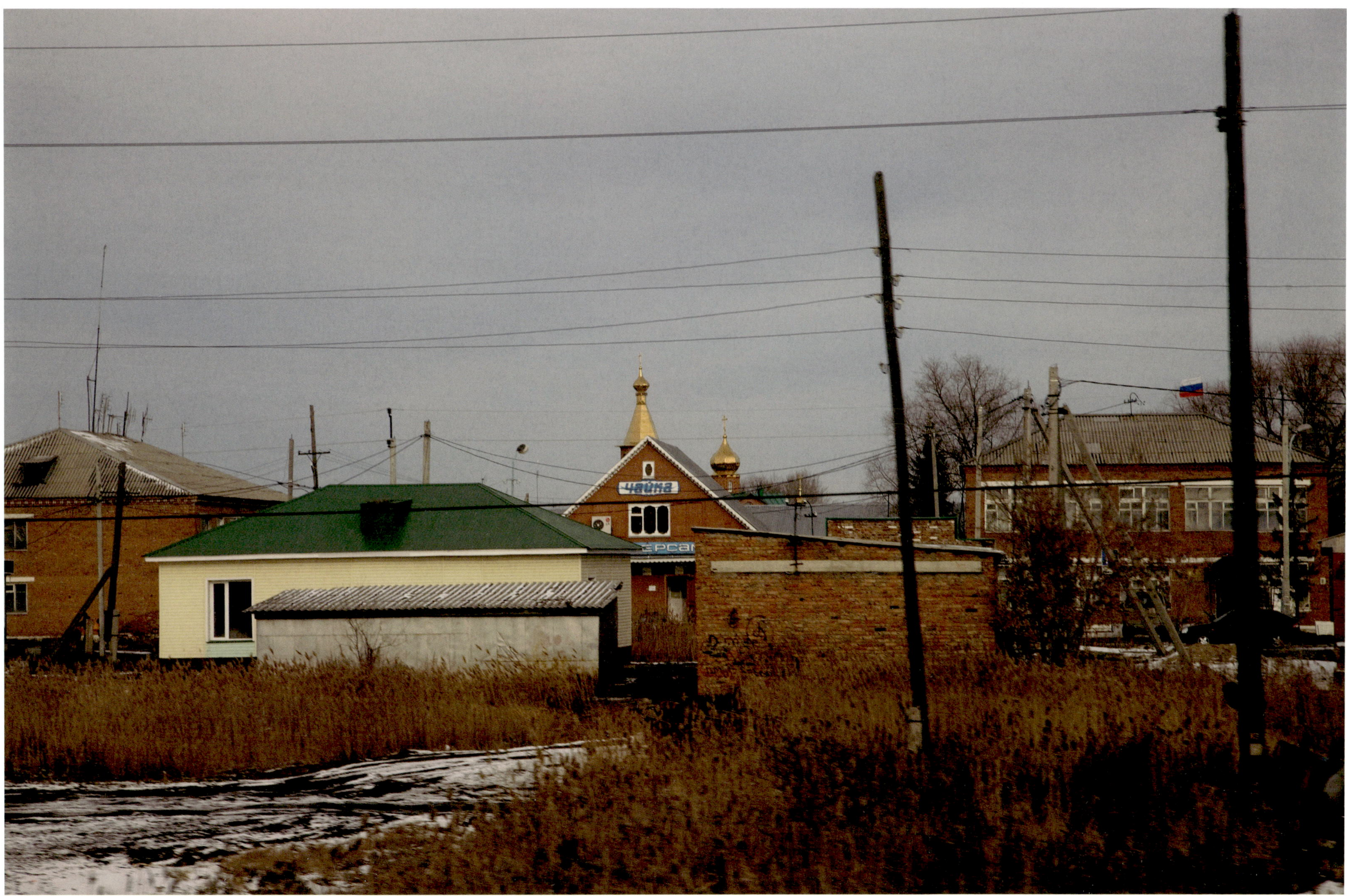

чайка

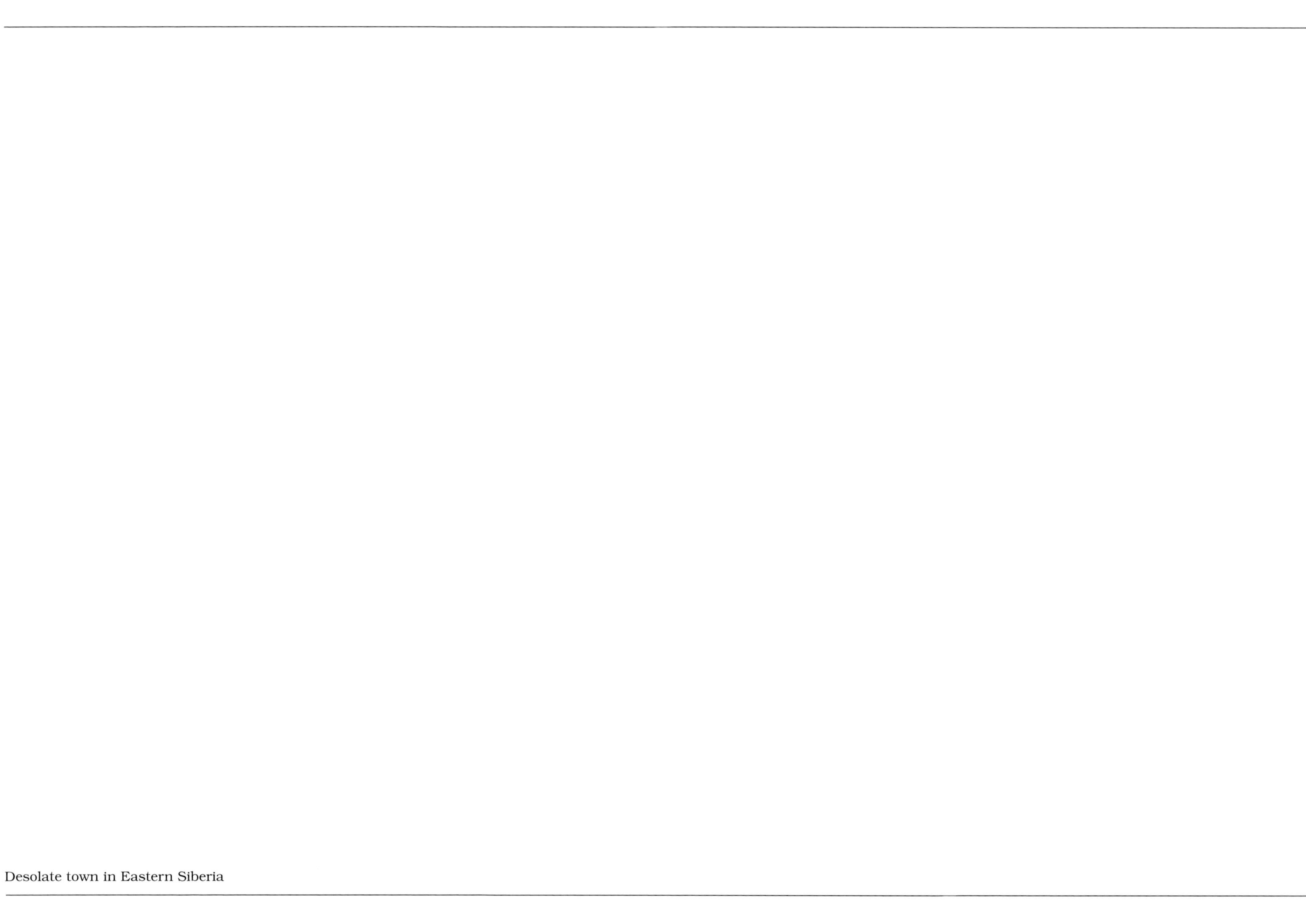

Desolate town in Eastern Siberia

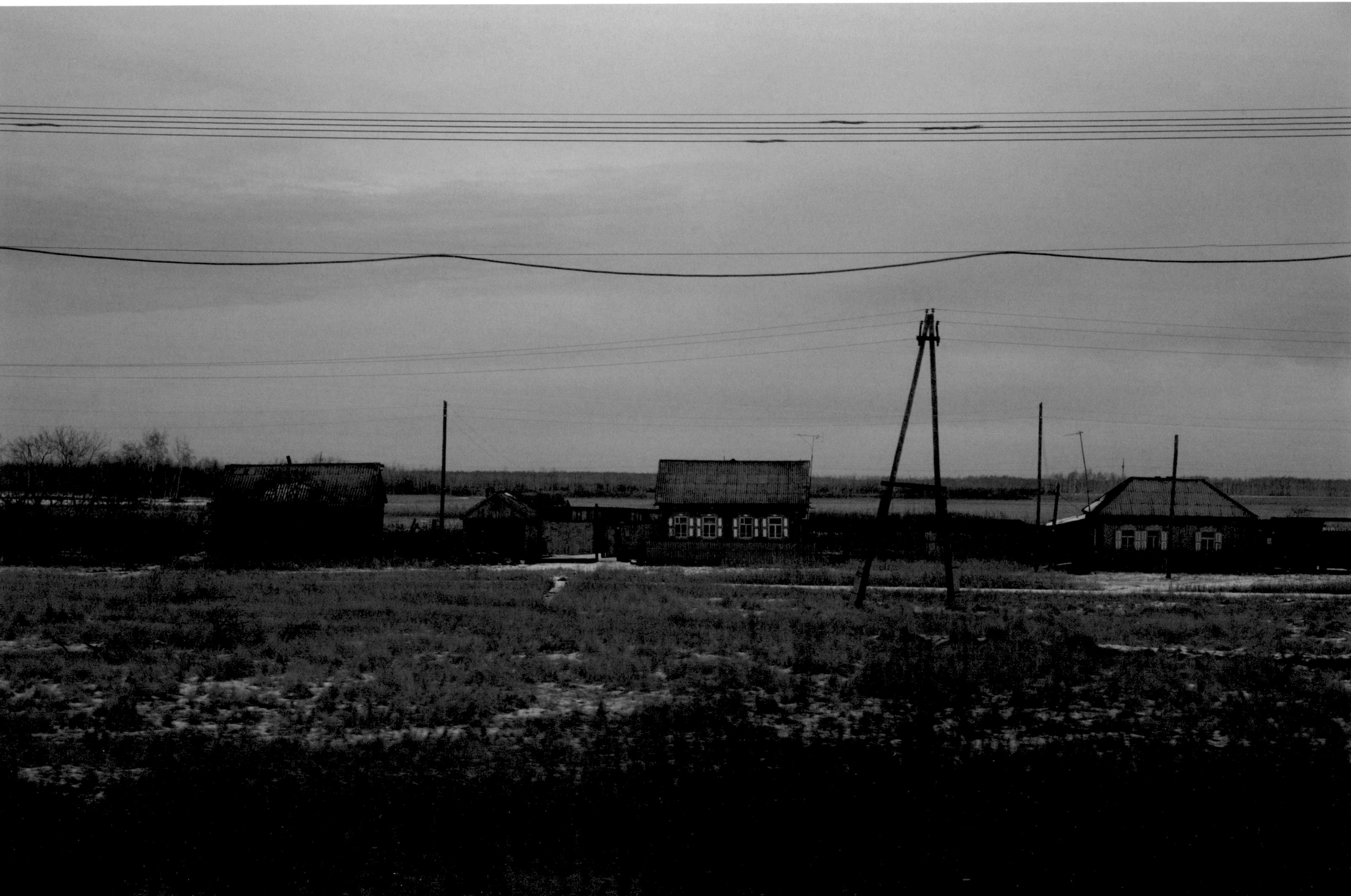

Snow-covered Siberian village

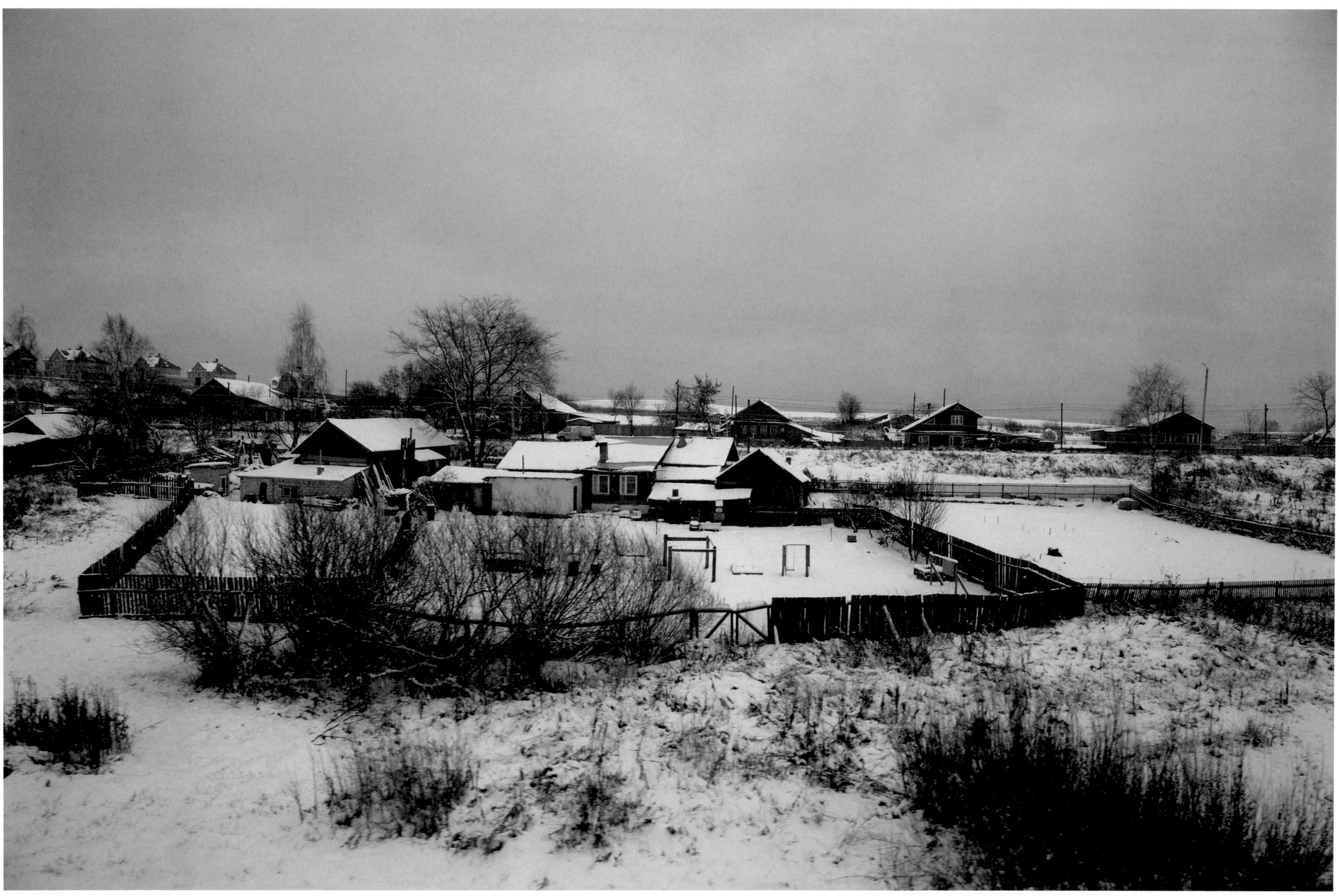

Siberian village

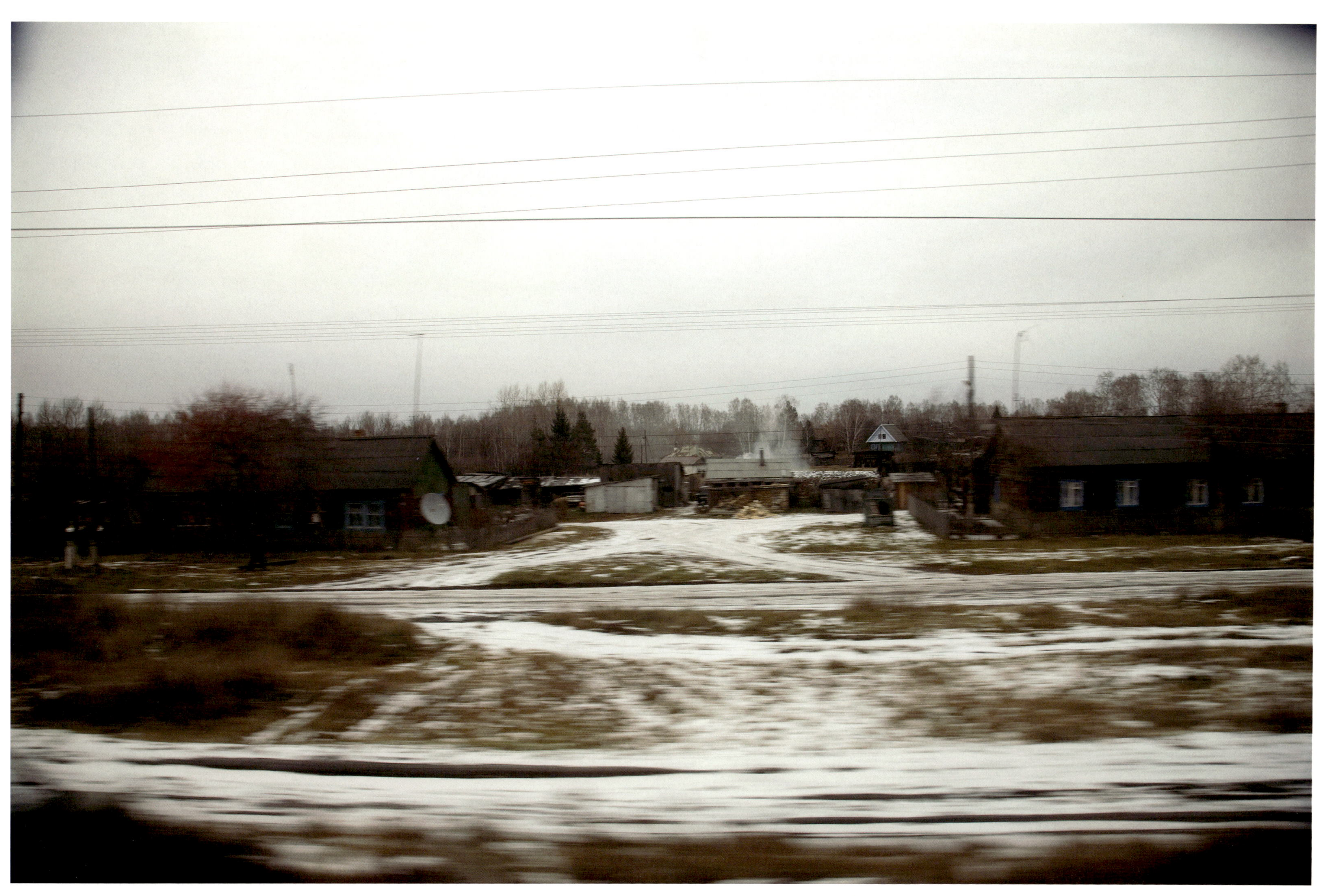

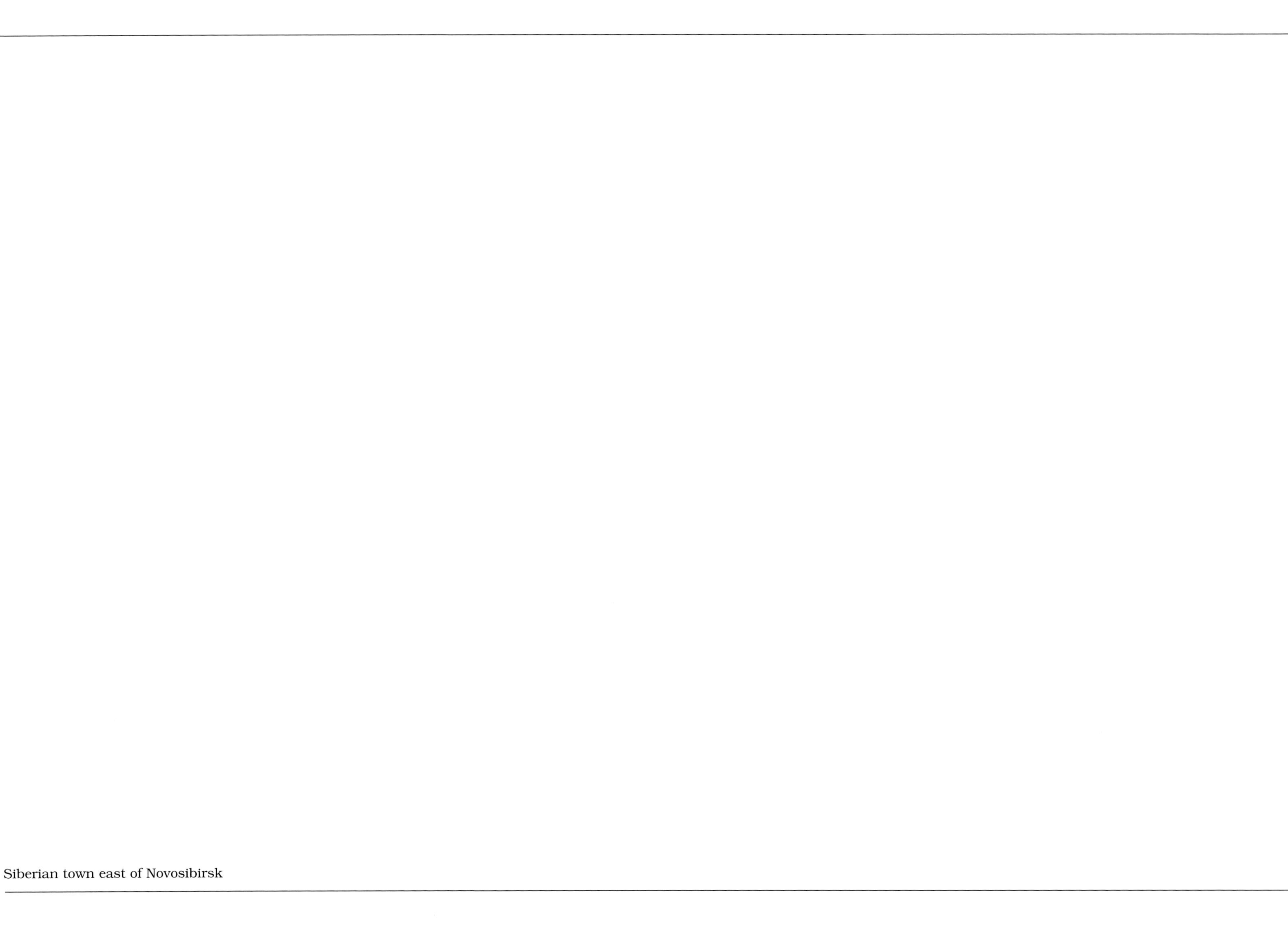

Siberian town east of Novosibirsk

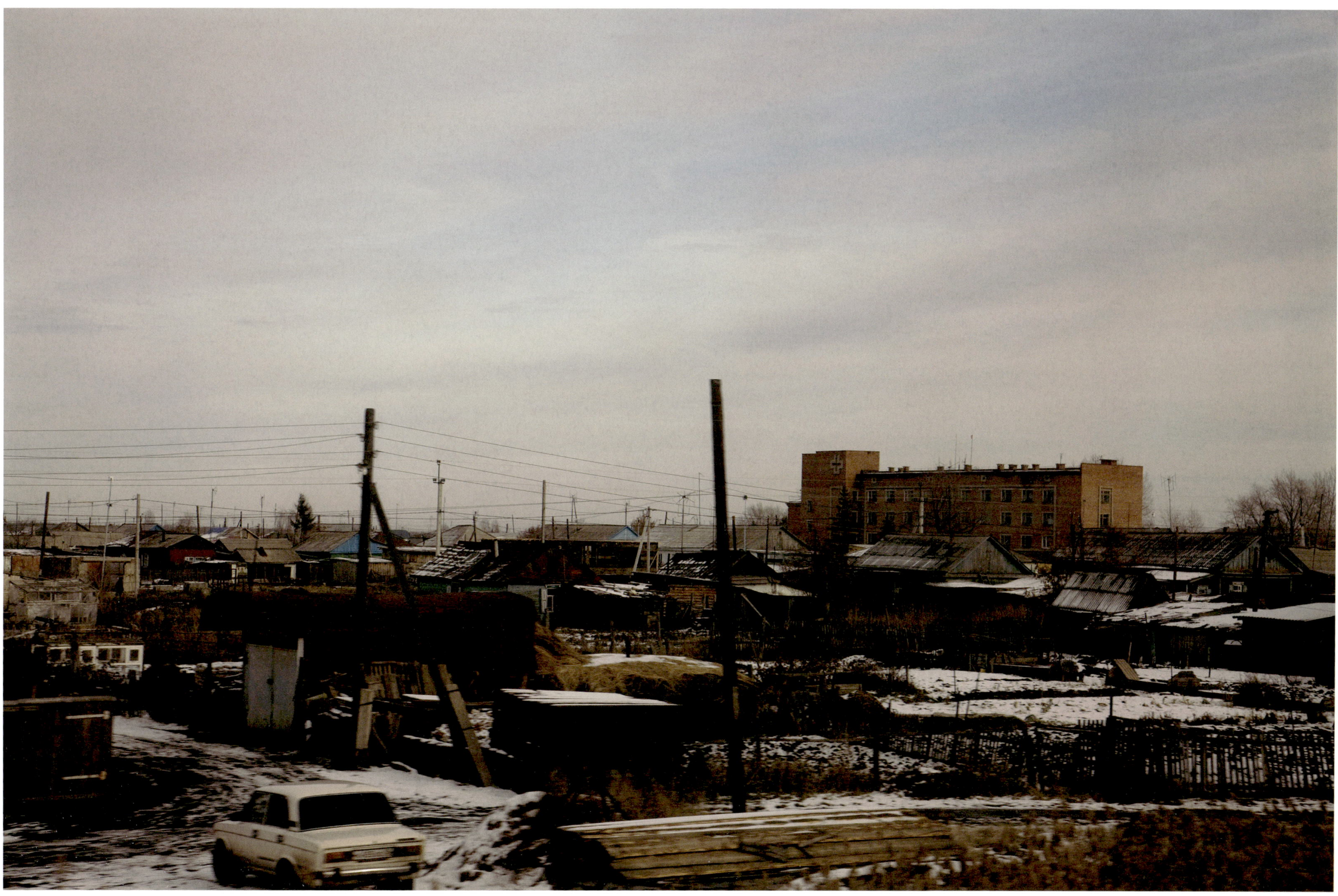

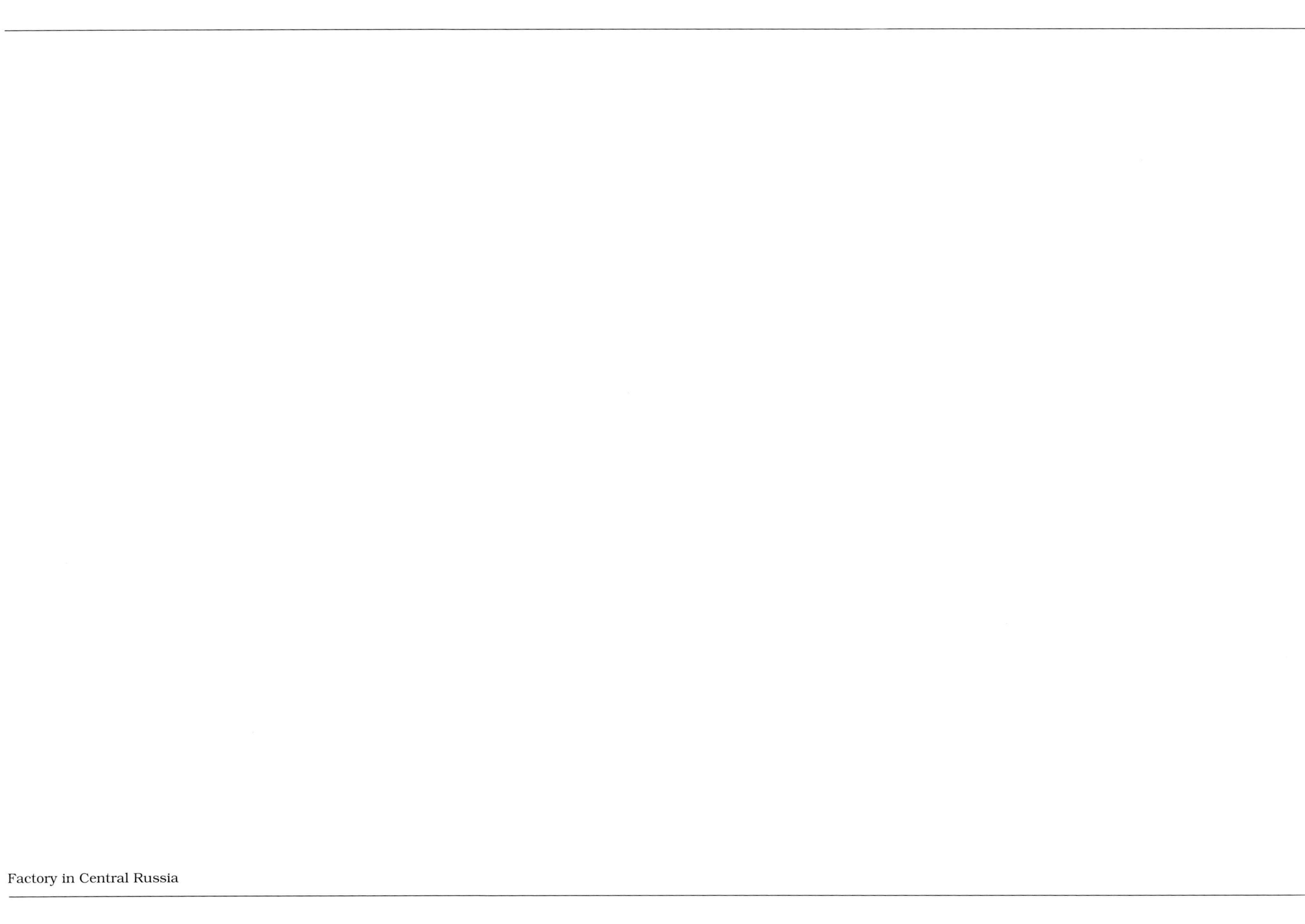

Factory in Central Russia

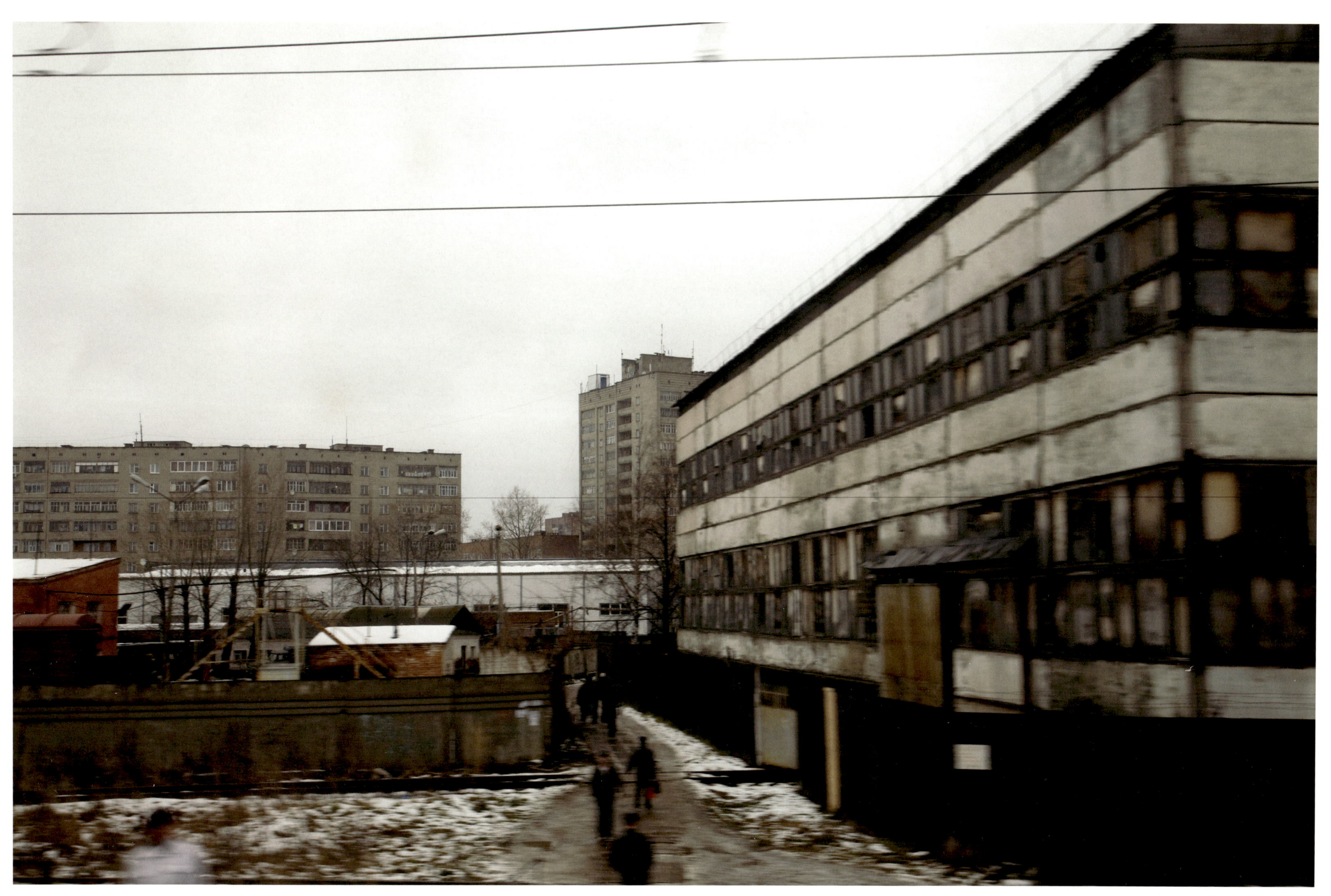

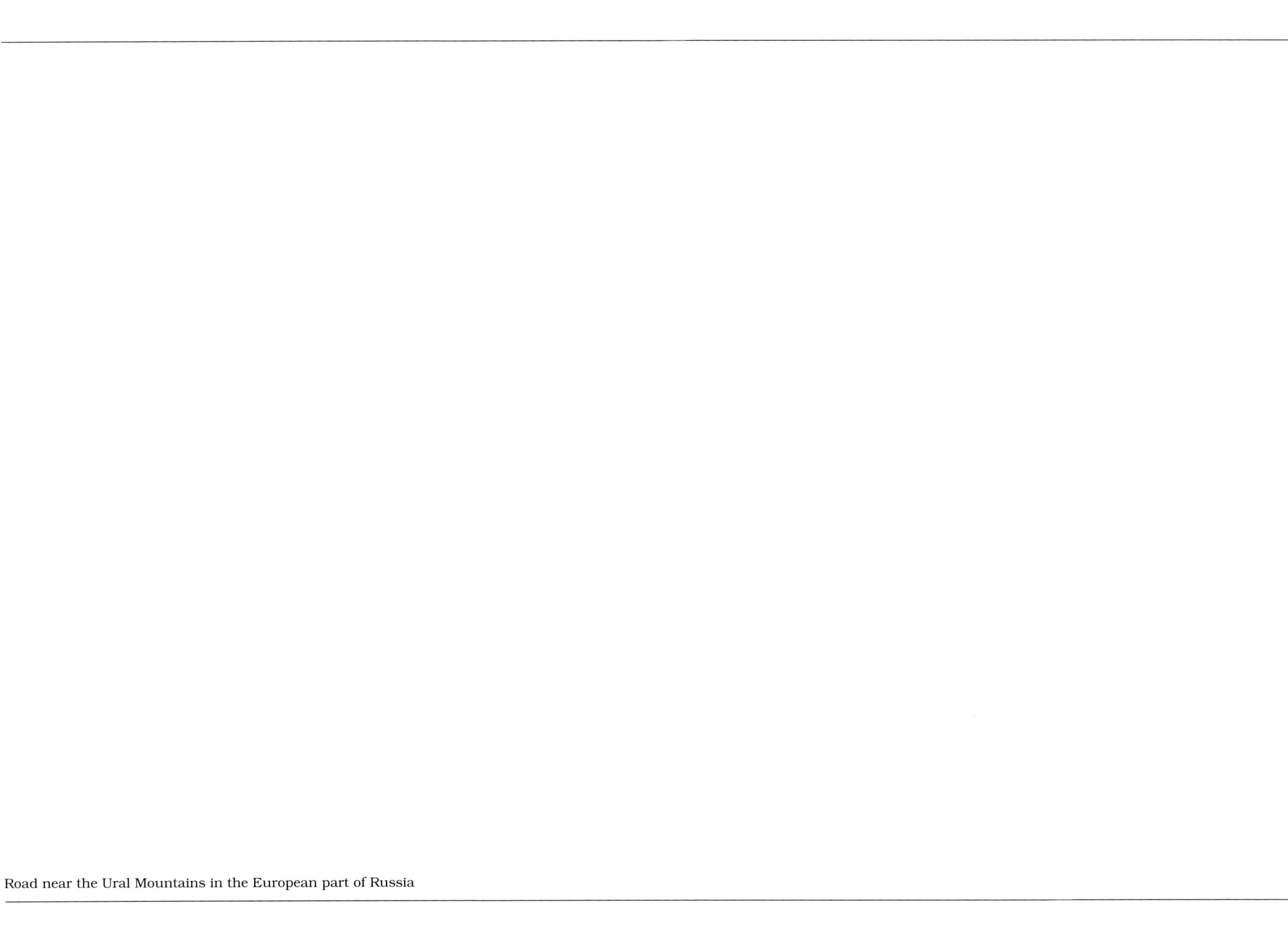

Road near the Ural Mountains in the European part of Russia

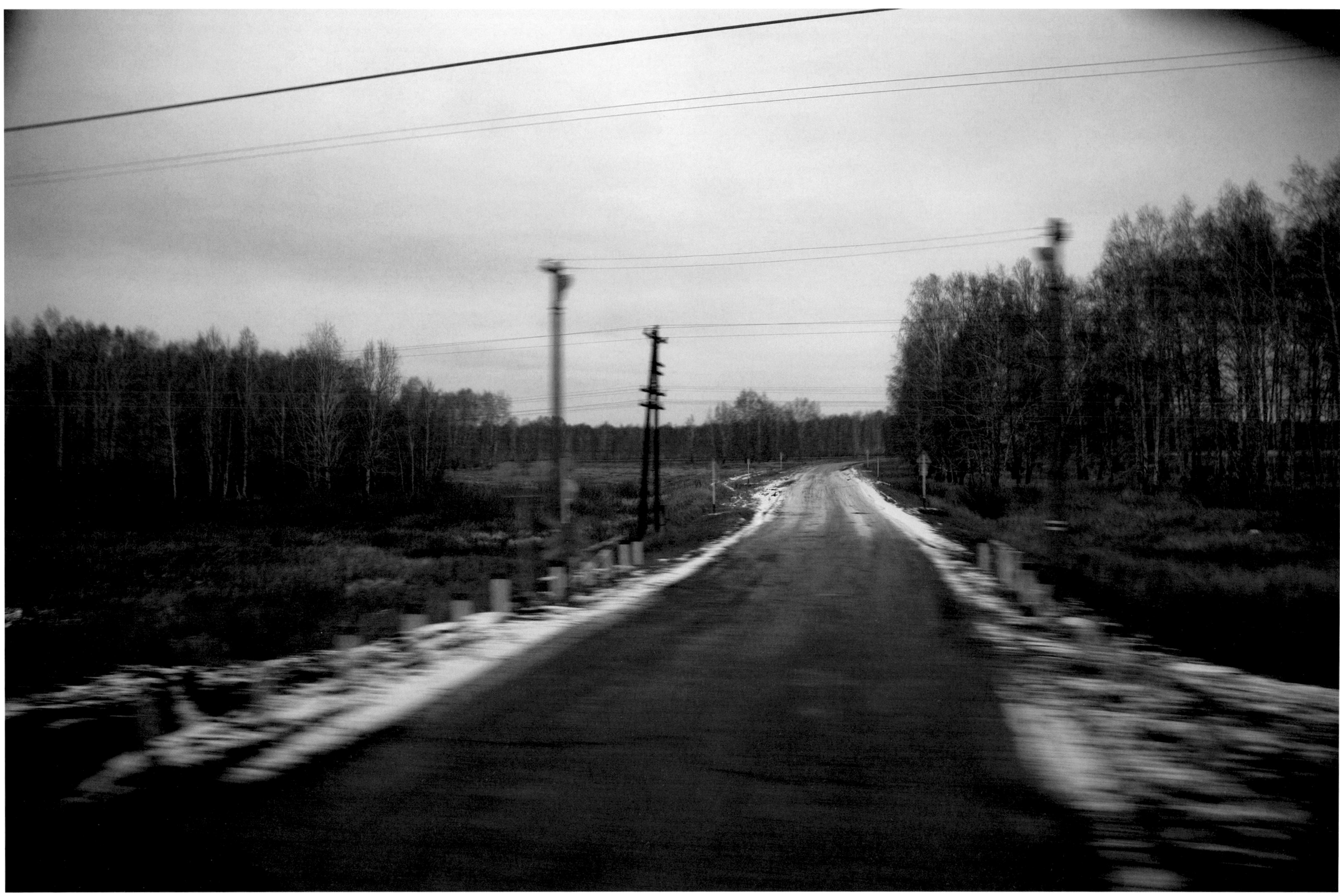

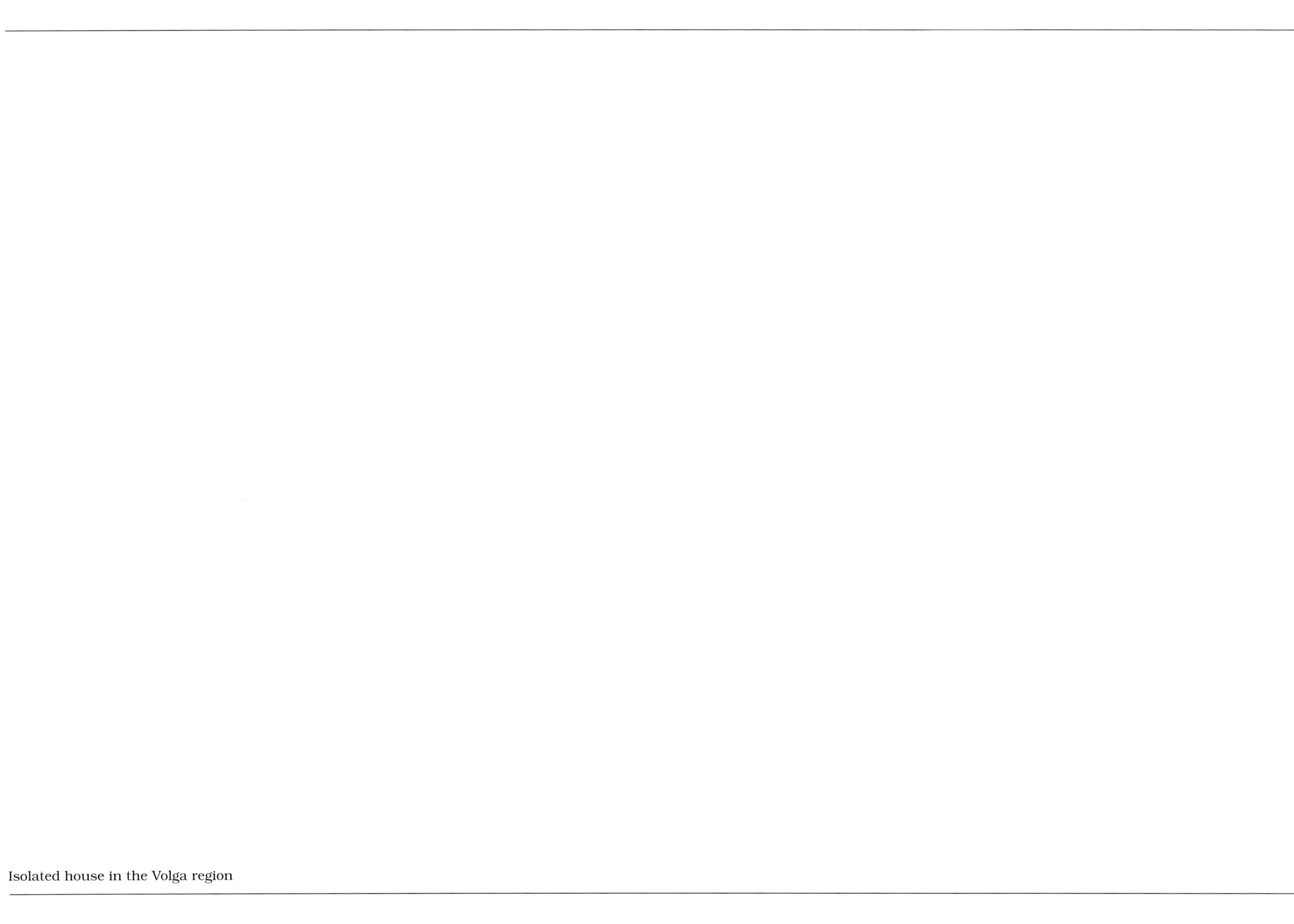

Isolated house in the Volga region

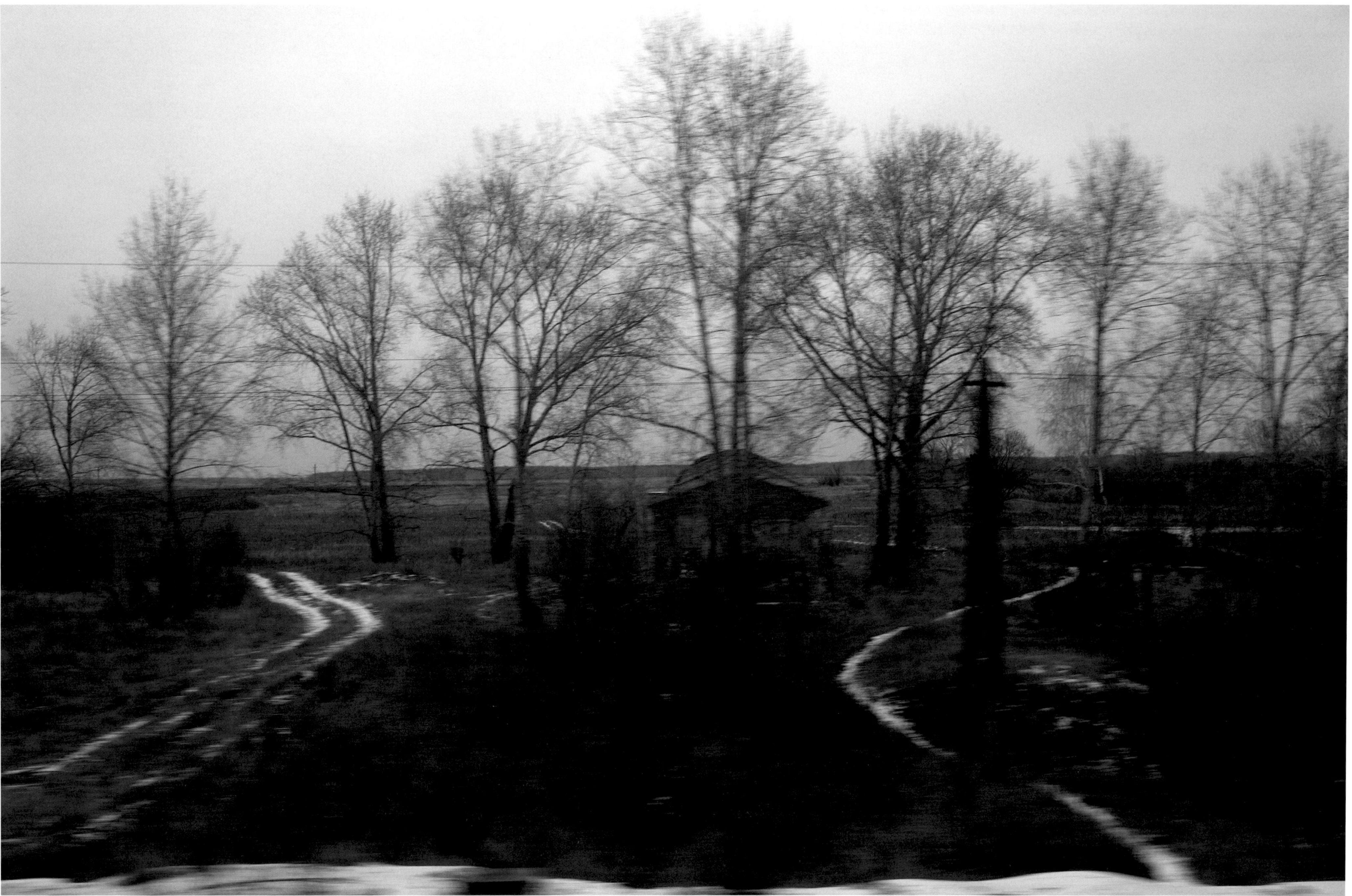

Nightfall in Eastern Siberia

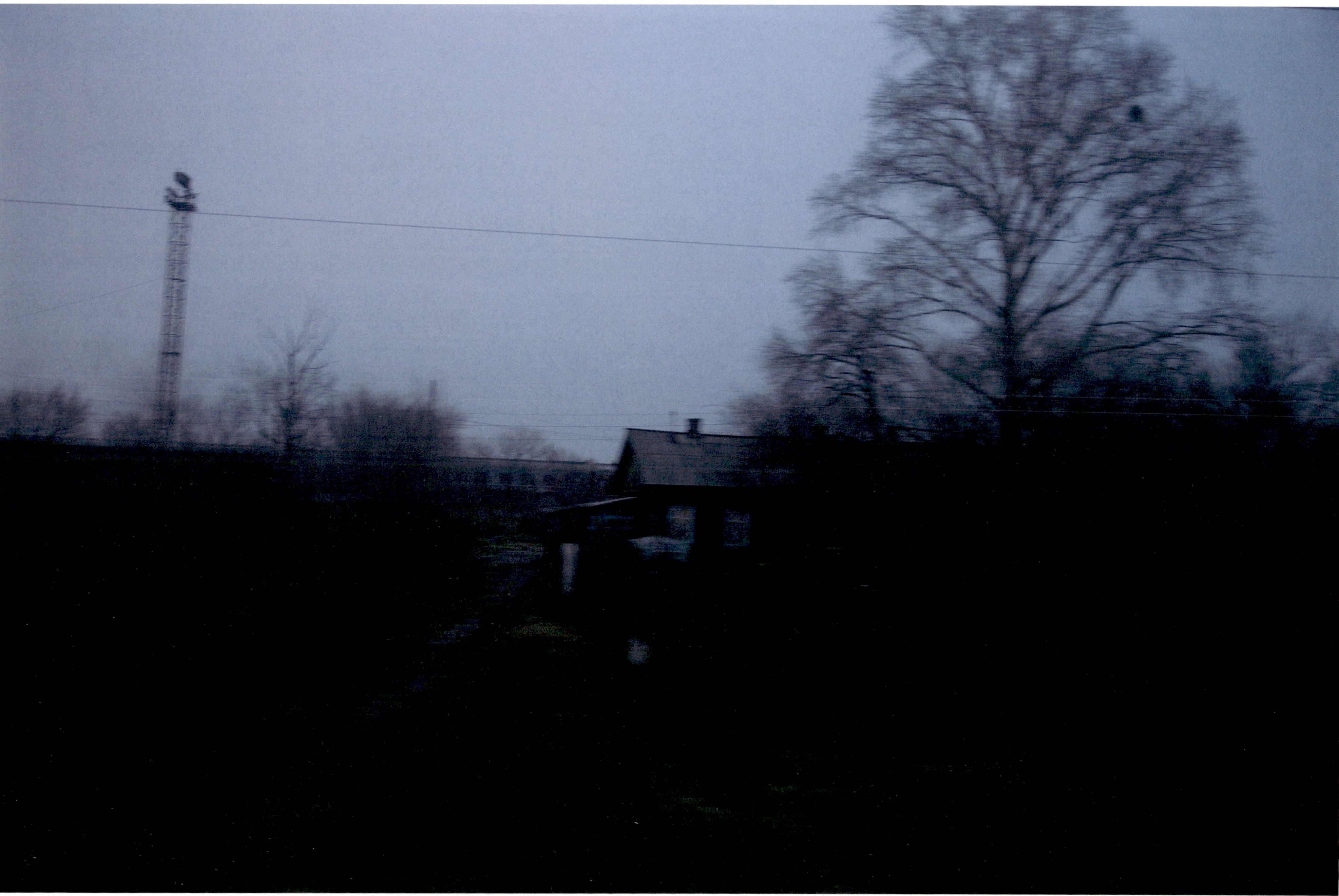

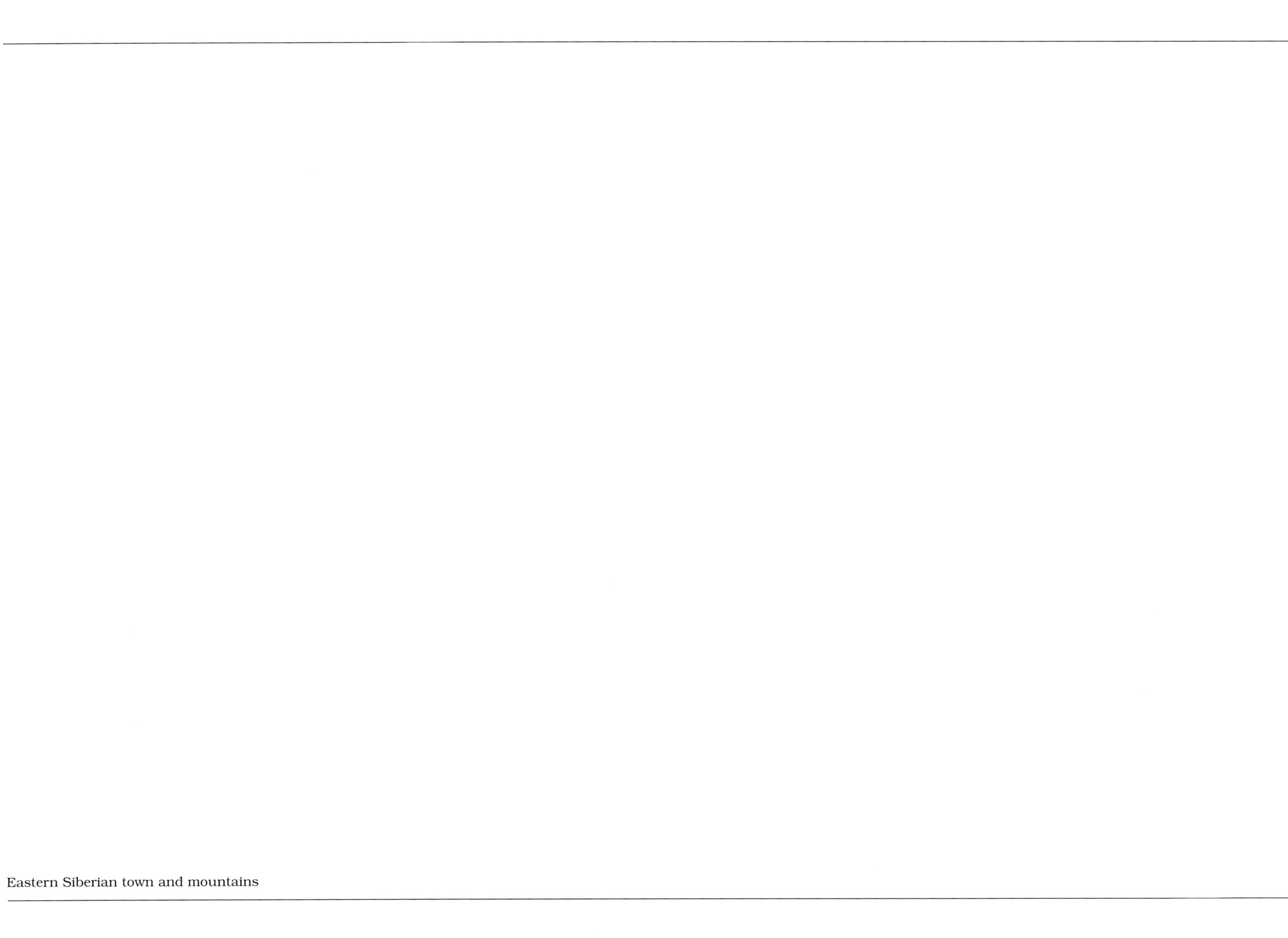

Eastern Siberian town and mountains

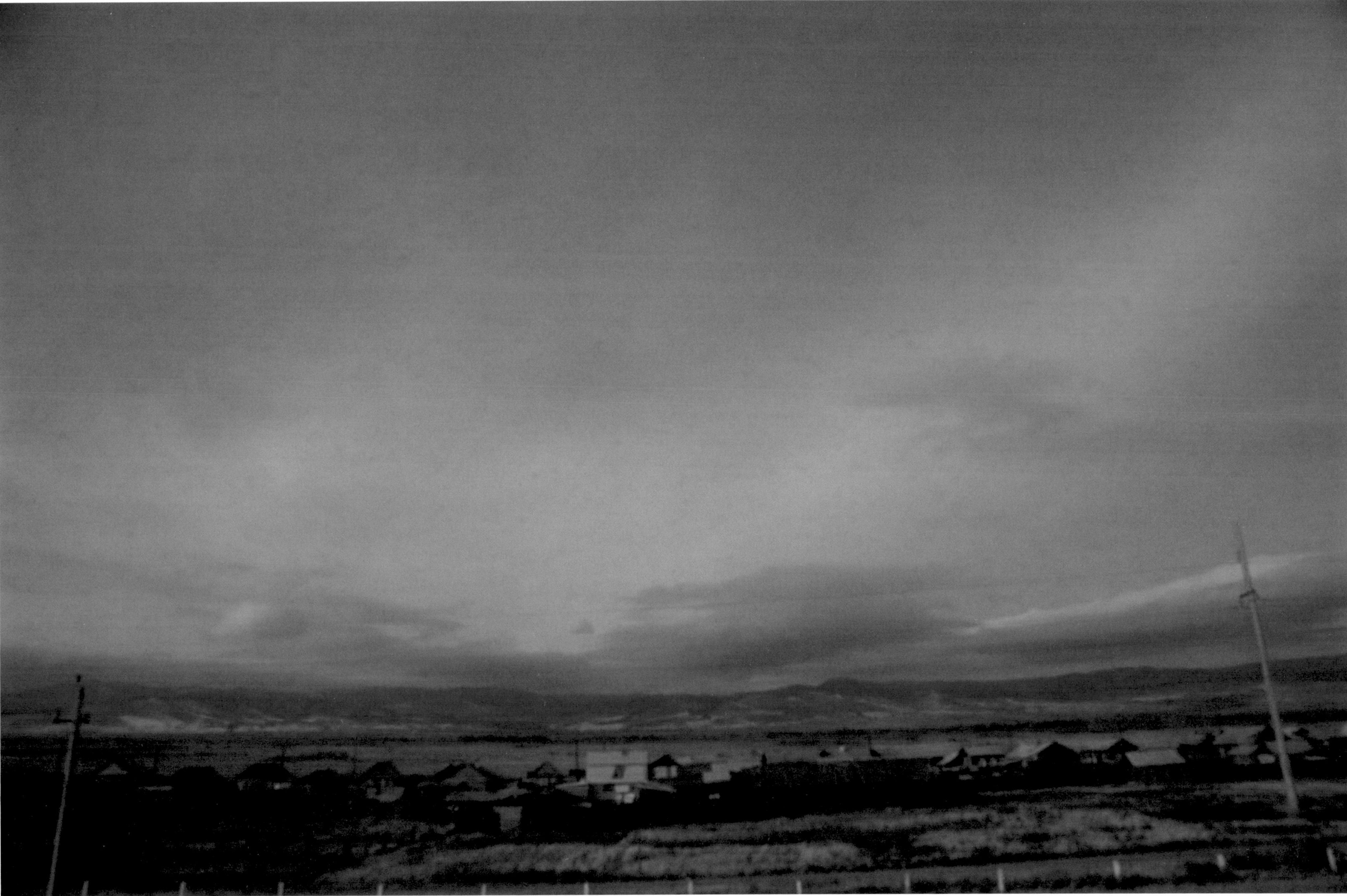

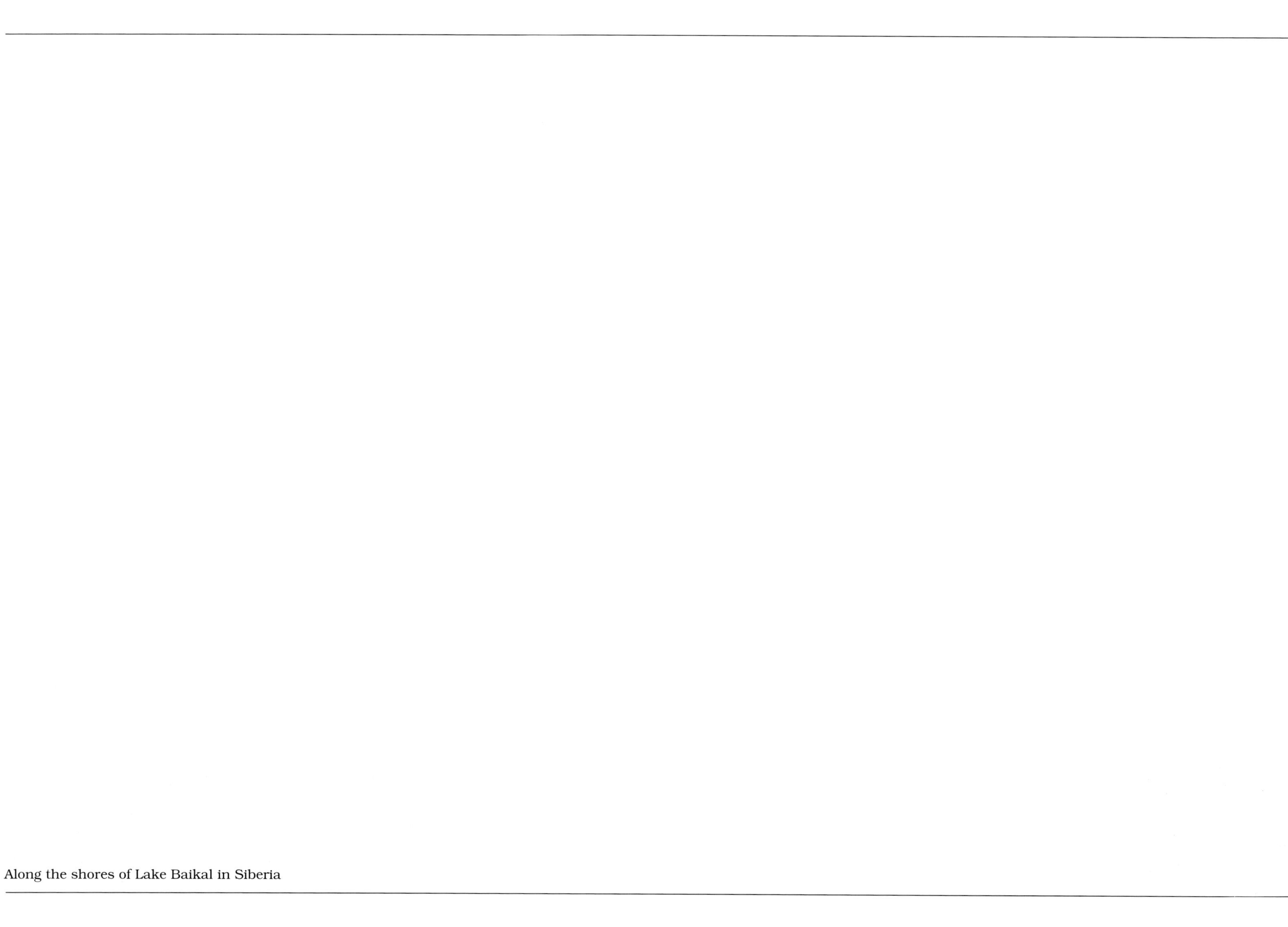

Along the shores of Lake Baikal in Siberia

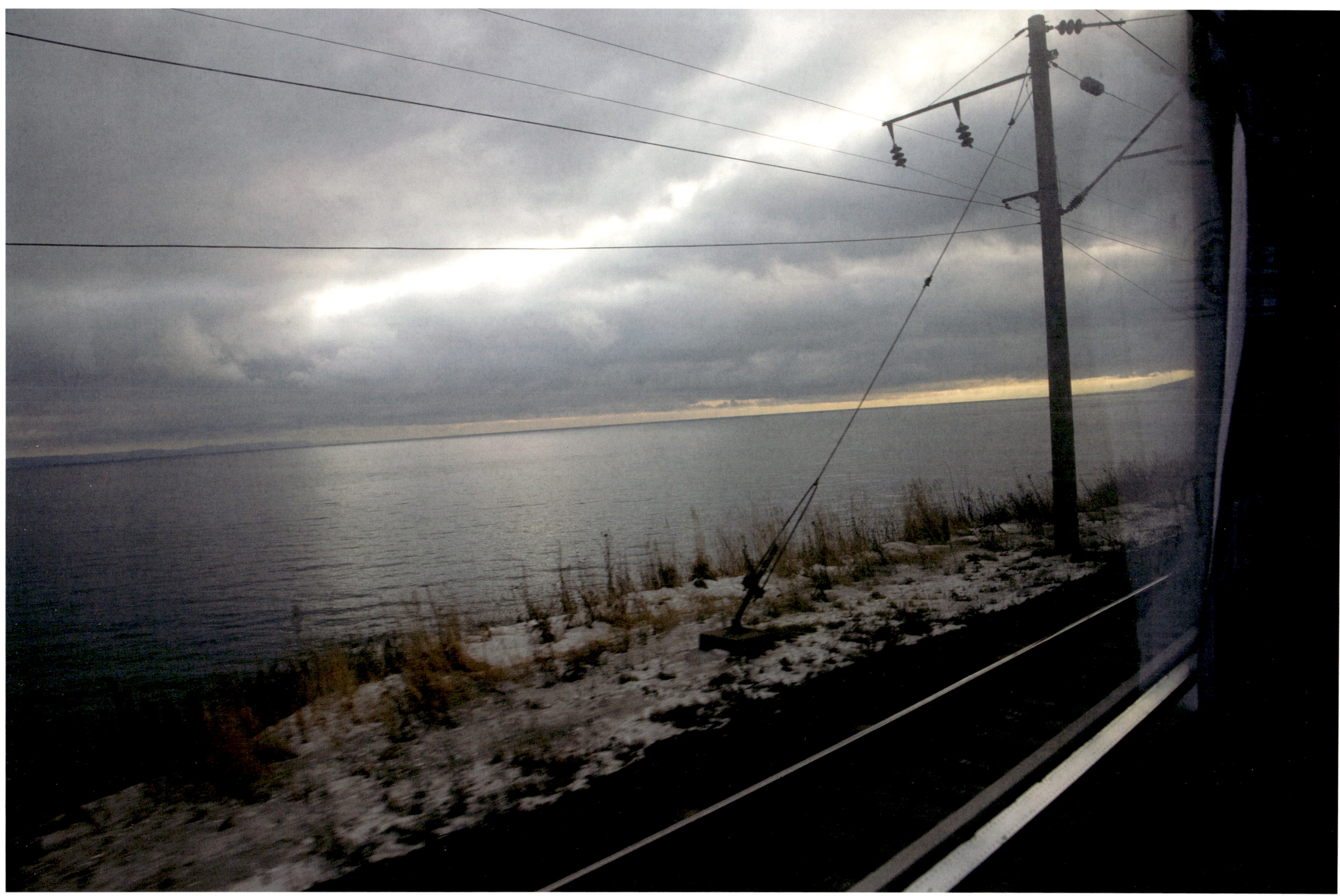

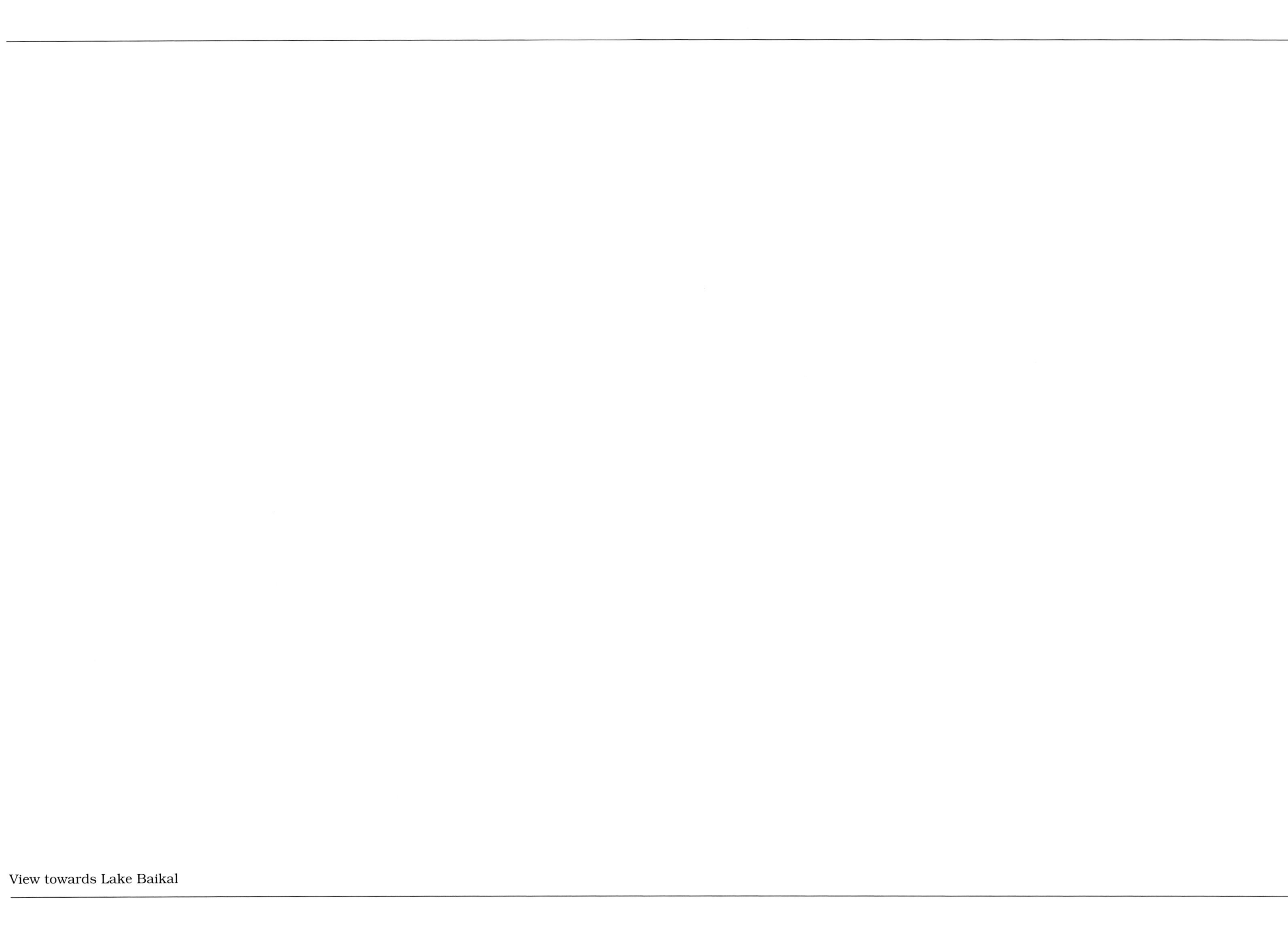

View towards Lake Baikal

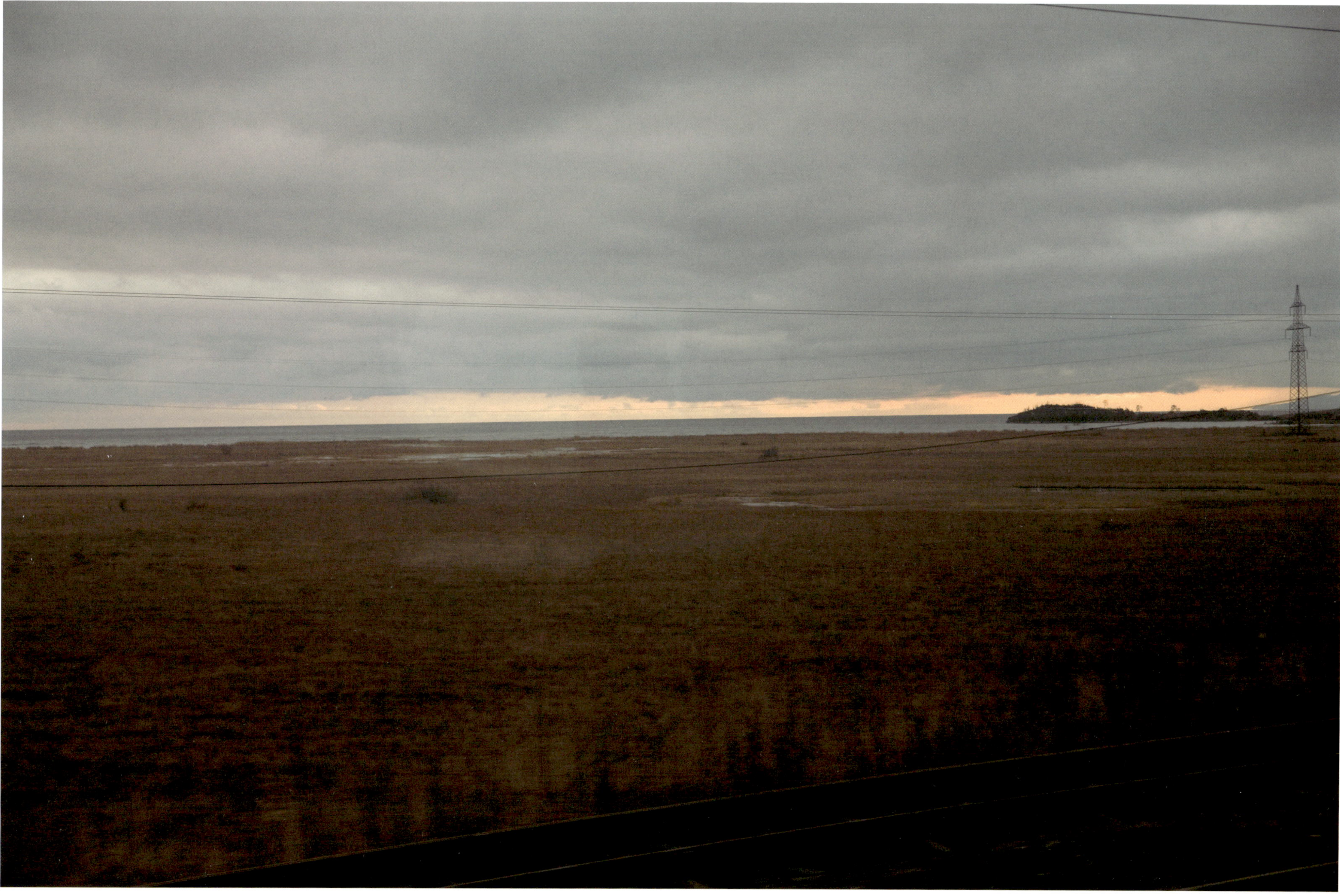

The vastness of Lake Baikal, the world's largest and deepest lake

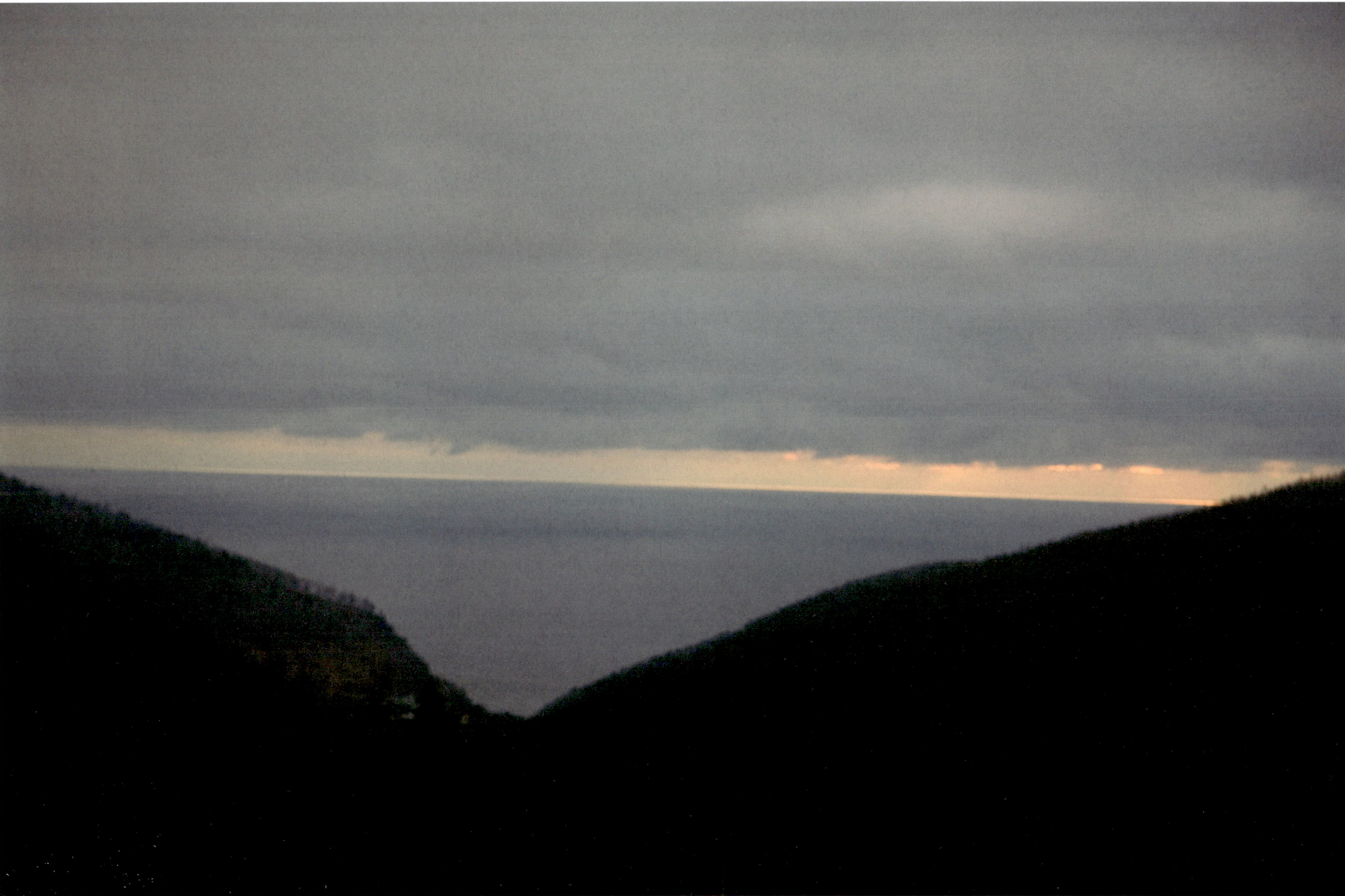

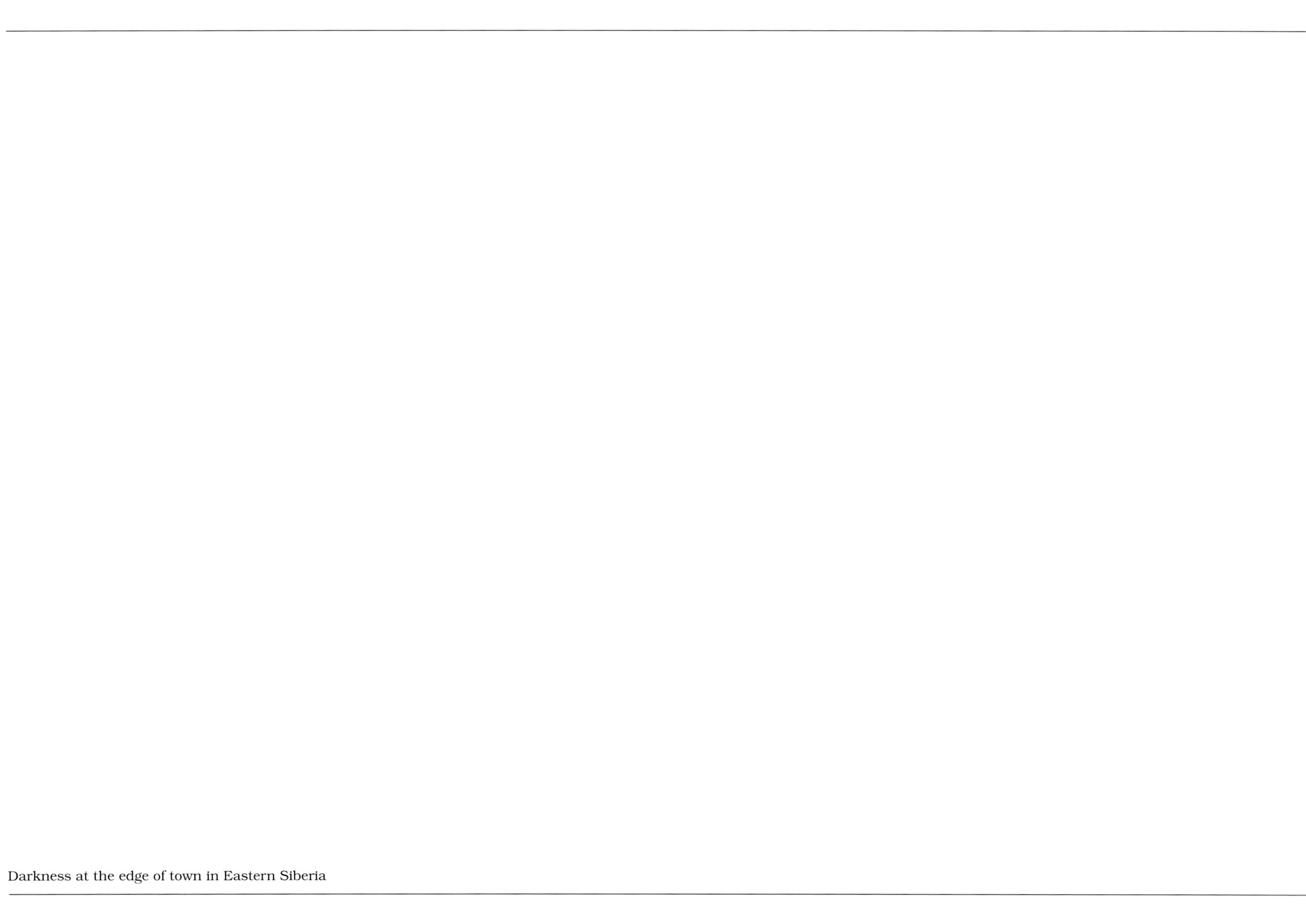

Darkness at the edge of town in Eastern Siberia

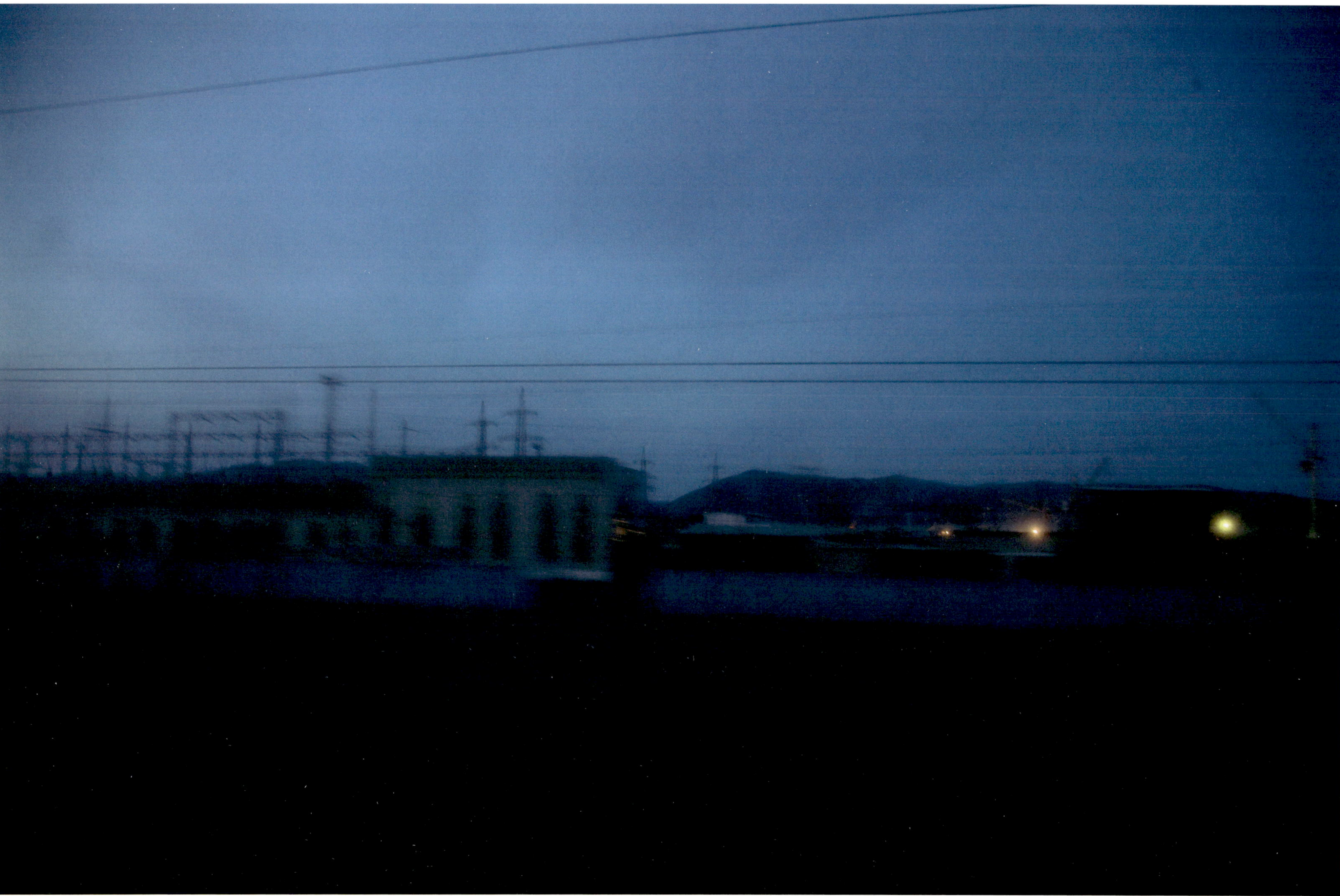

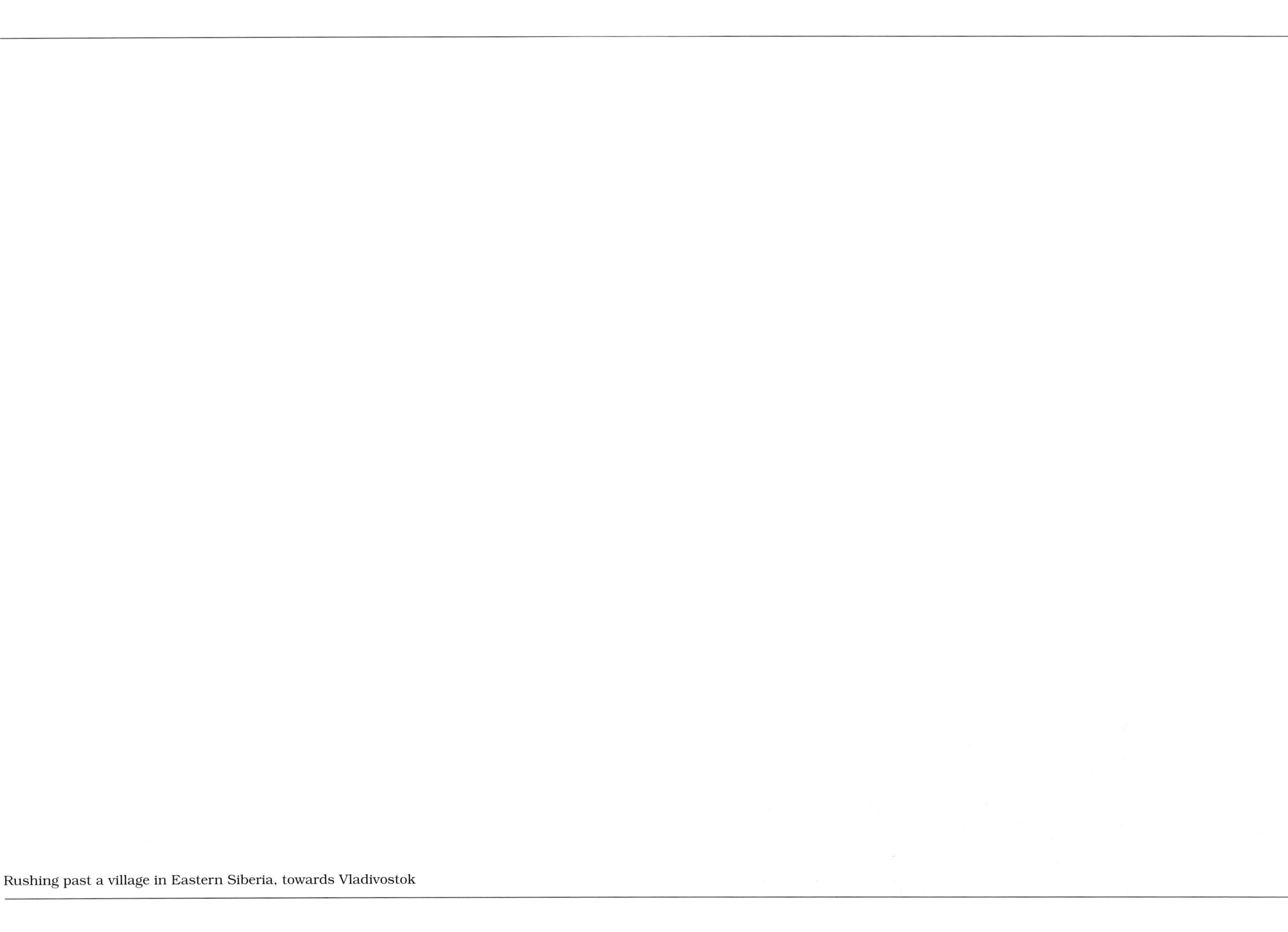

Rushing past a village in Eastern Siberia, towards Vladivostok

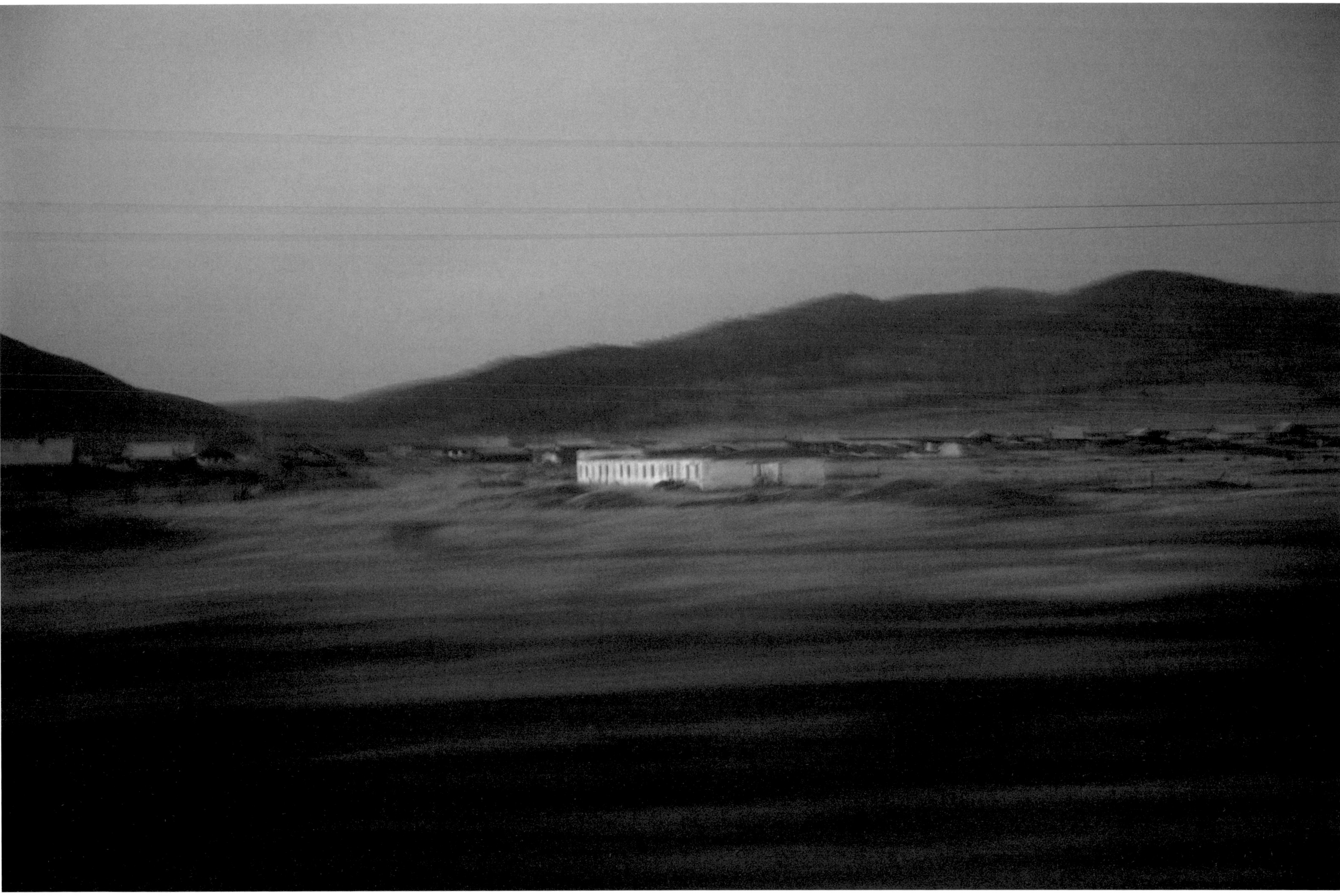

Far Eastern Russia at twilight

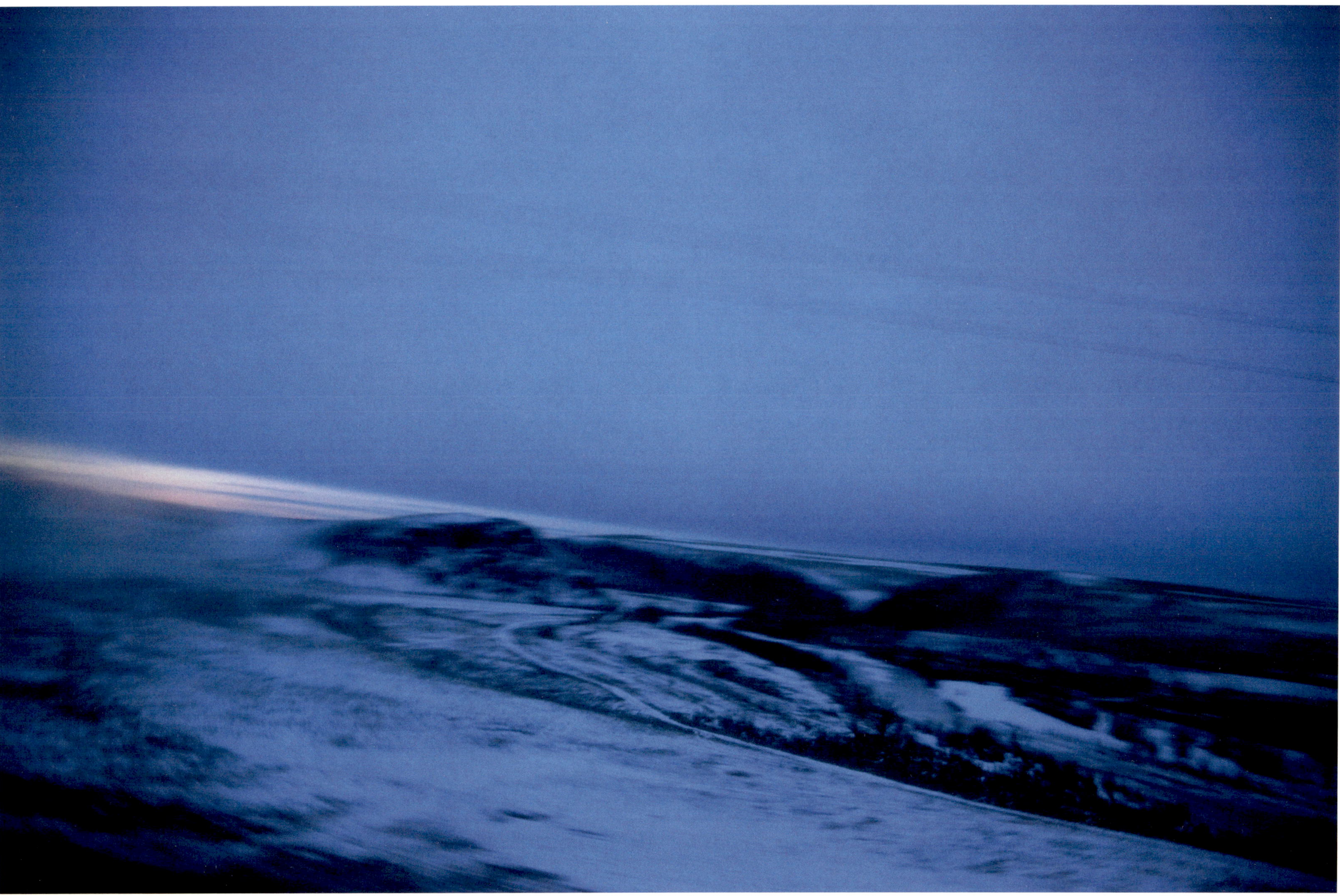

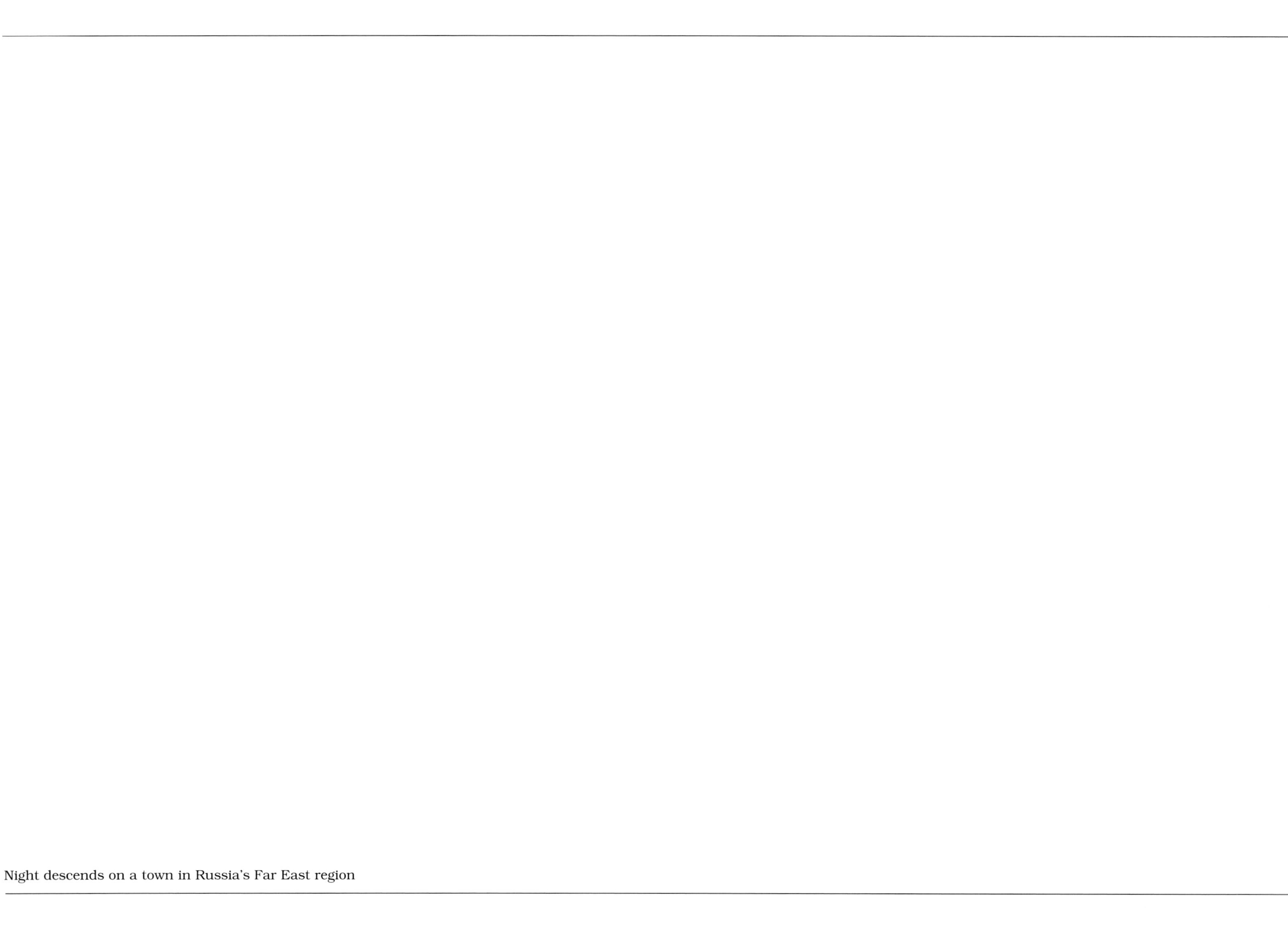

Night descends on a town in Russia's Far East region

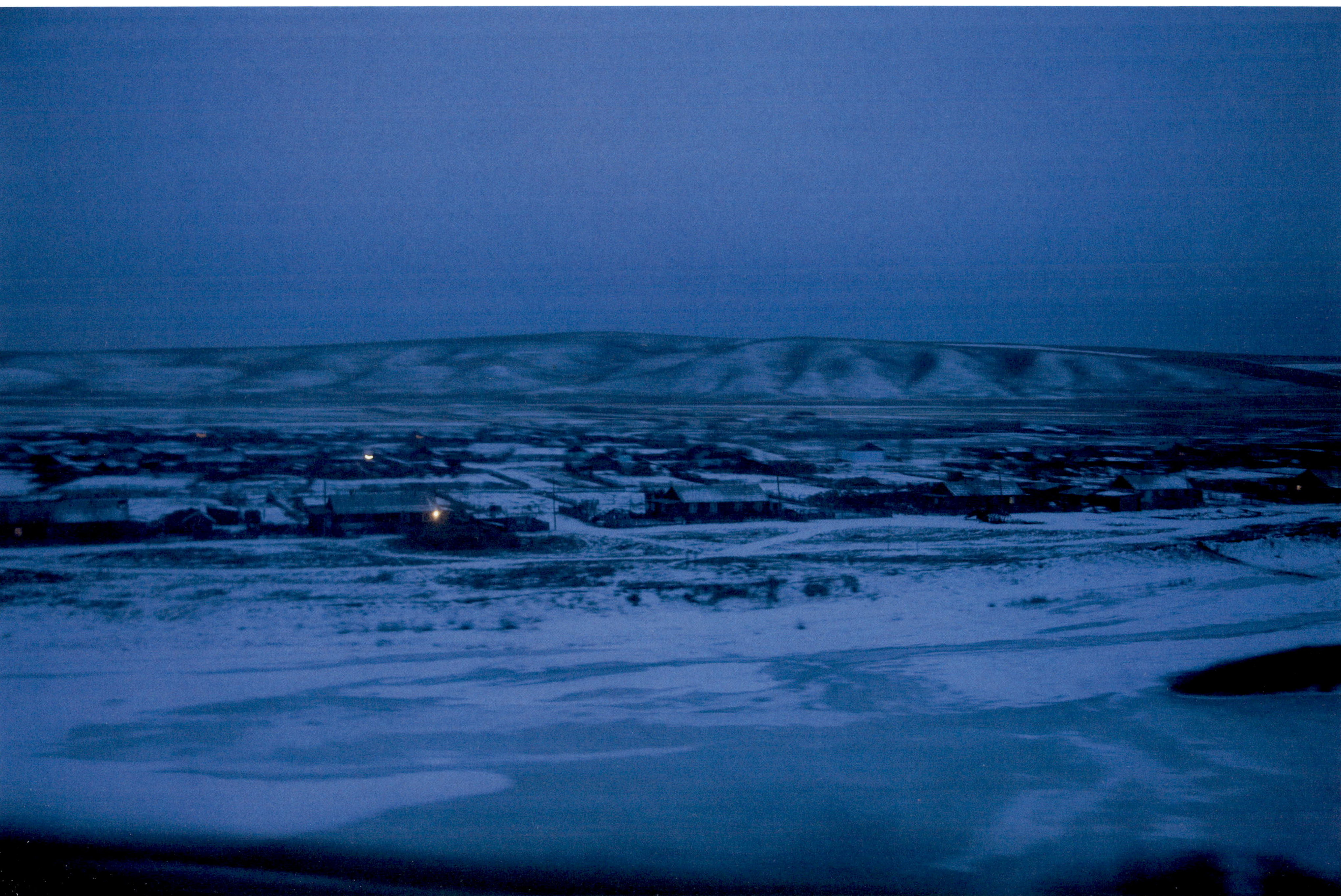

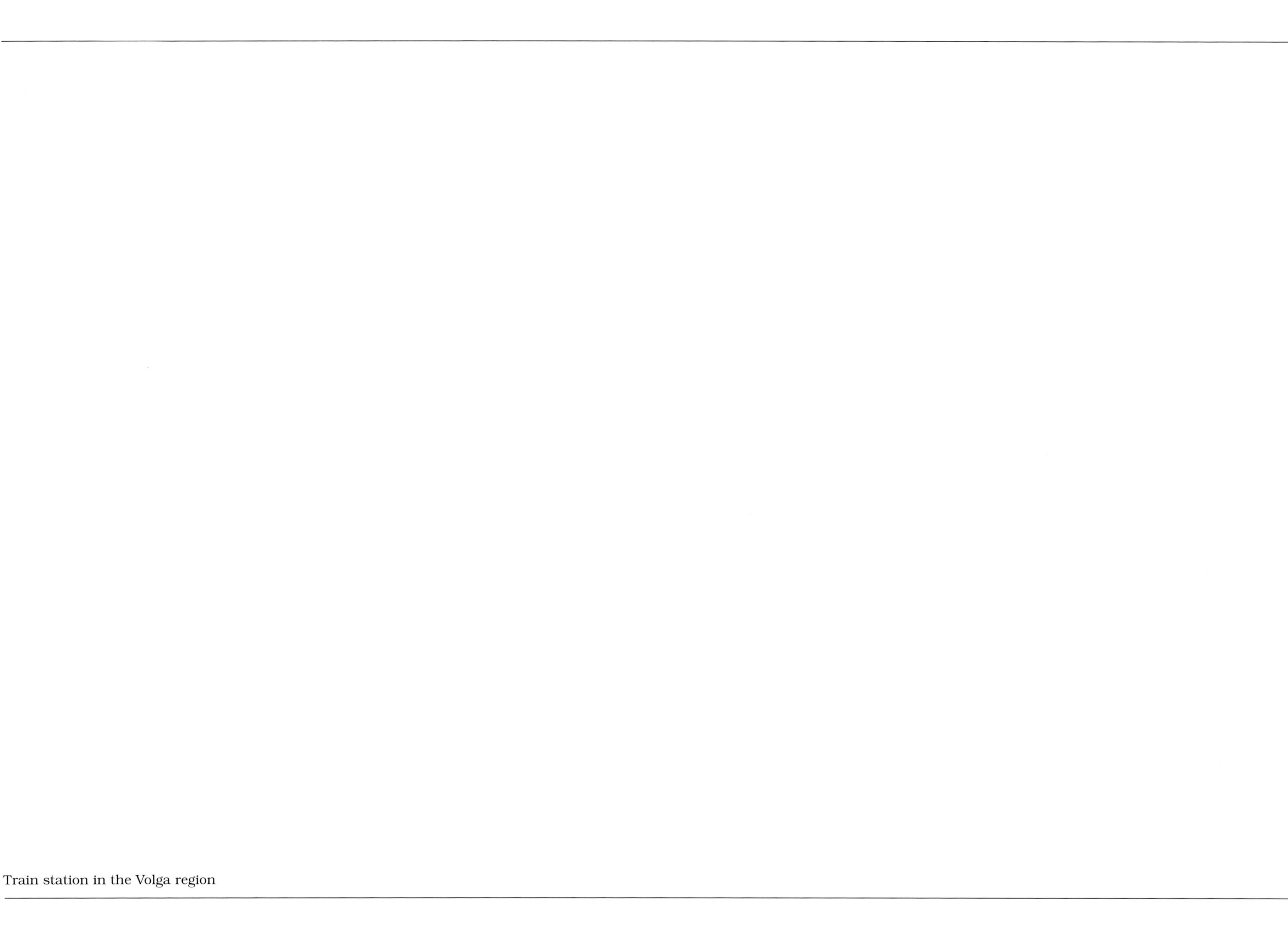

Train station in the Volga region

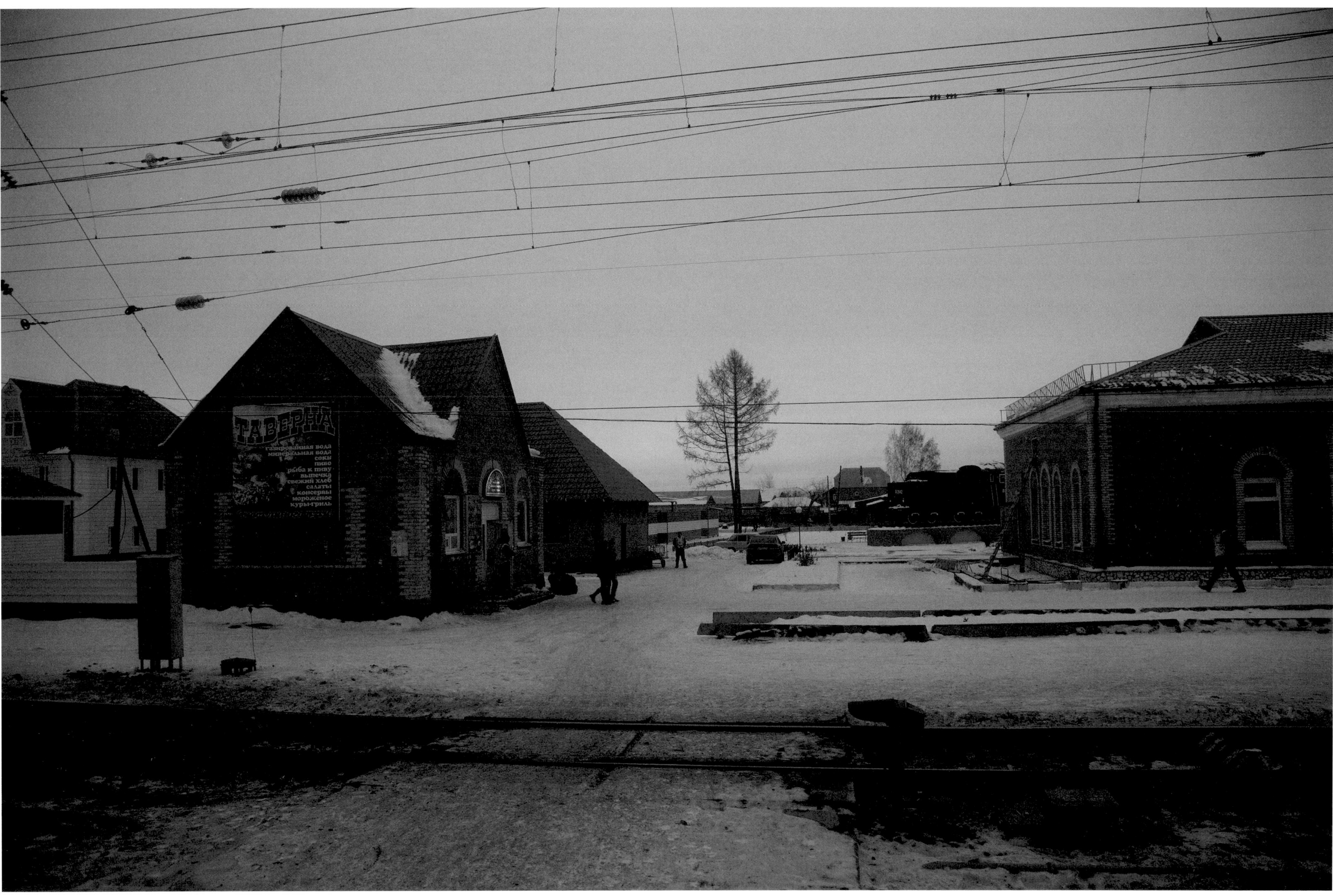
ТАВЕРНА
газированная вода
минеральная вода
соки
пиво
рыба к пиву
выпечка
свежий хлеб
салаты
консервы
мороженое
куры-гриль

Green building adds colour to Siberian village towards Vladivostok

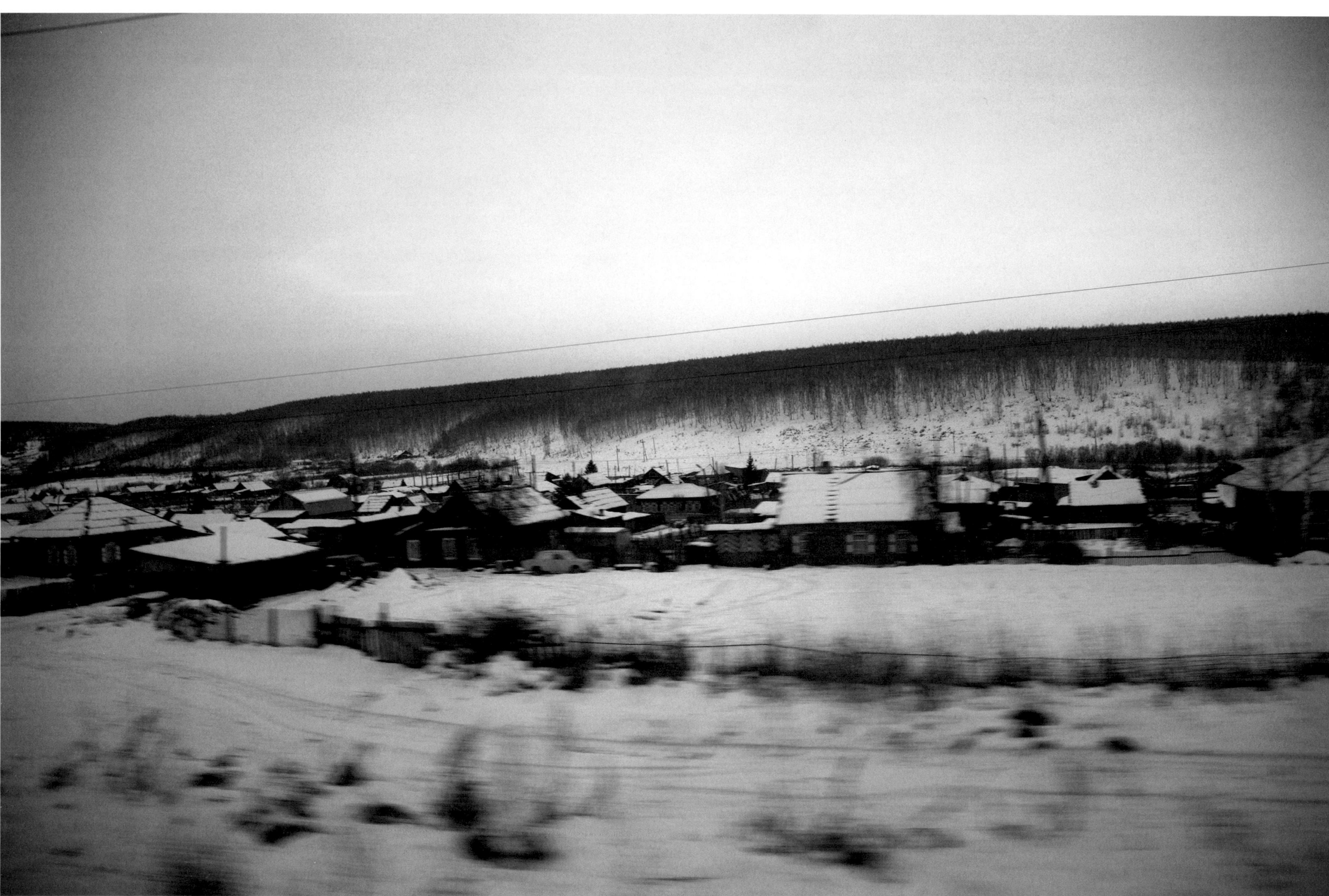

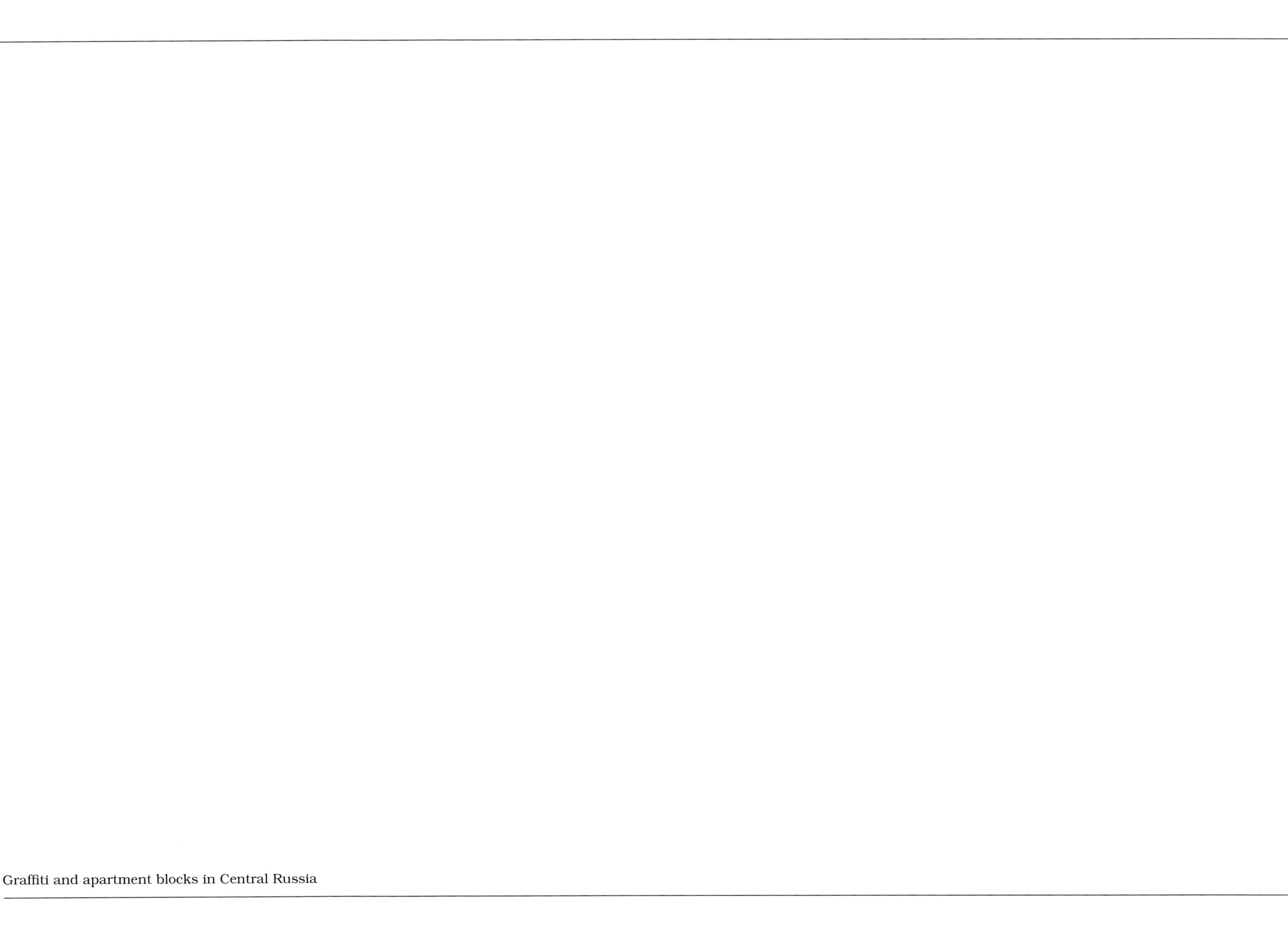

Graffiti and apartment blocks in Central Russia

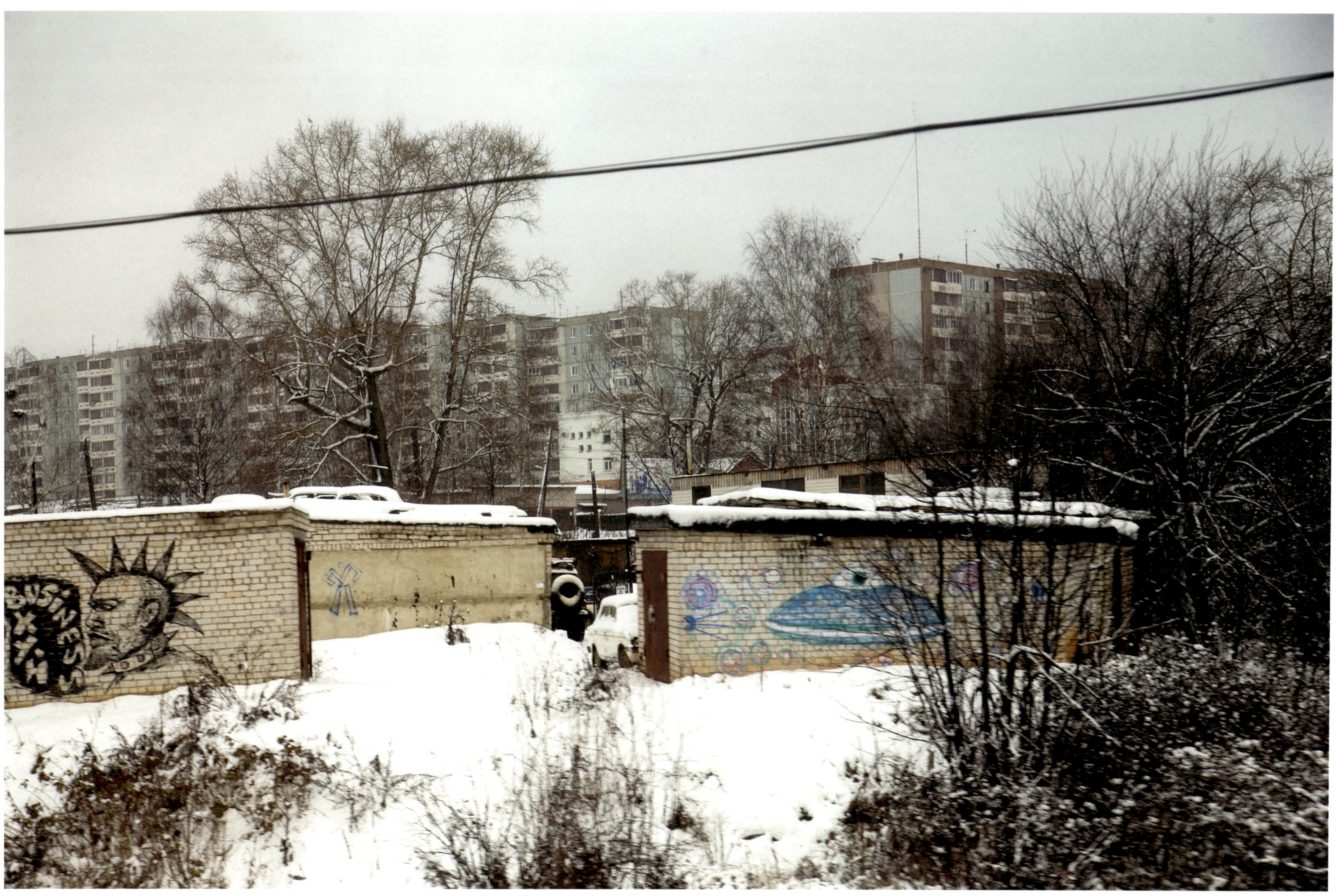
BUSINESS

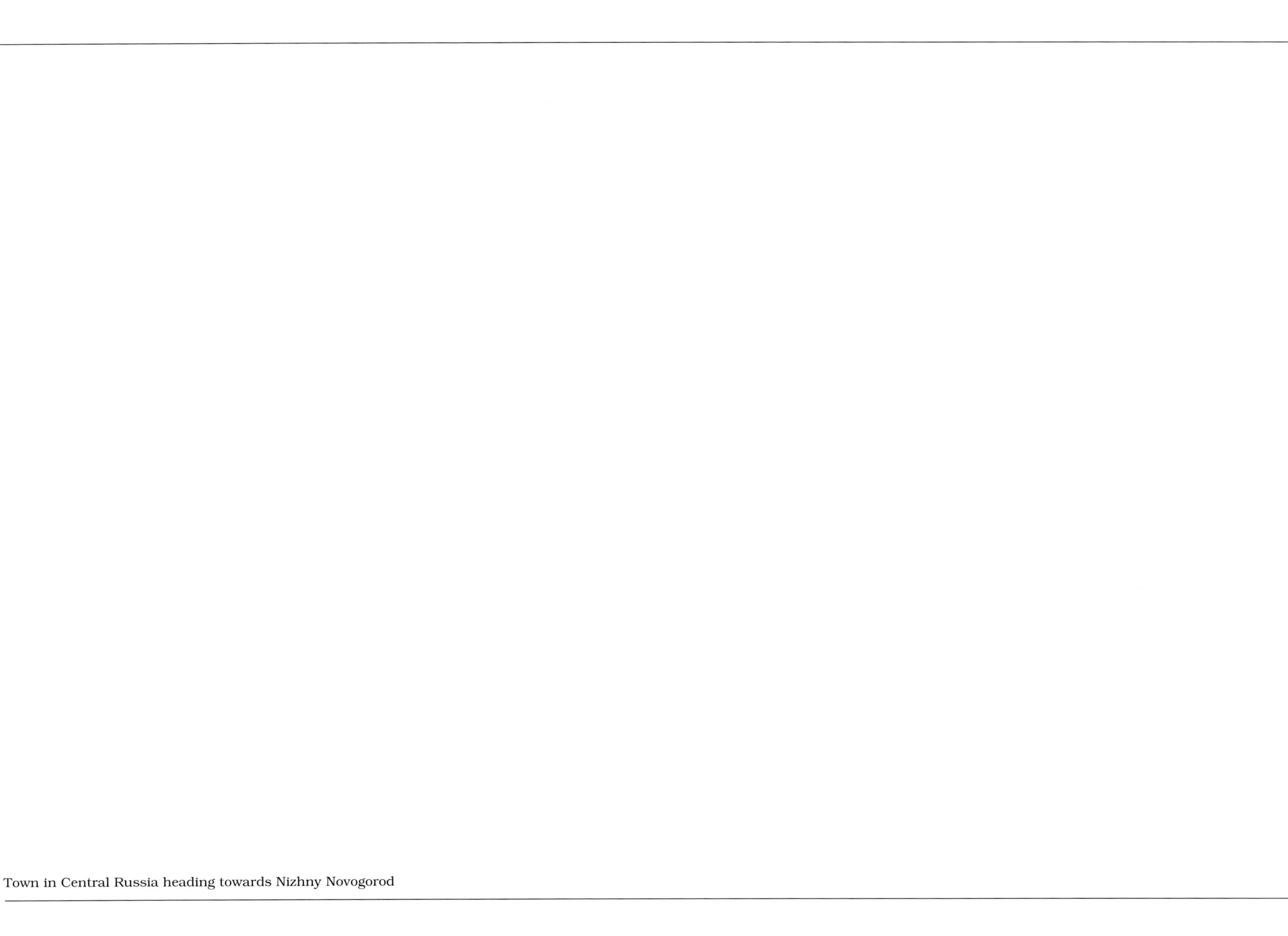

Town in Central Russia heading towards Nizhny Novogorod

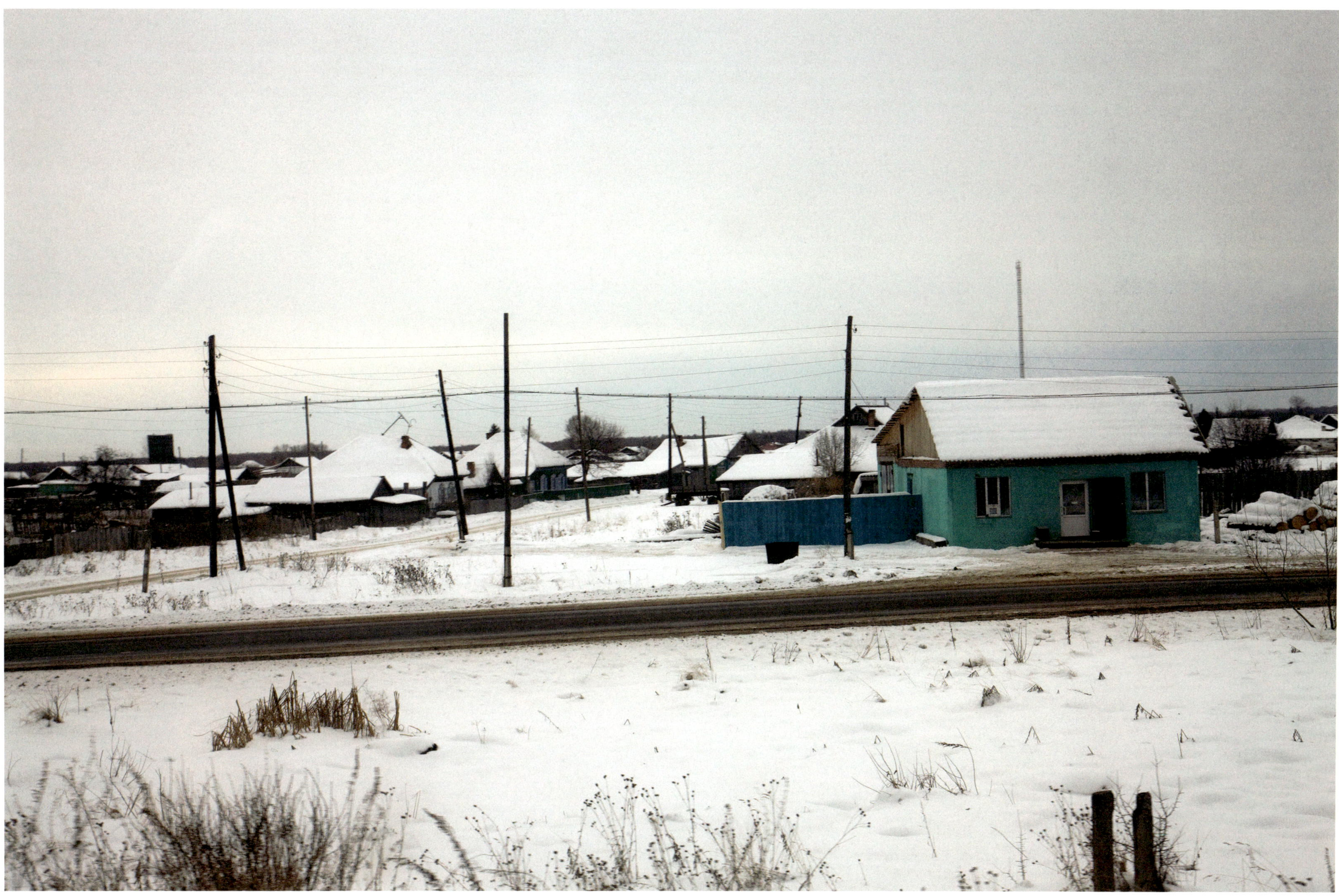

Village in Siberia

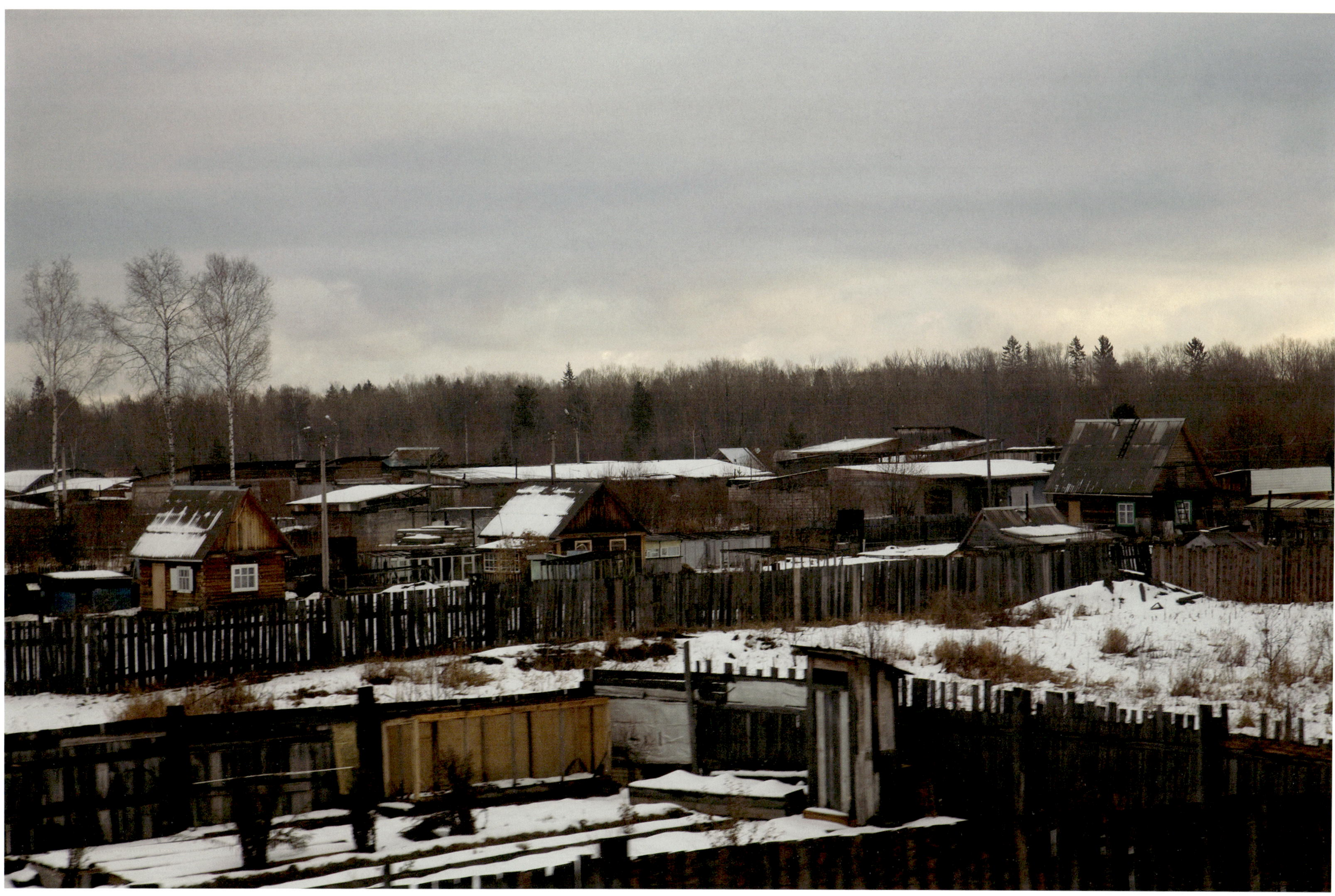

Village east of the Urals in Siberia

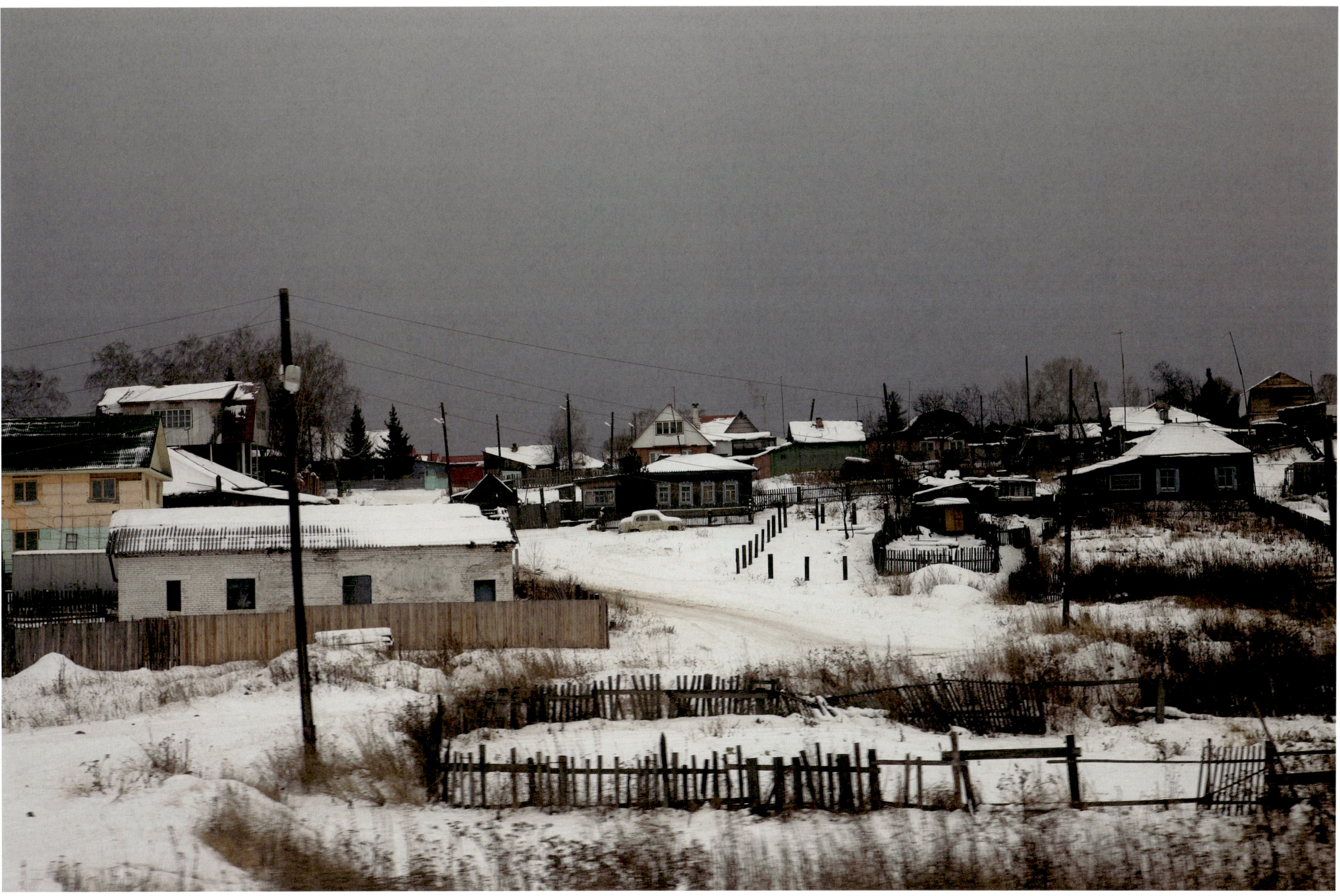

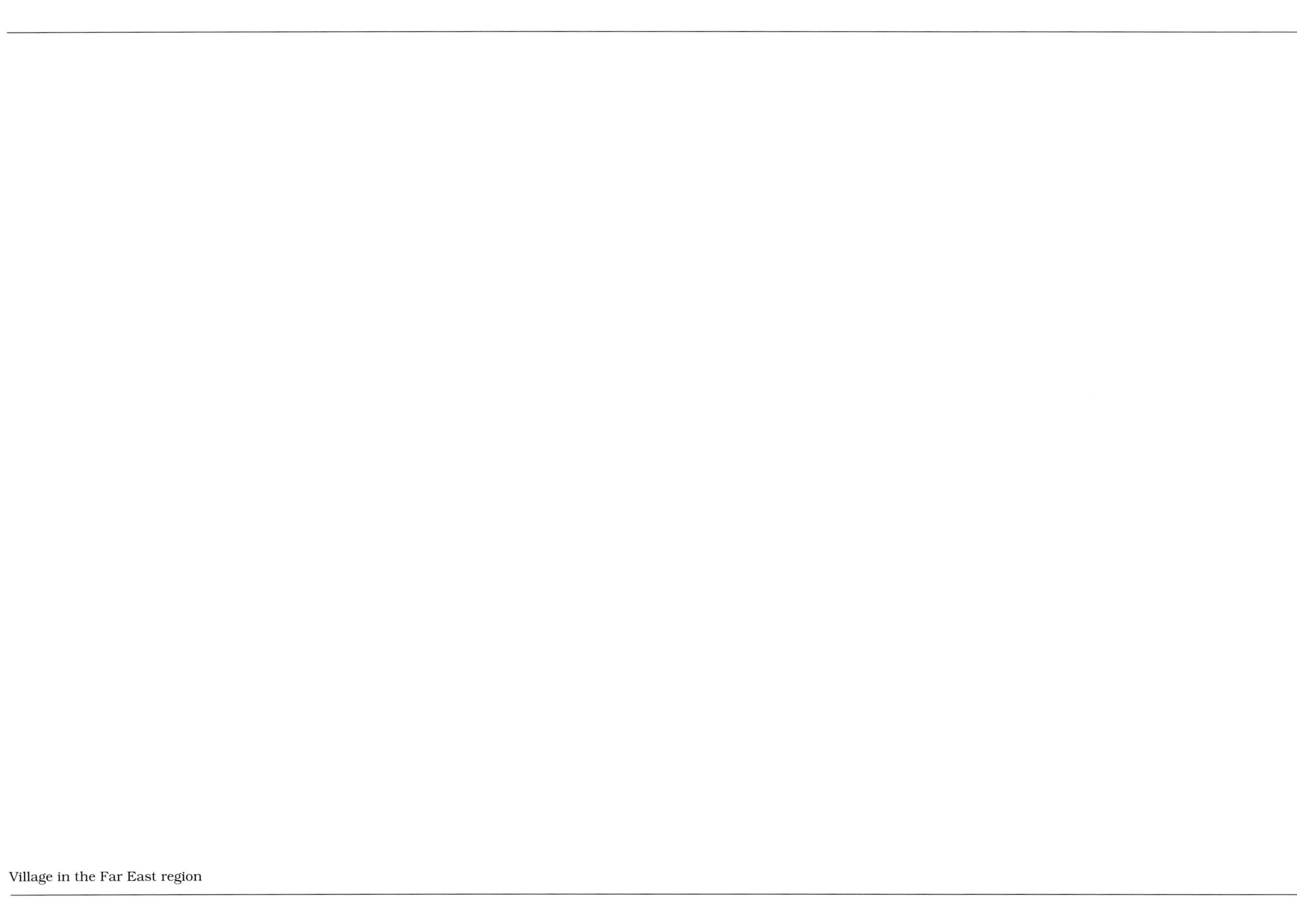

Village in the Far East region

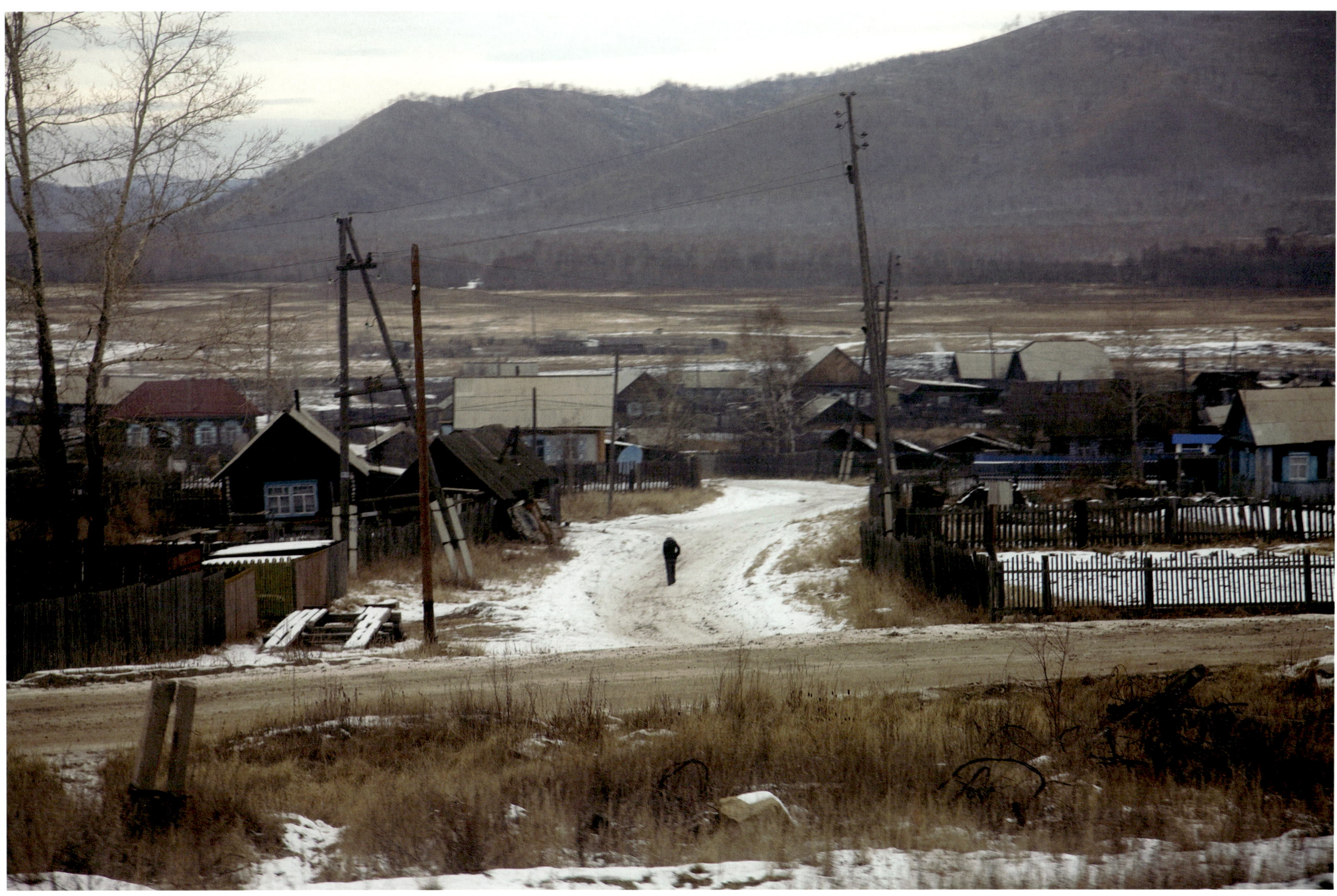

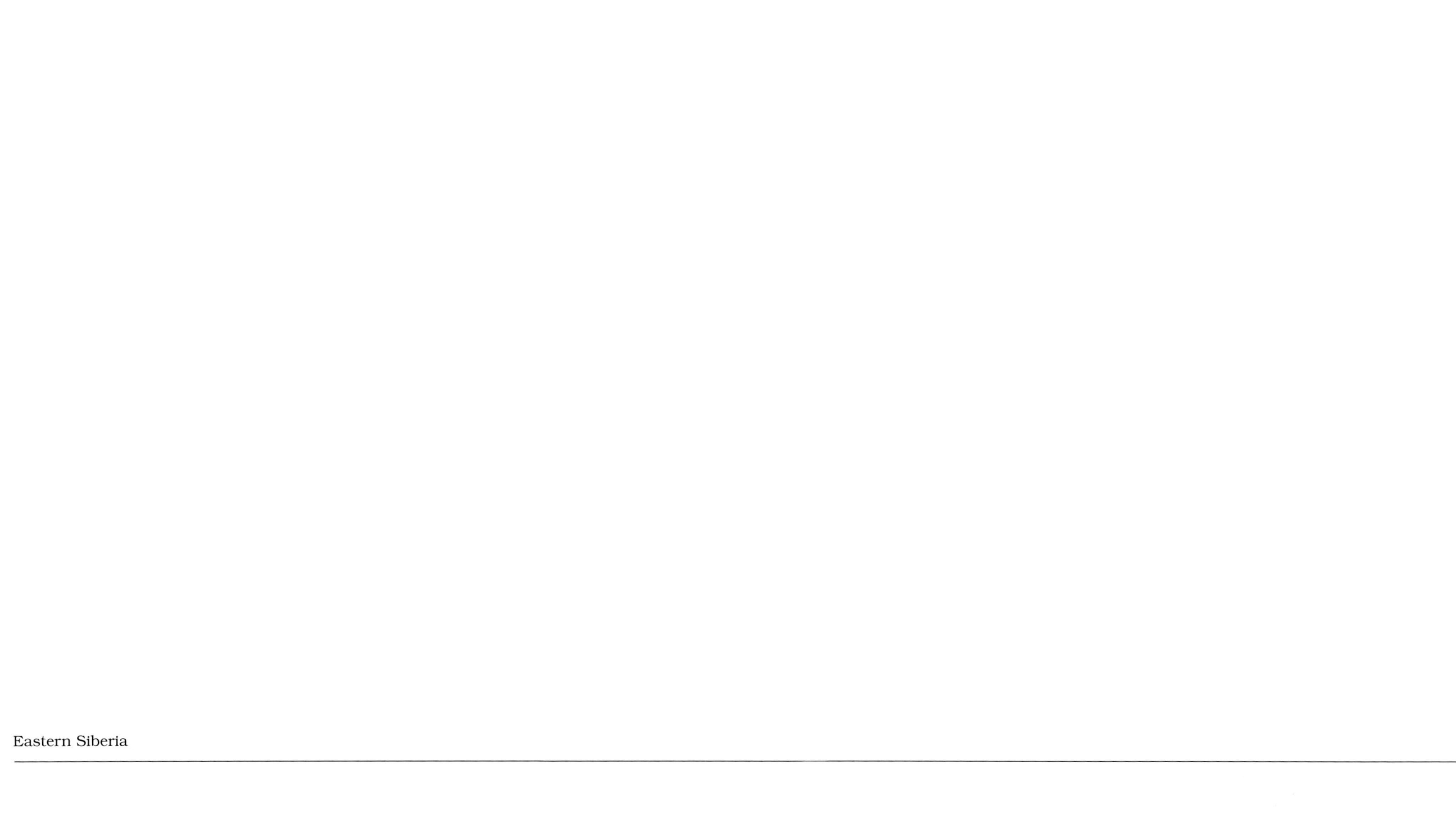

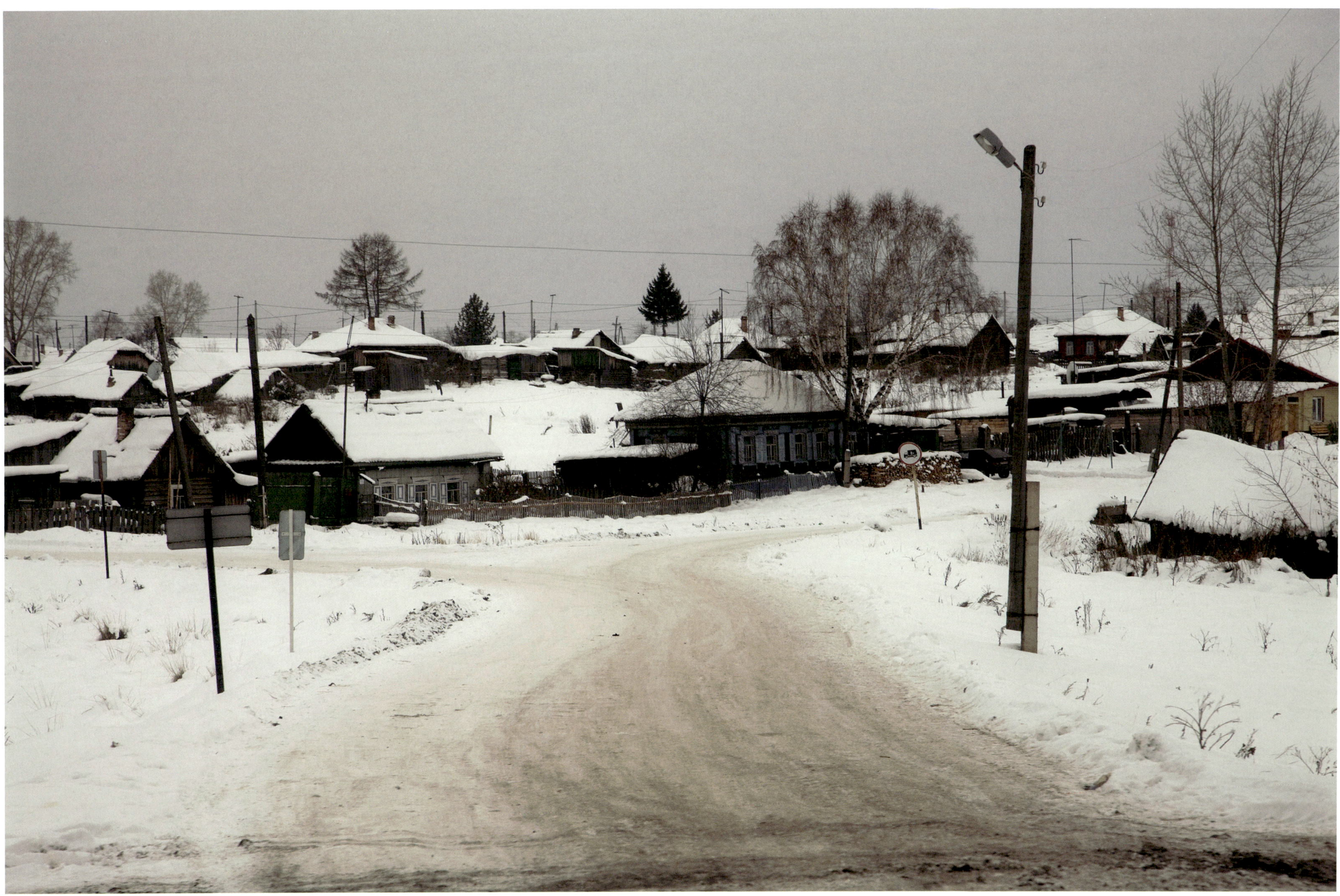

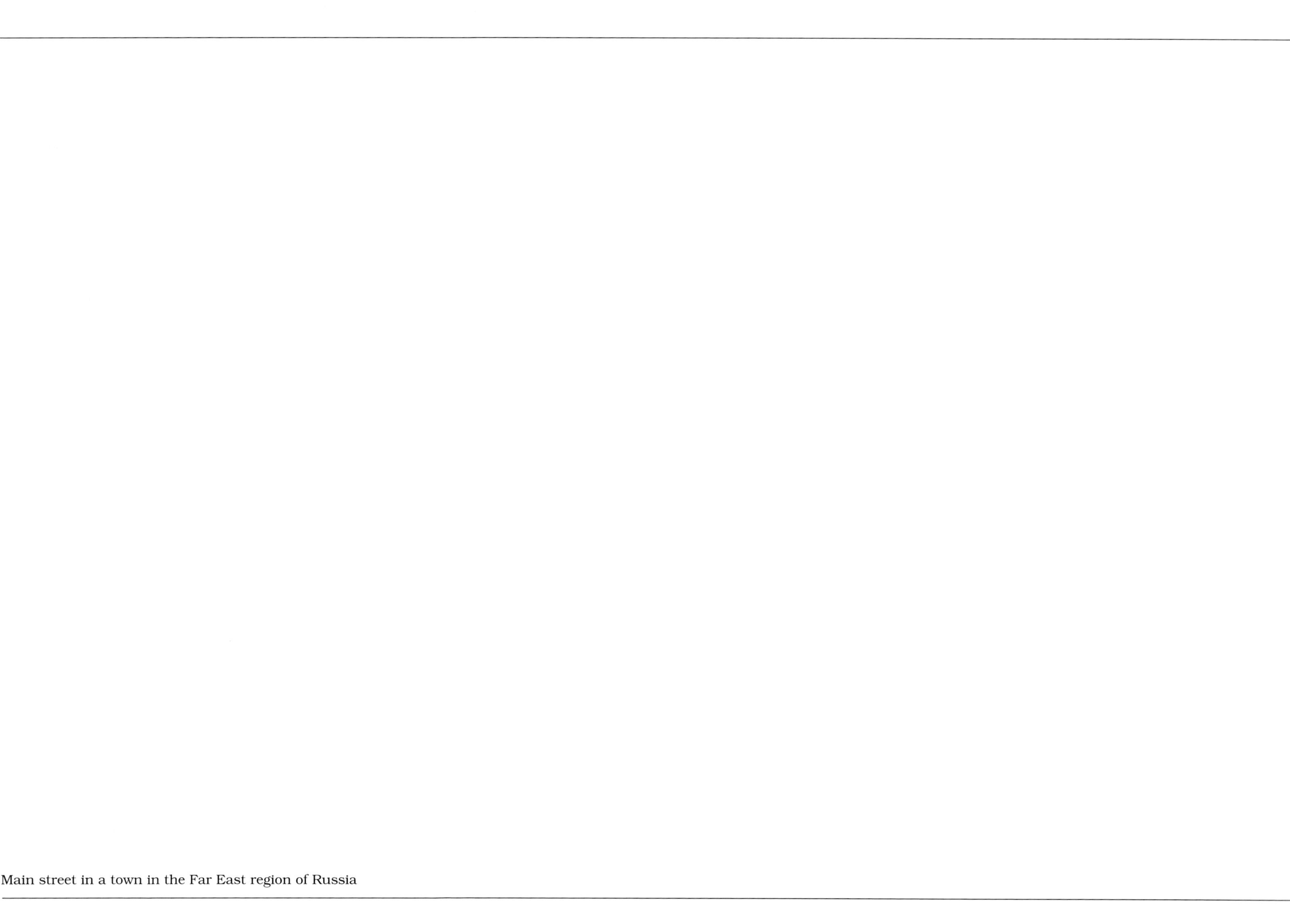

Main street in a town in the Far East region of Russia

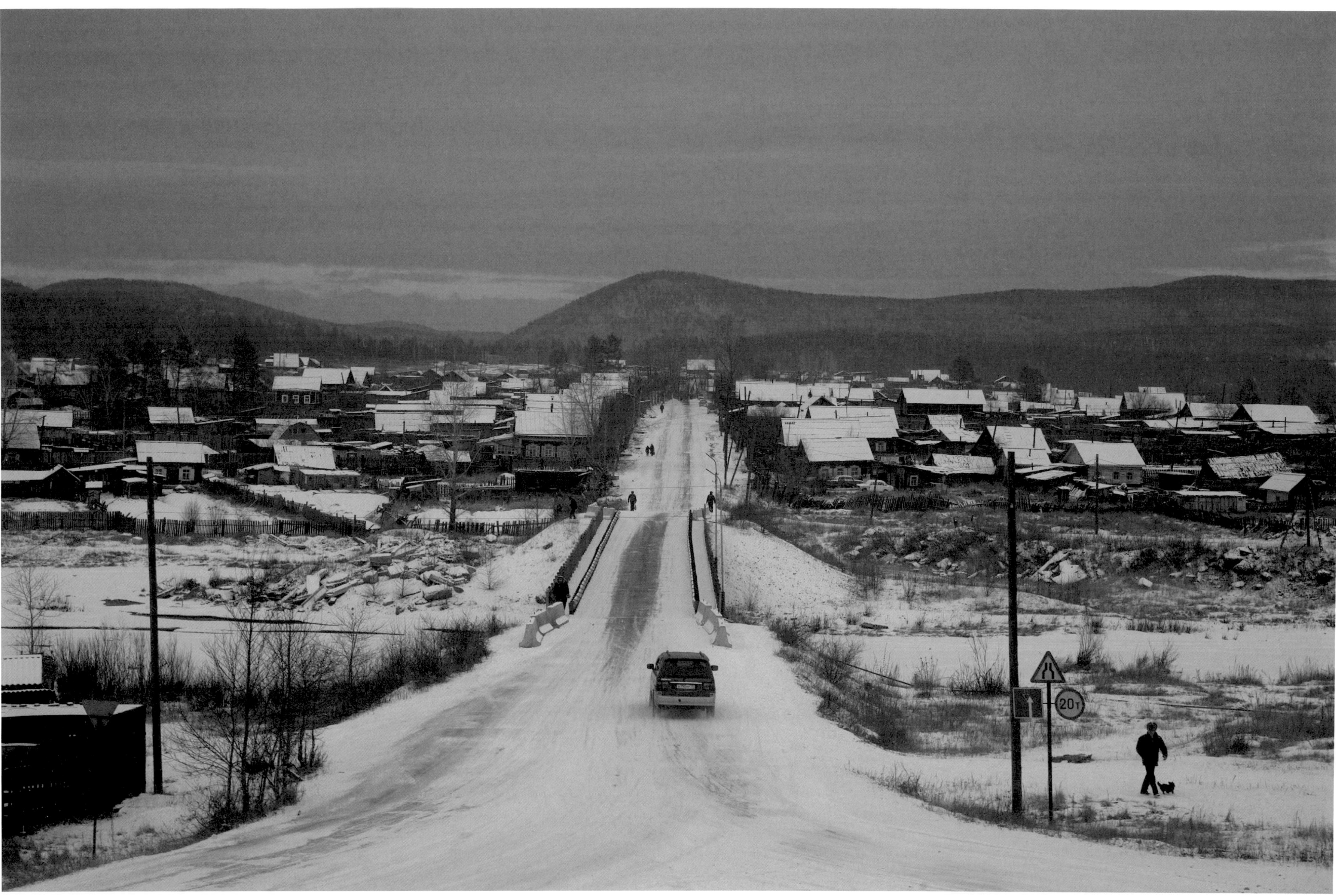

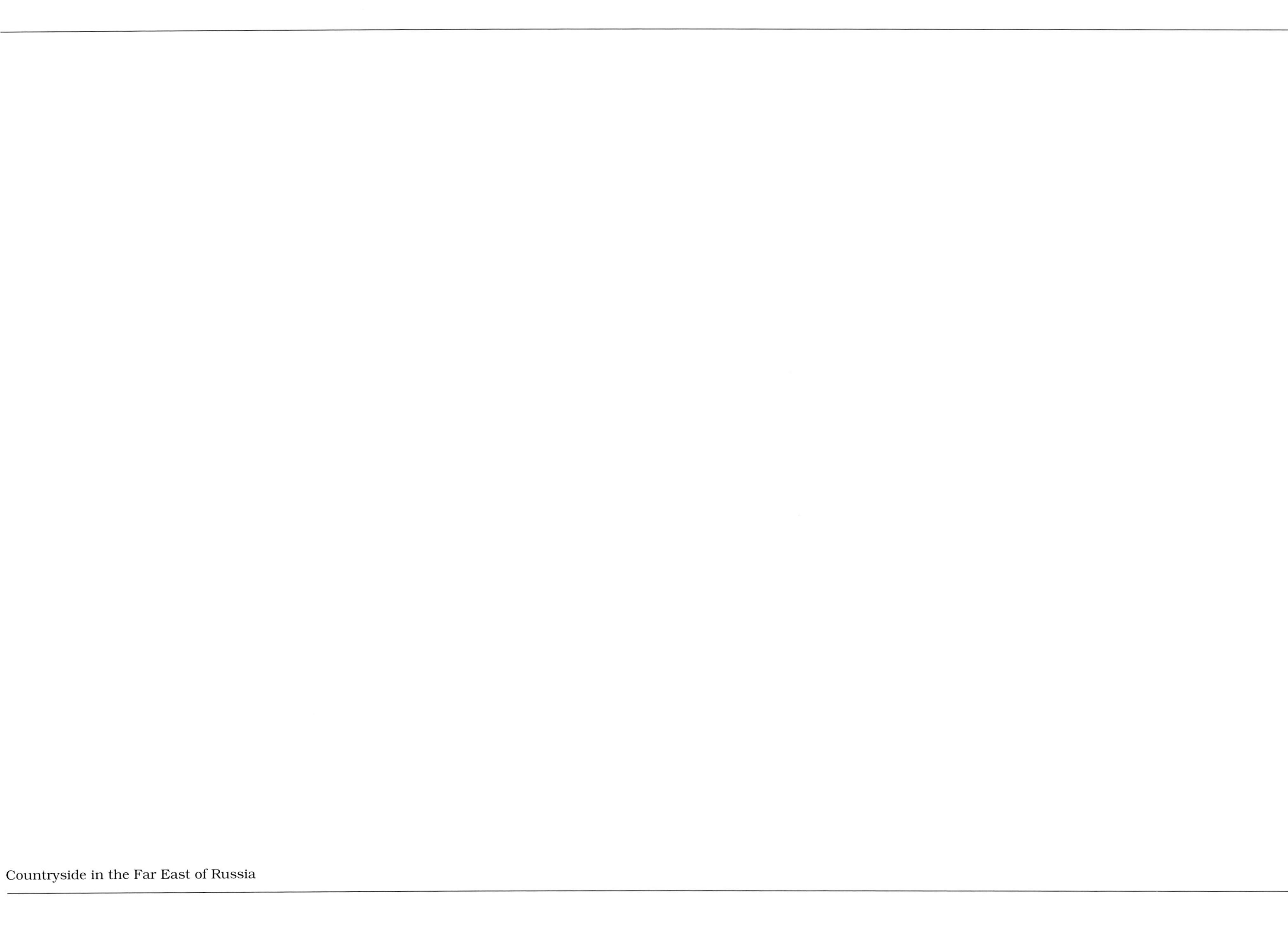

Countryside in the Far East of Russia

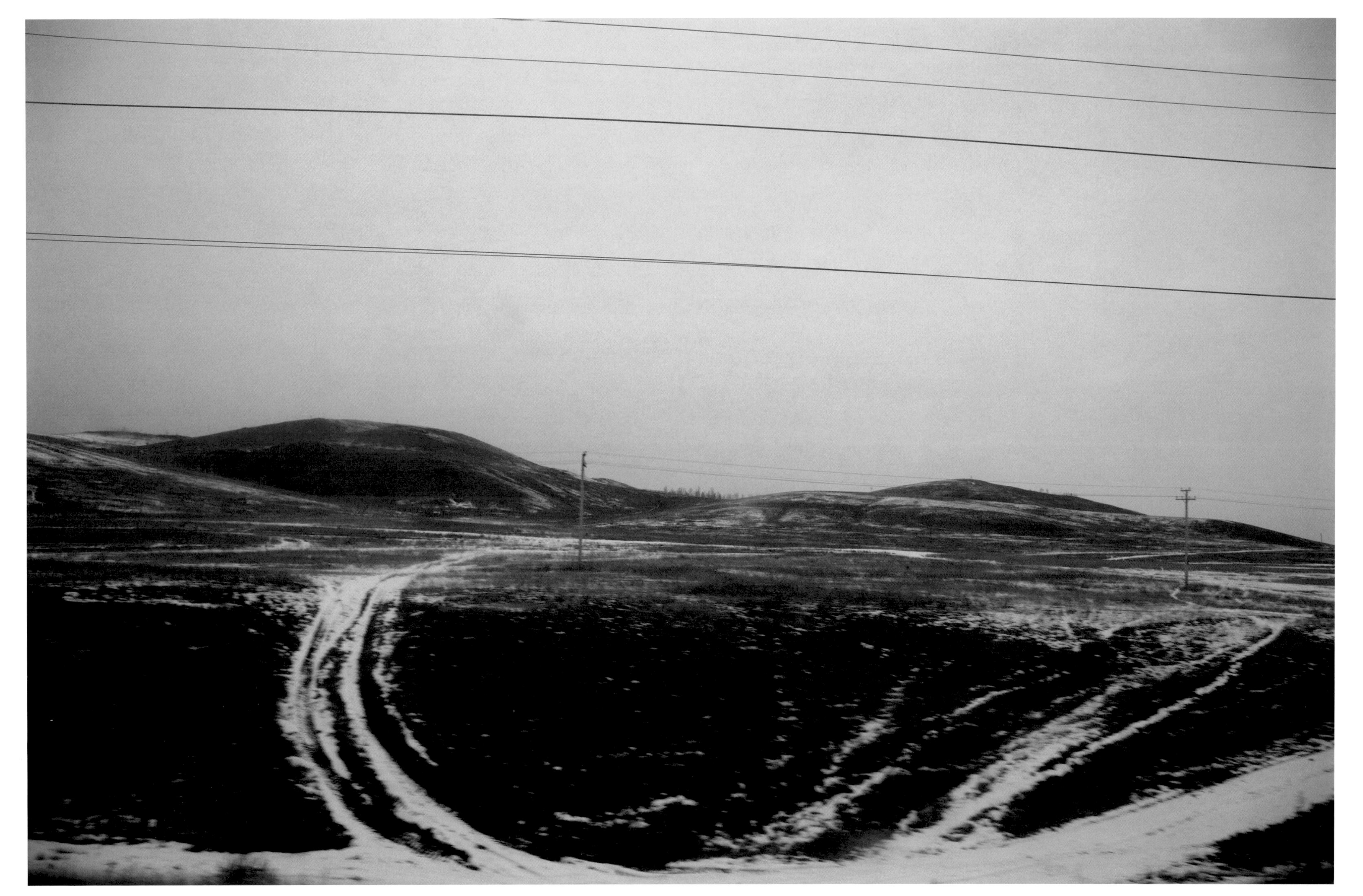

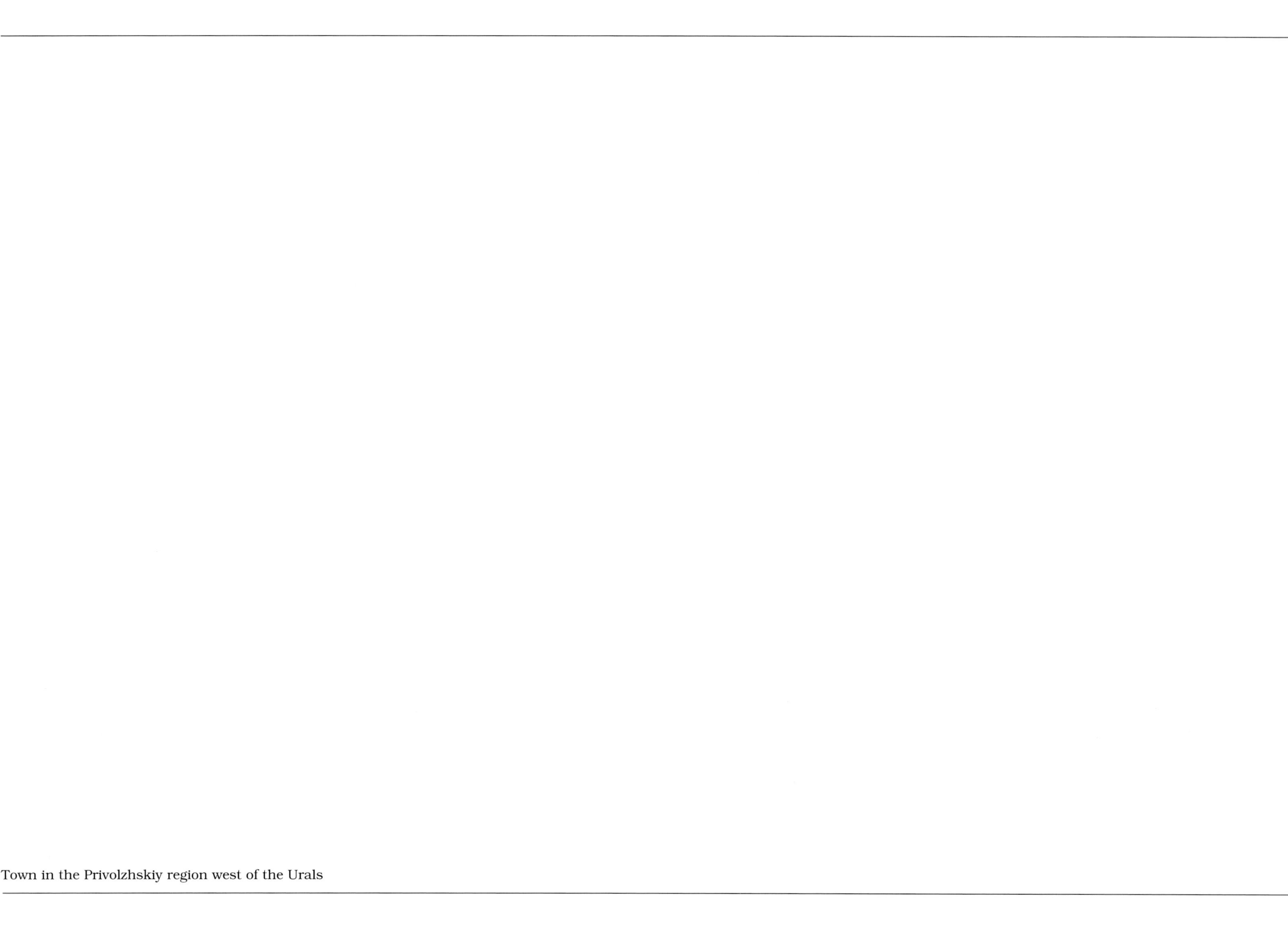

Town in the Privolzhskiy region west of the Urals

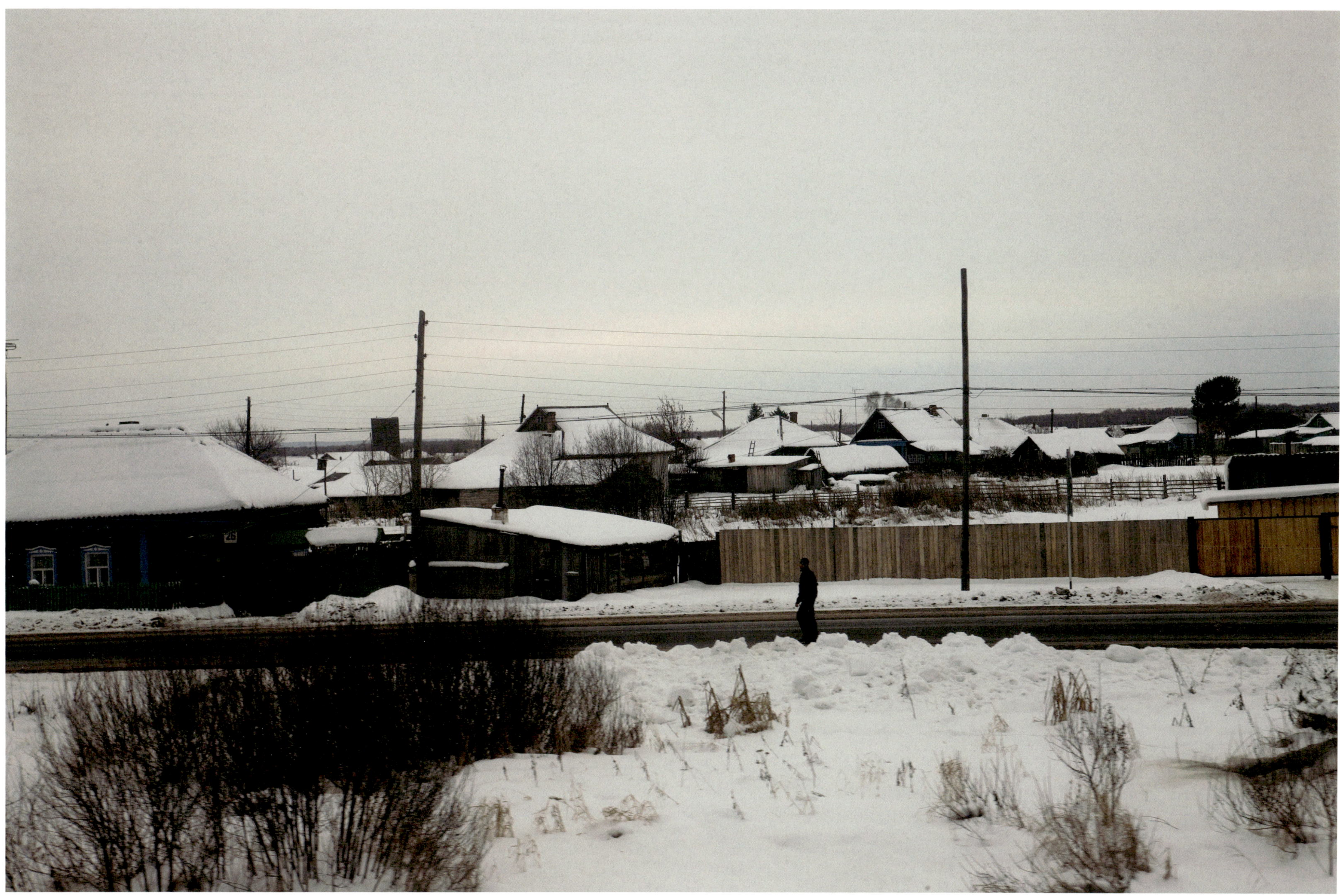

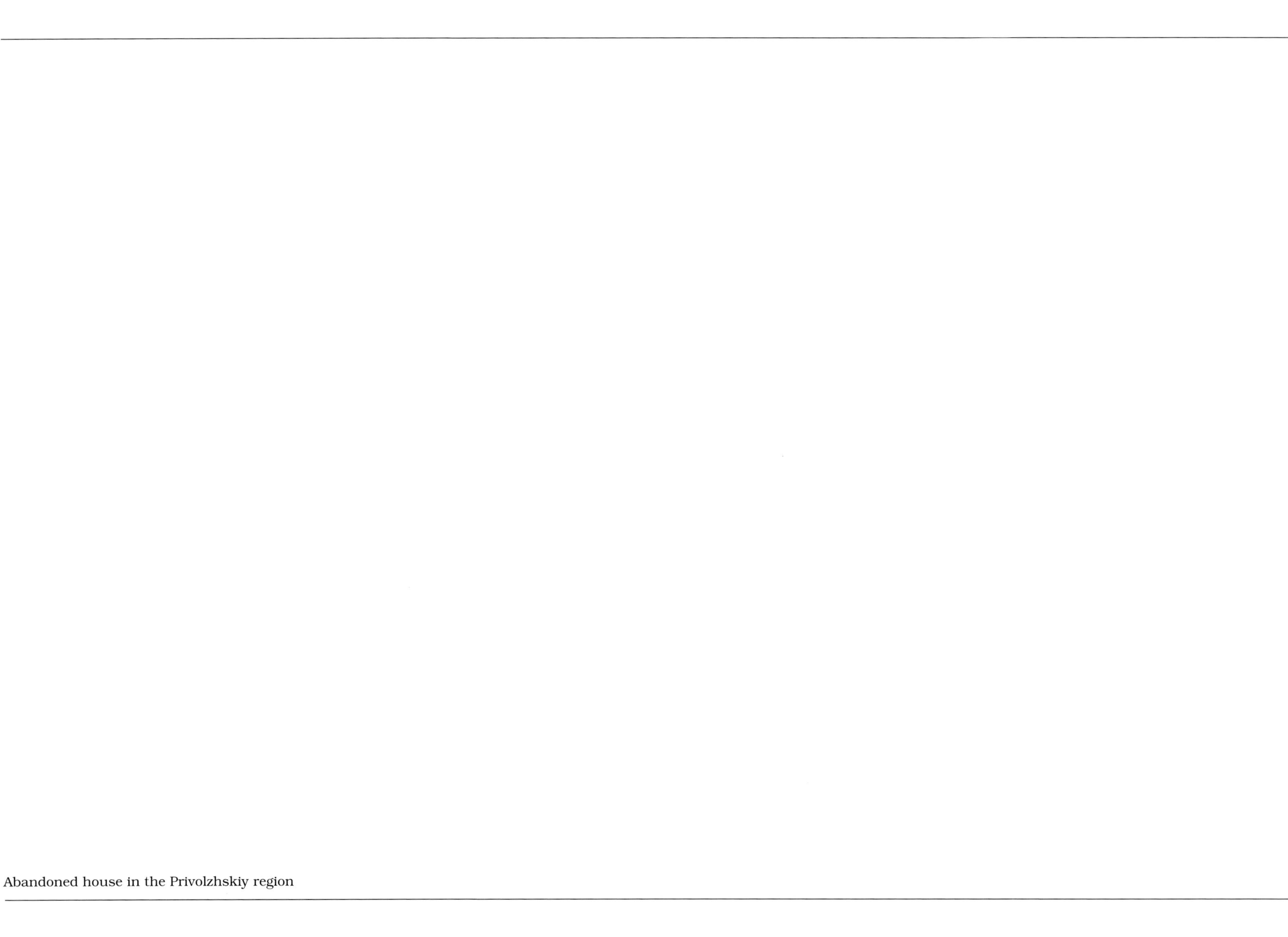

Abandoned house in the Privolzhskiy region

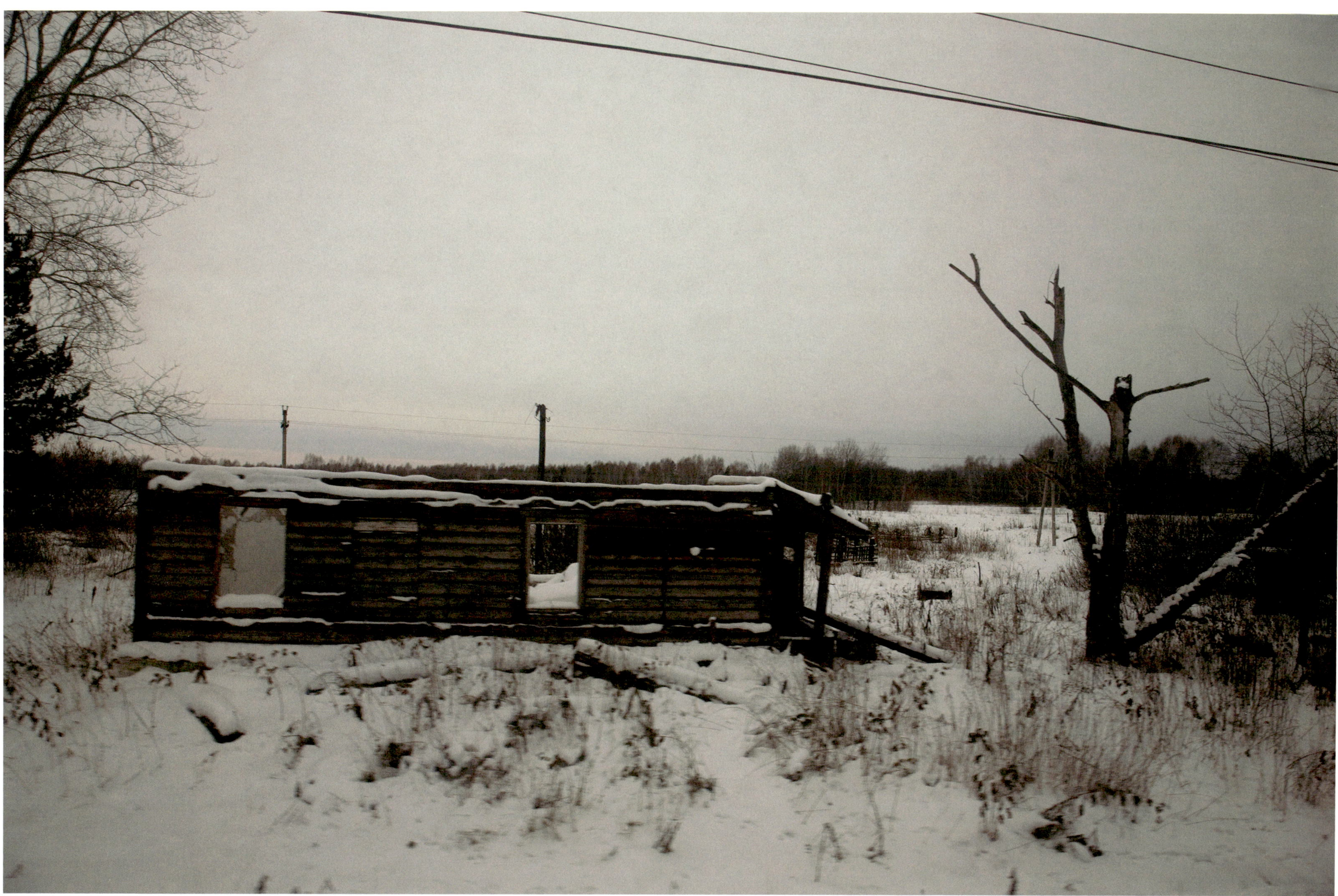

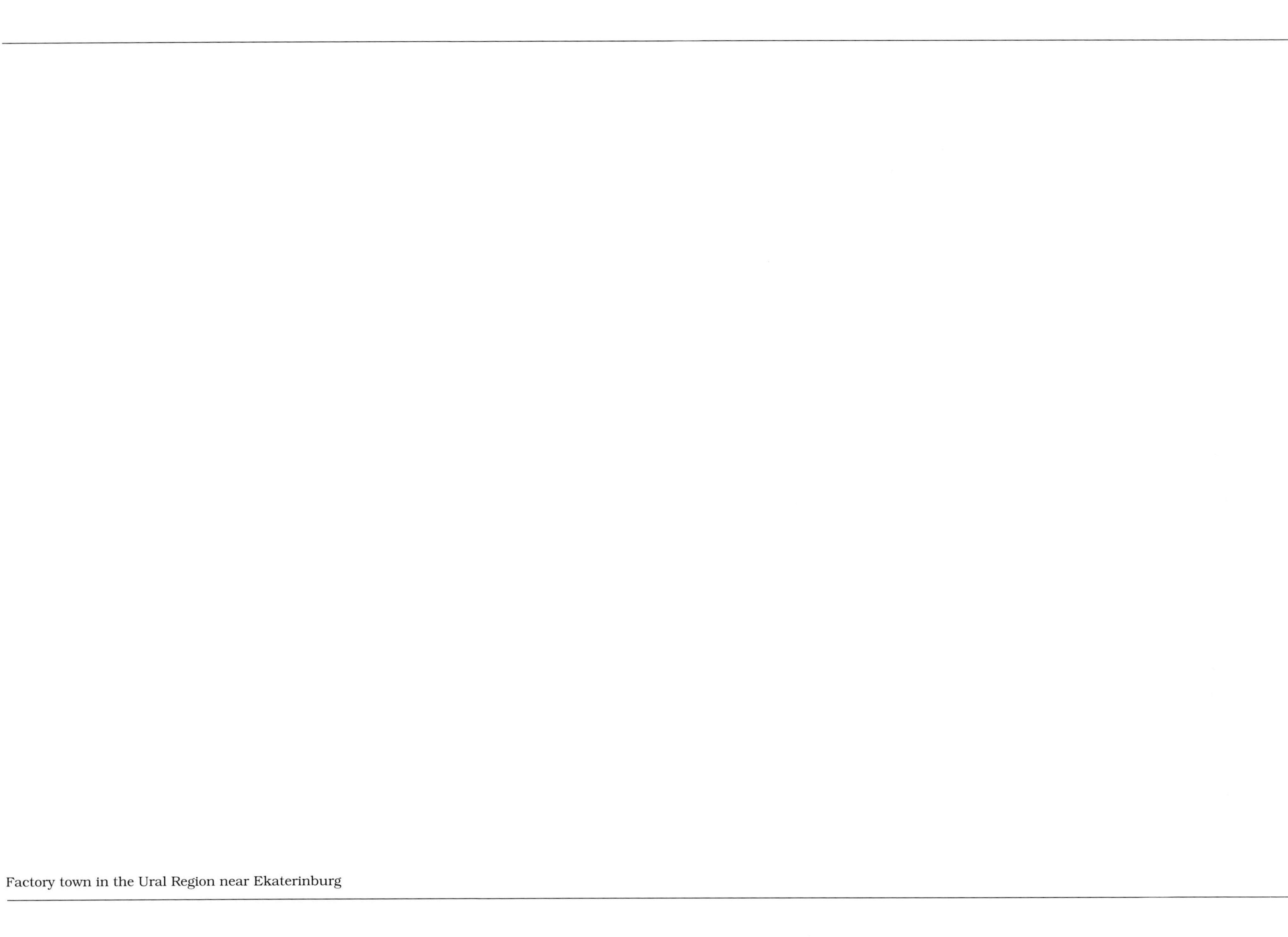

Factory town in the Ural Region near Ekaterinburg

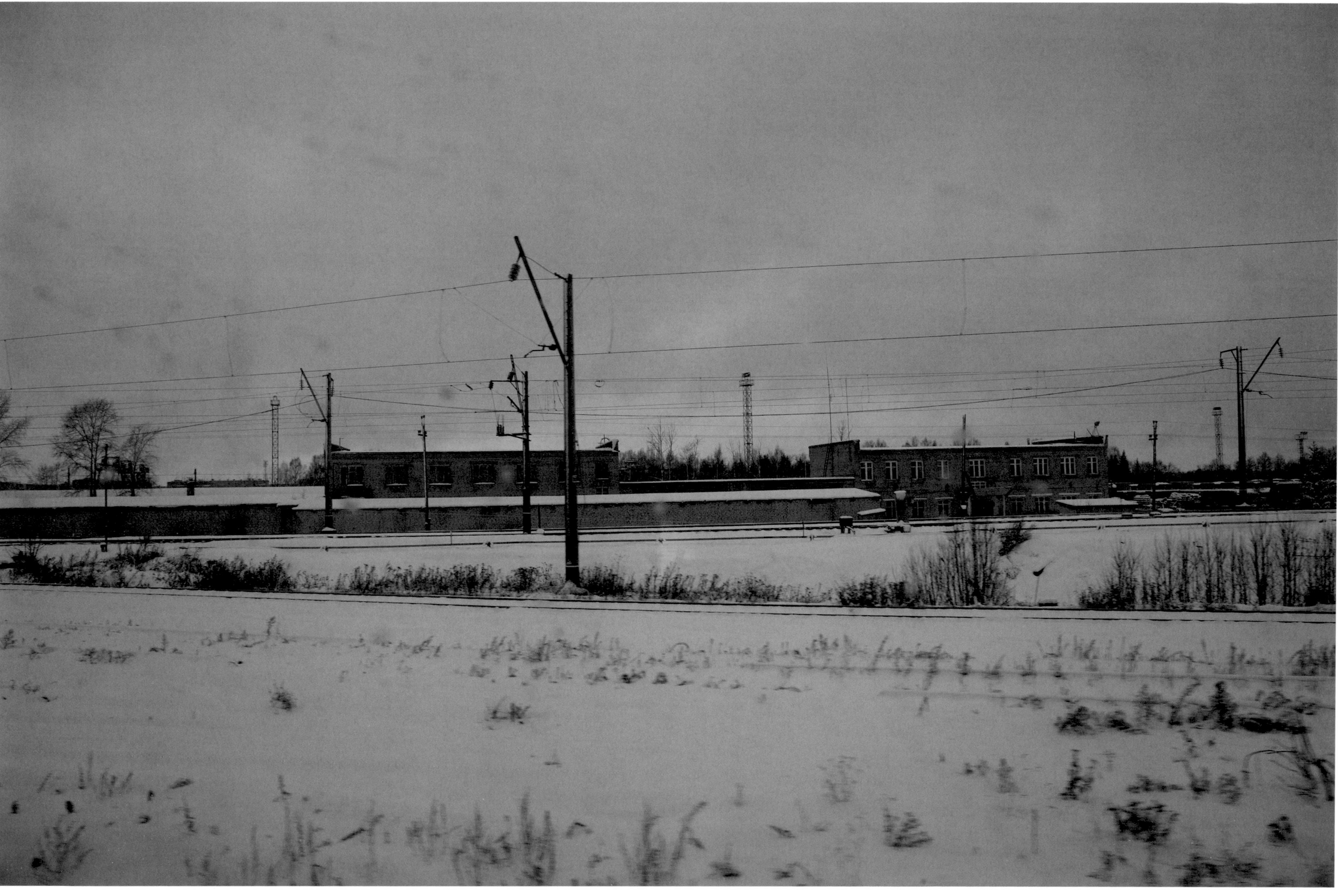

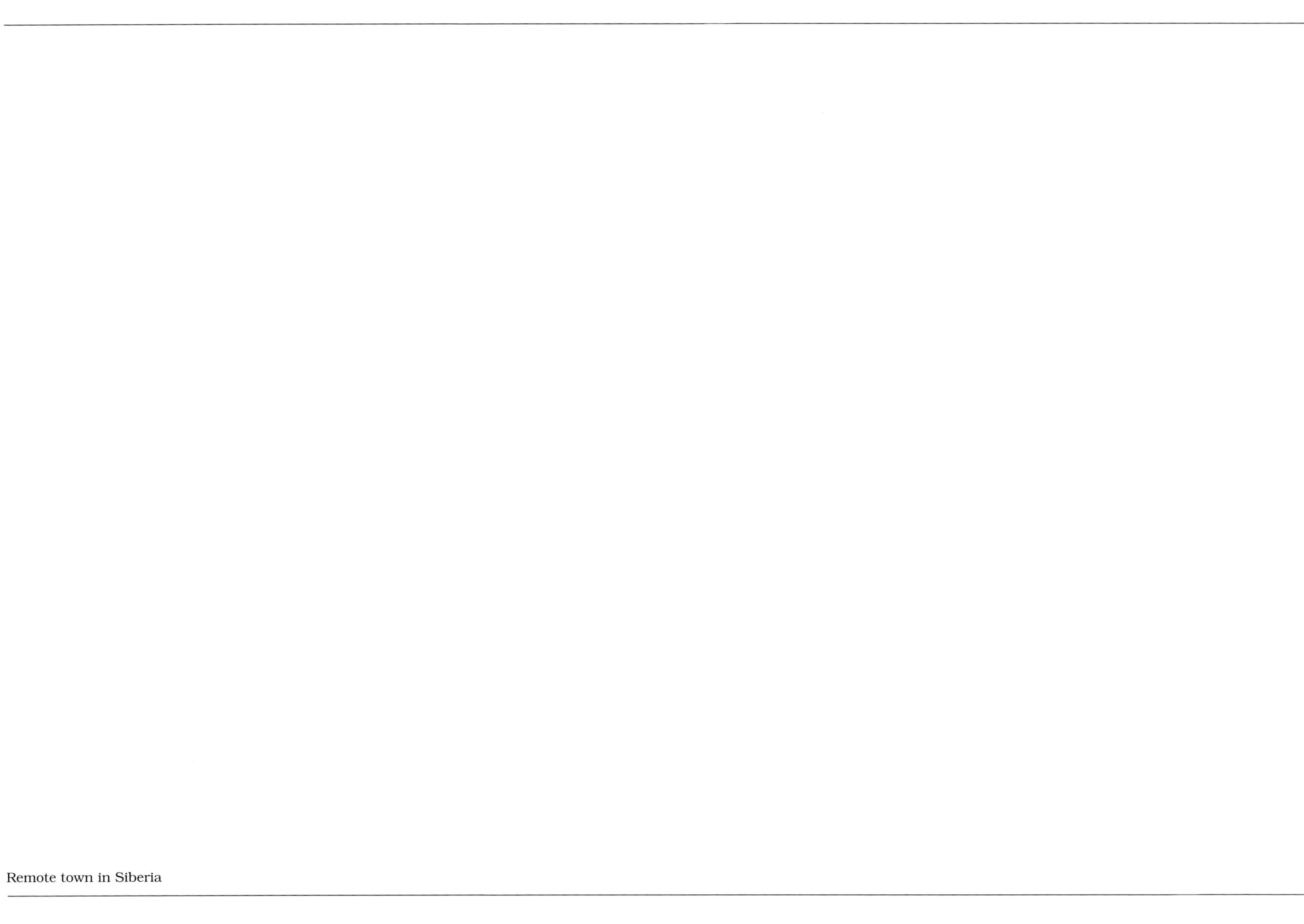

Remote town in Siberia

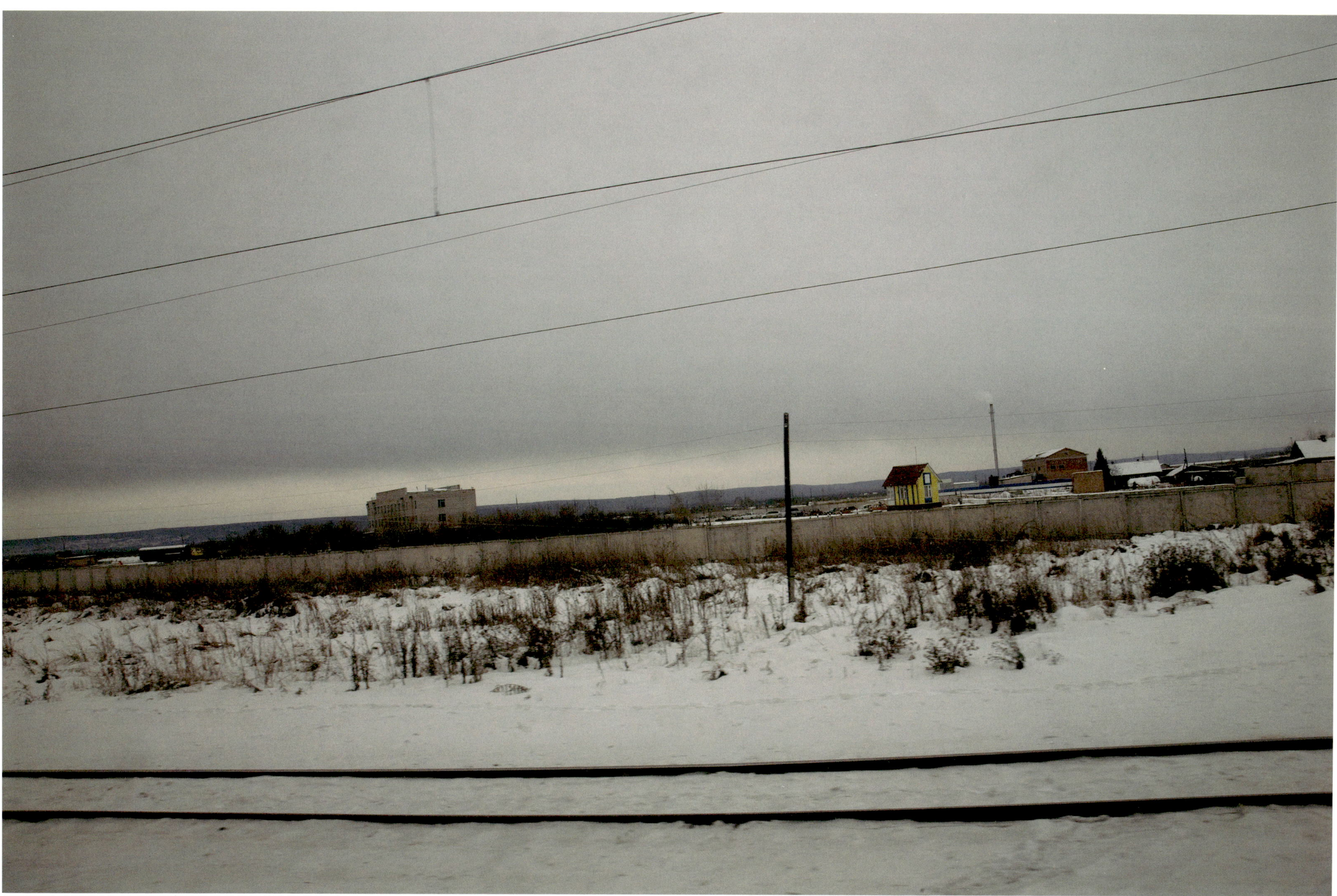

Remaining smokestack in the Far East

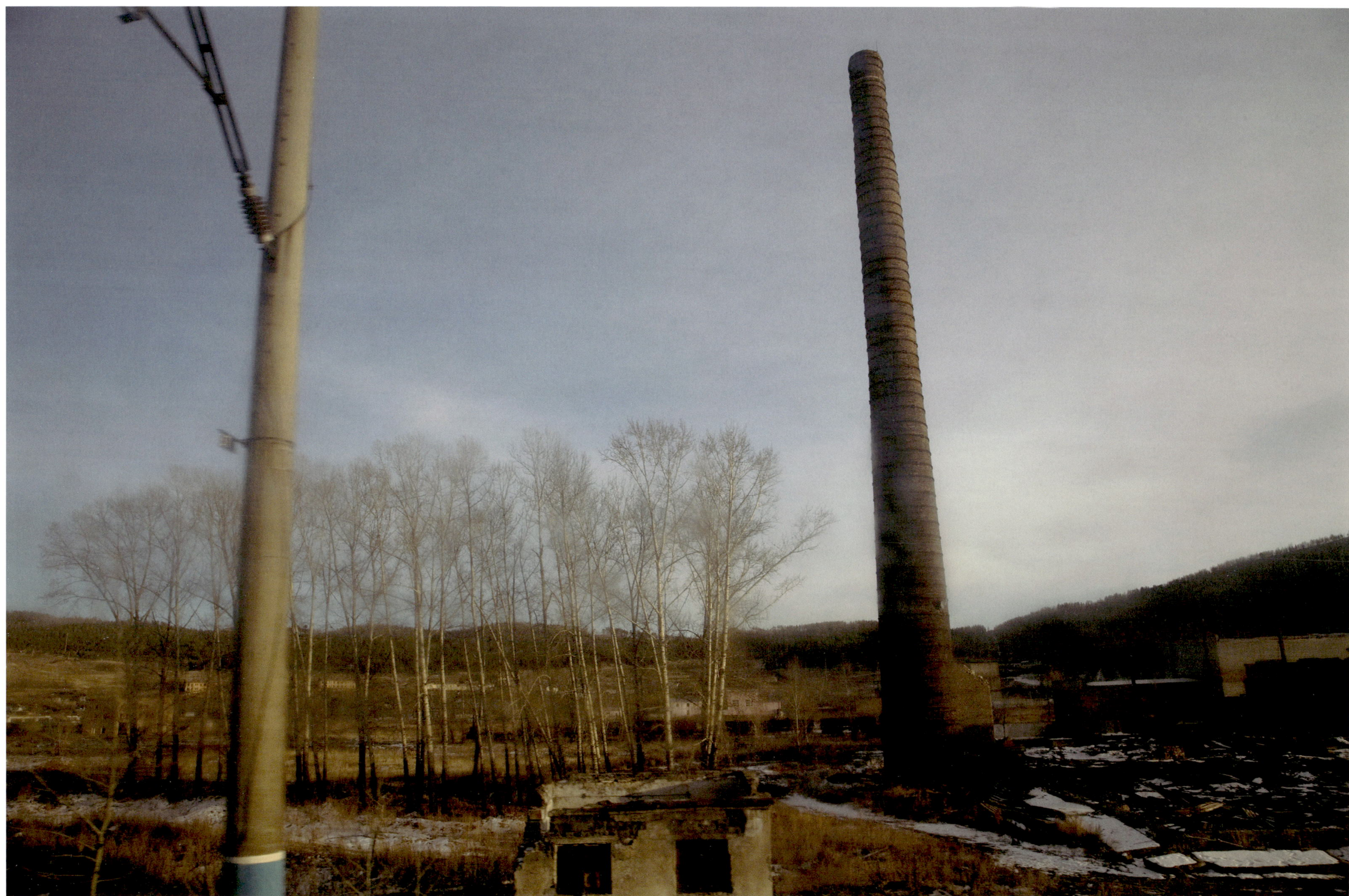

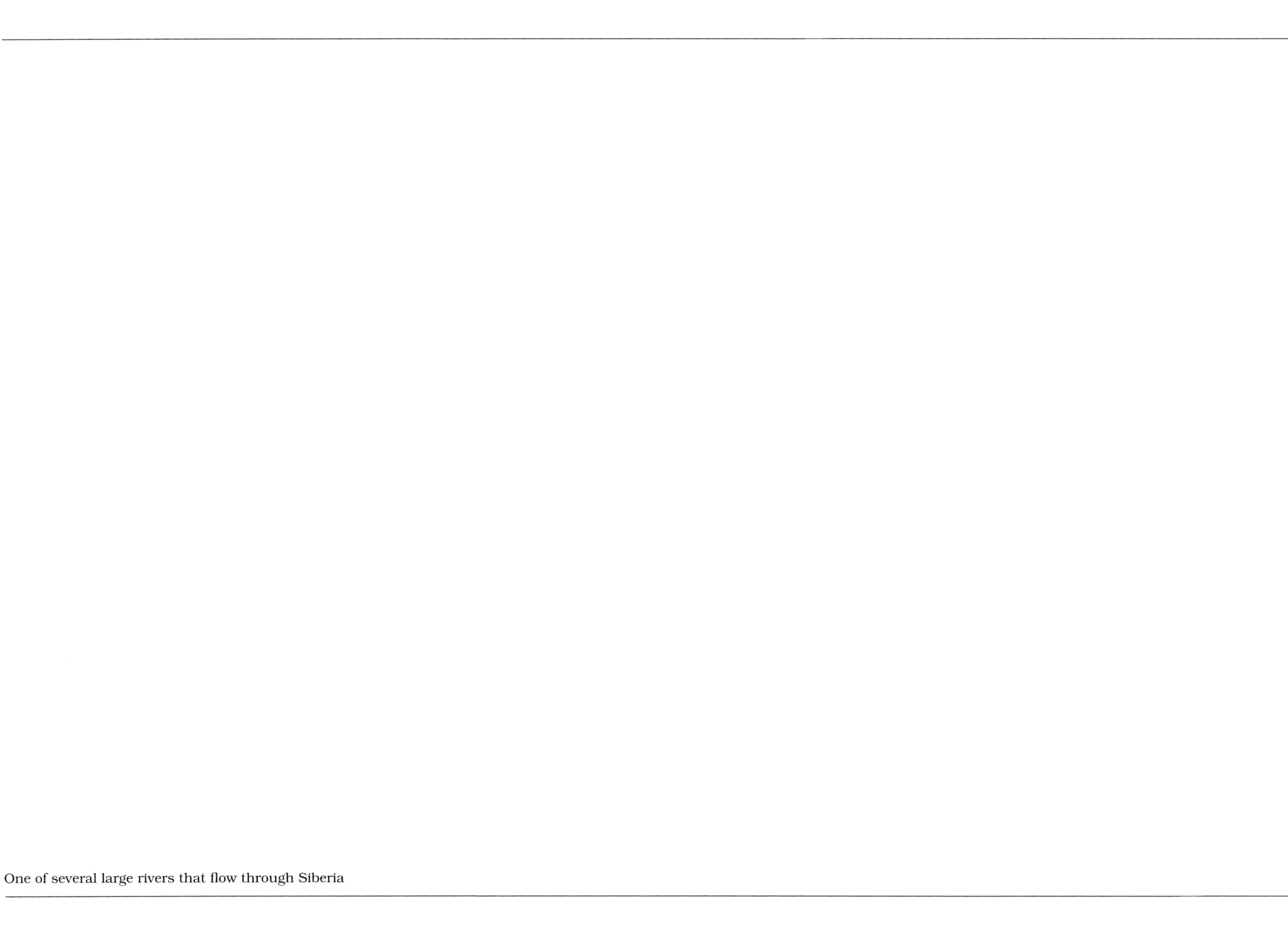

One of several large rivers that flow through Siberia

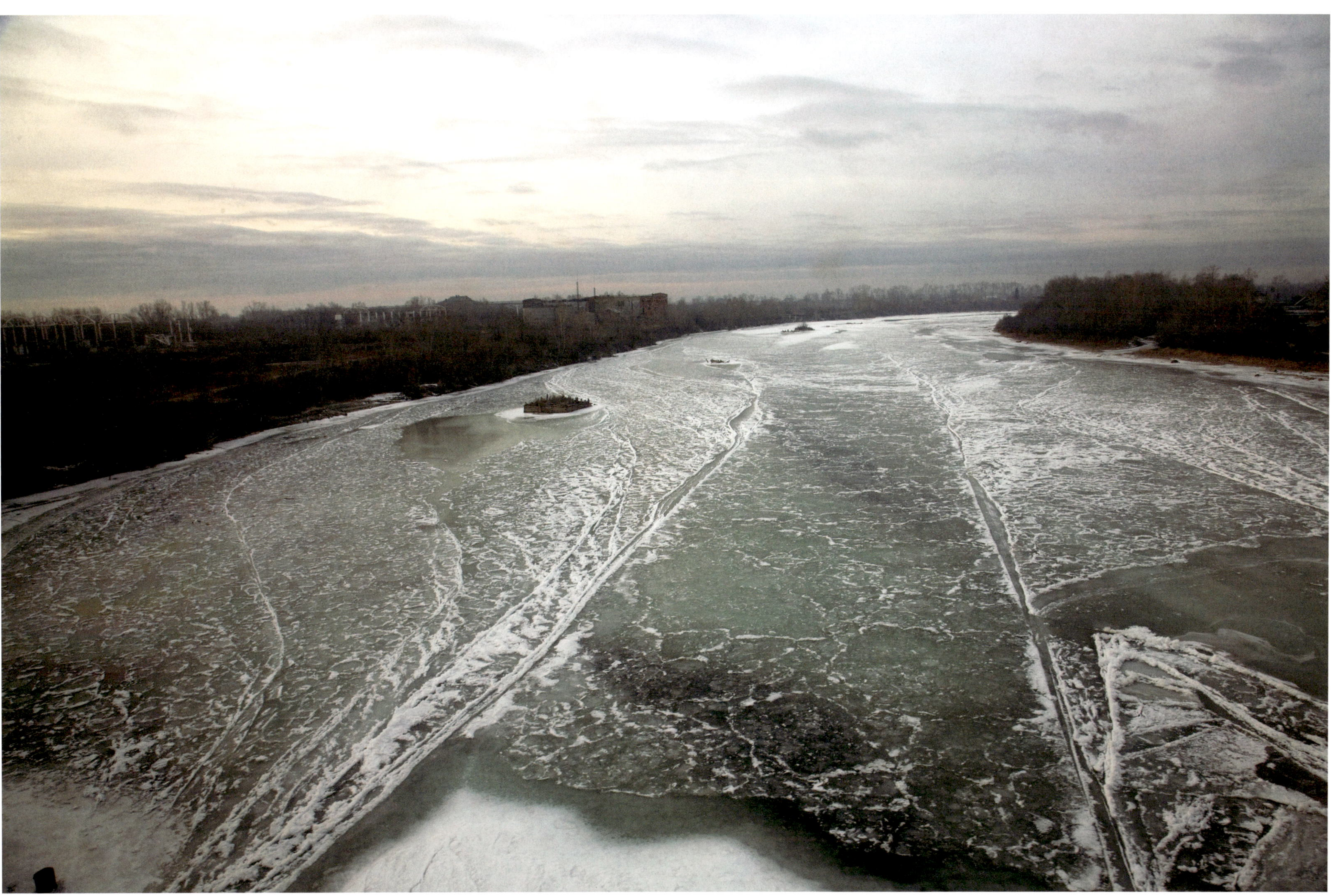

Near Lake Baikal

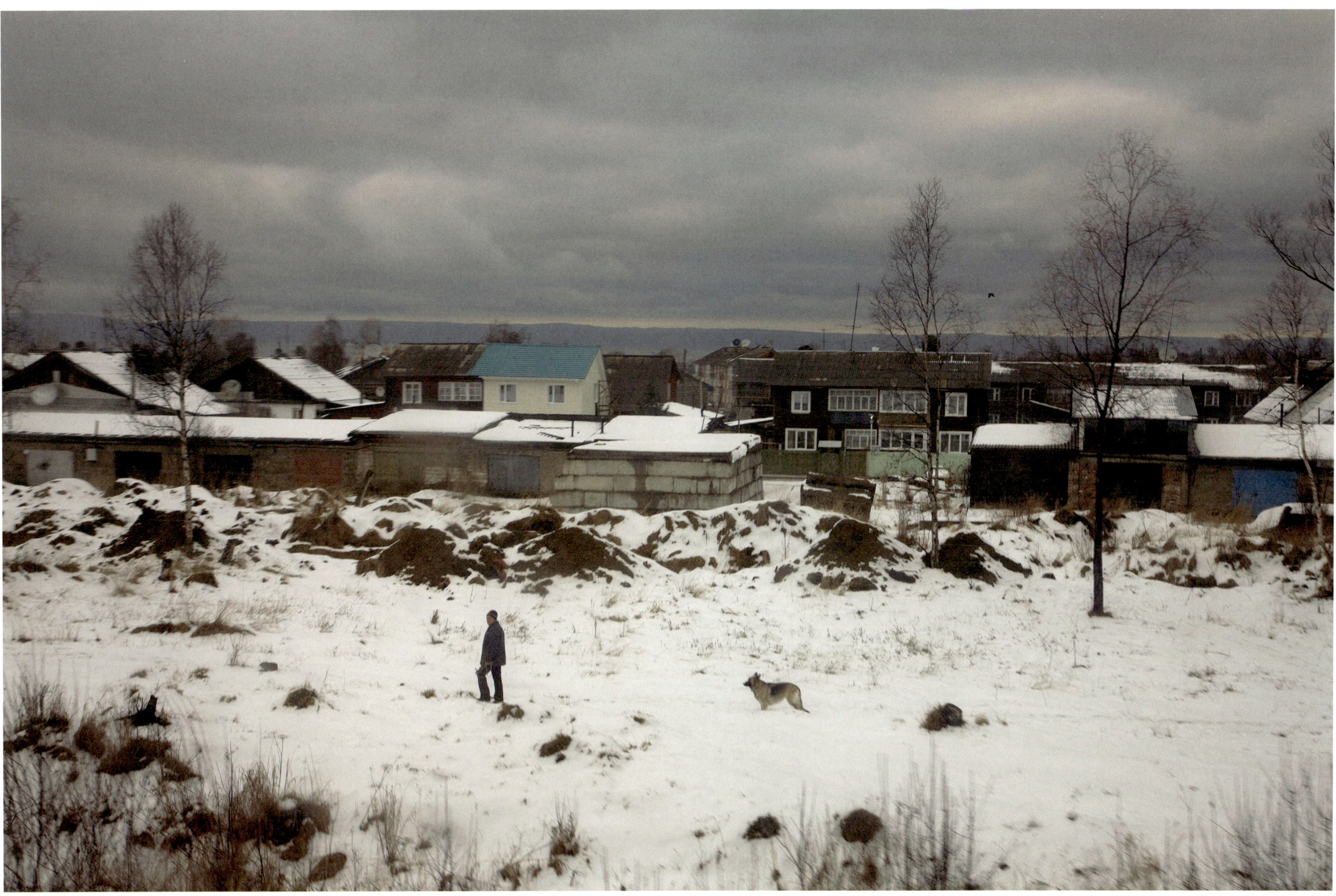

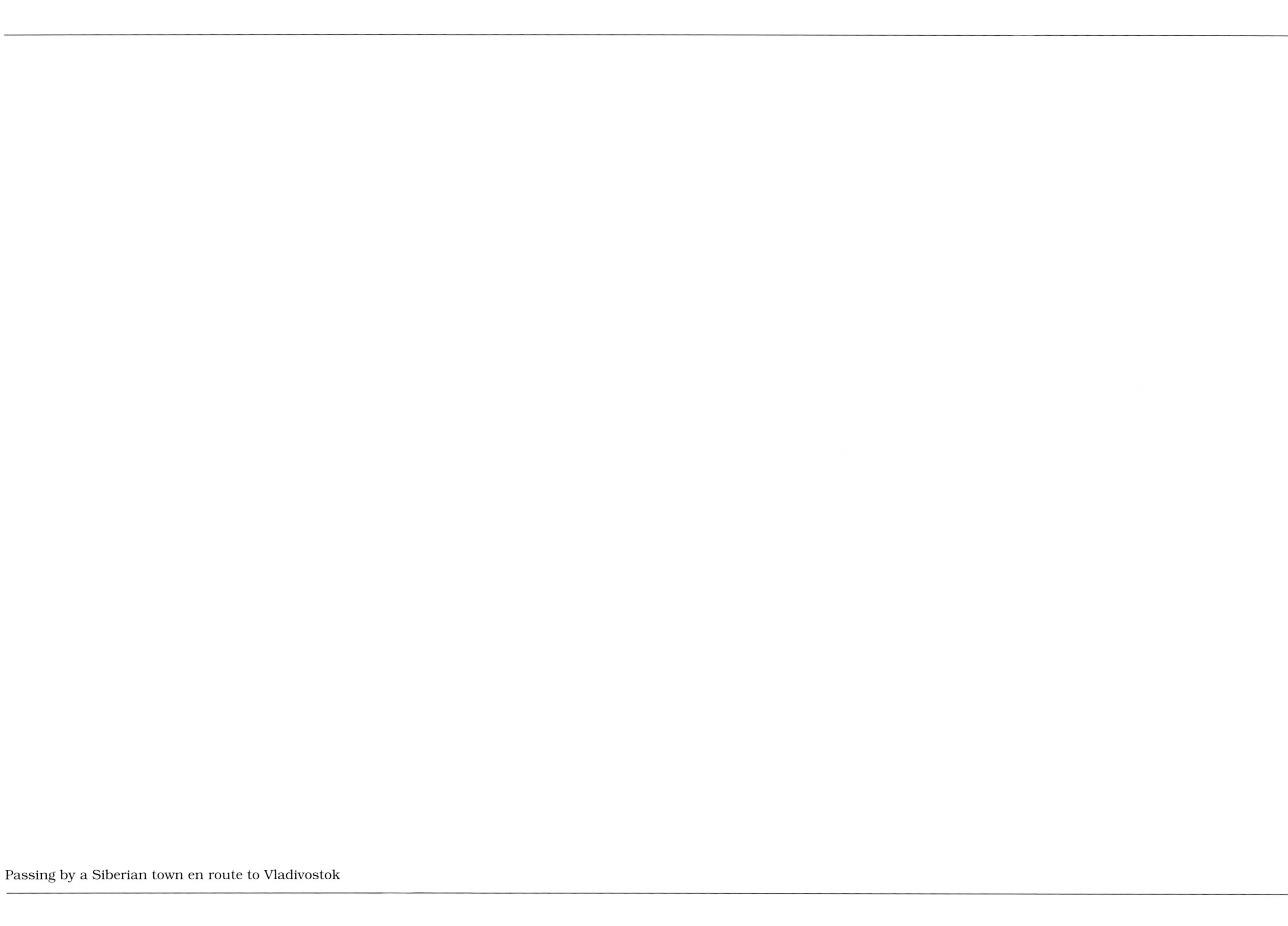

Passing by a Siberian town en route to Vladivostok

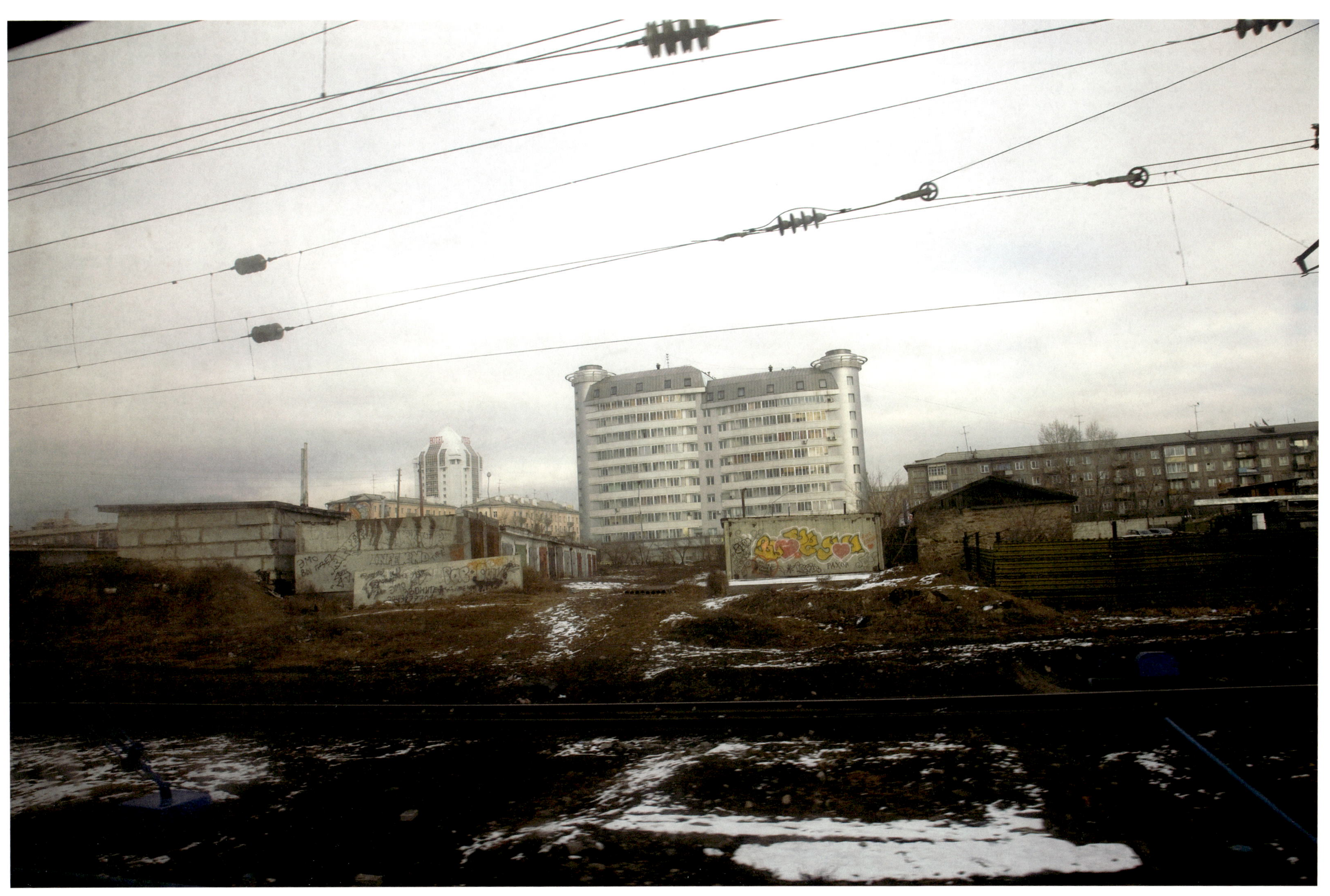

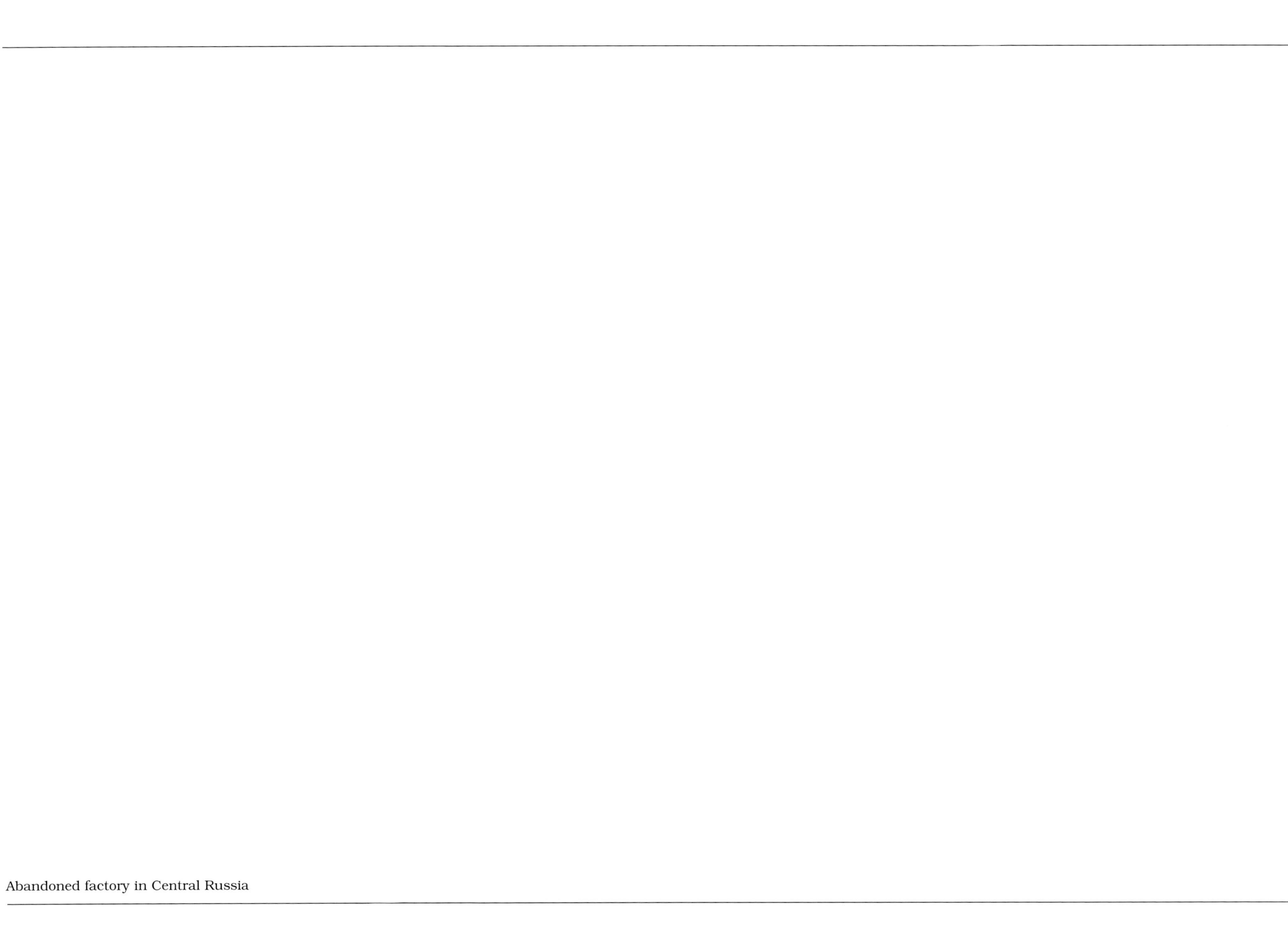

Abandoned factory in Central Russia

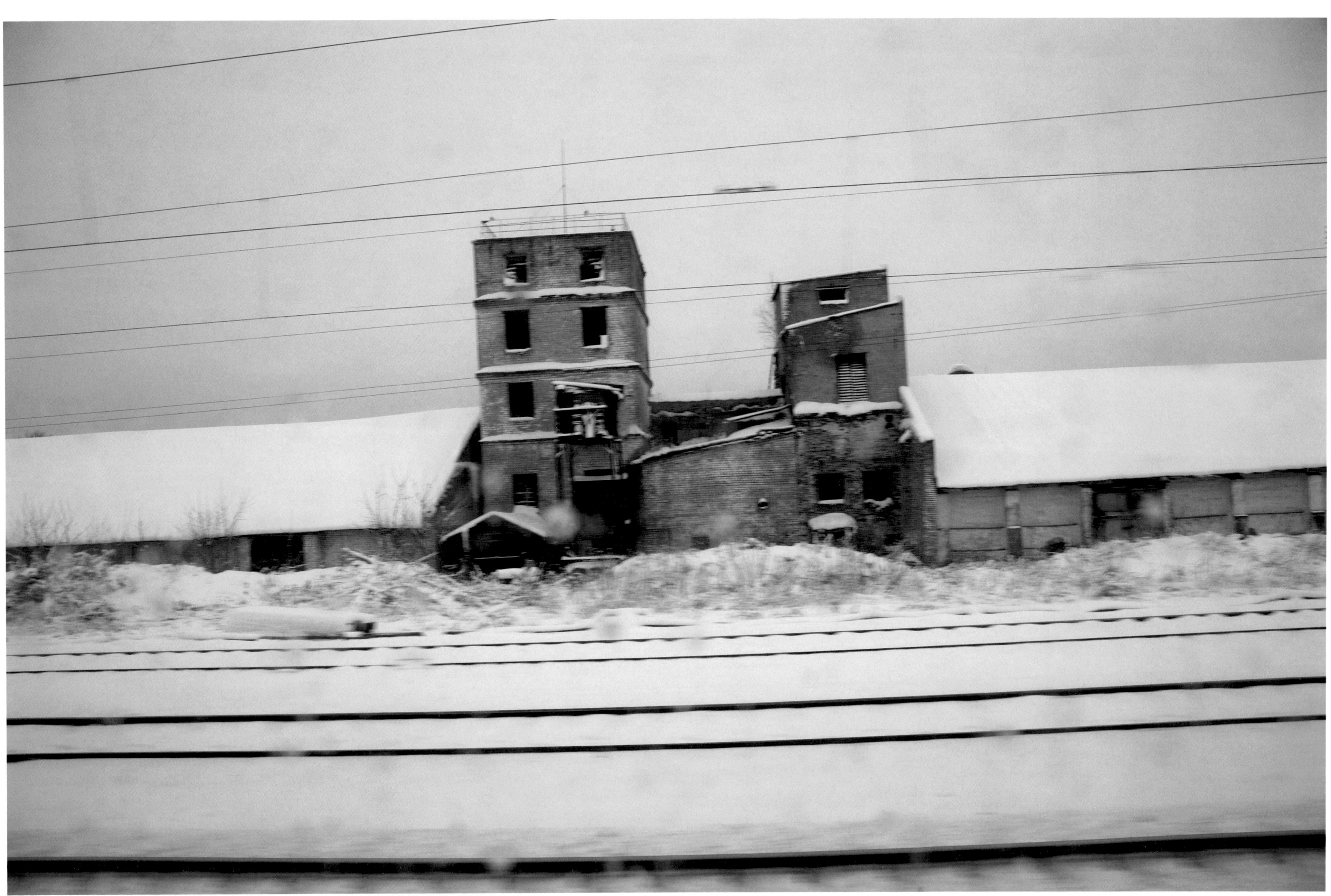

Industrial area west of the Urals

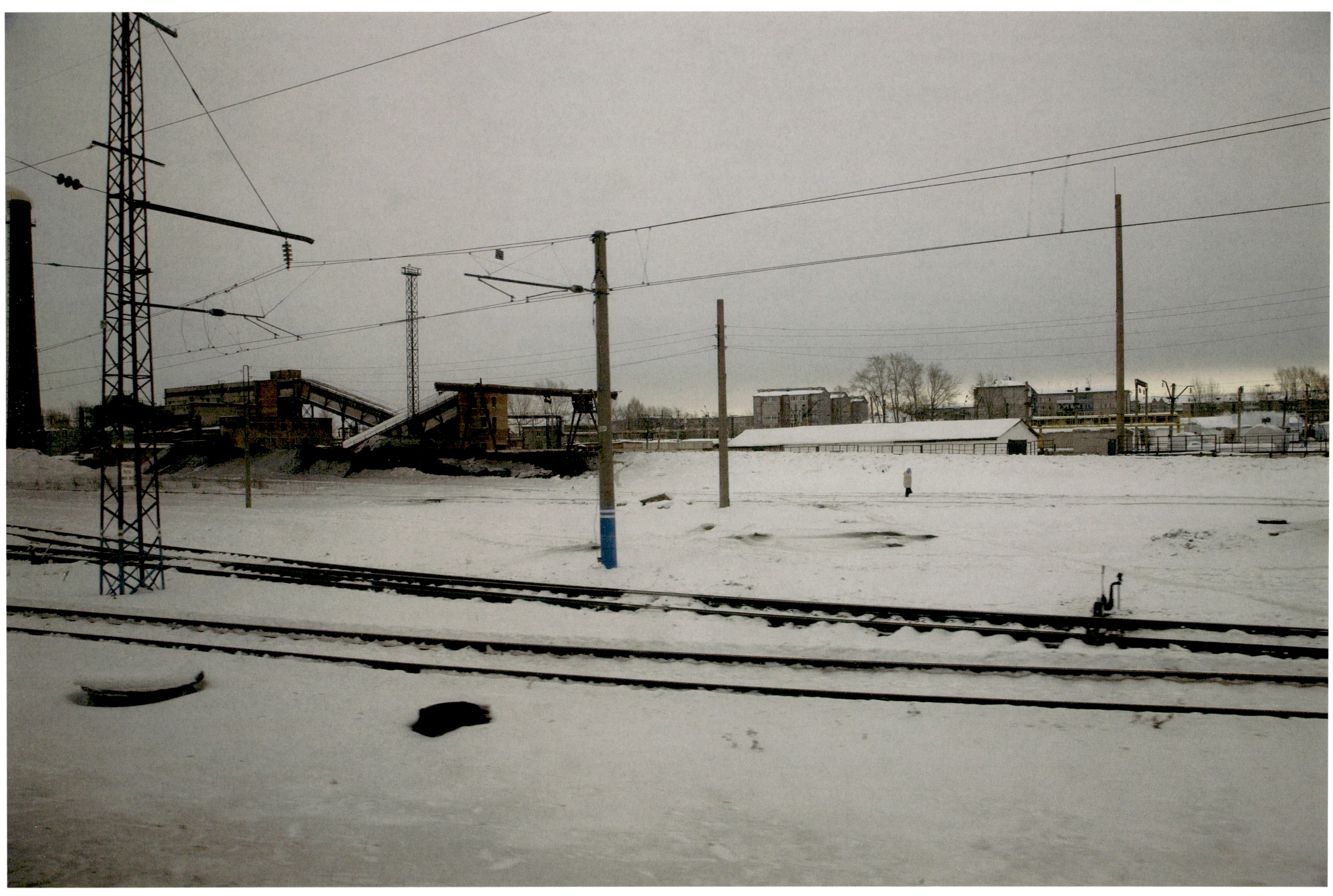

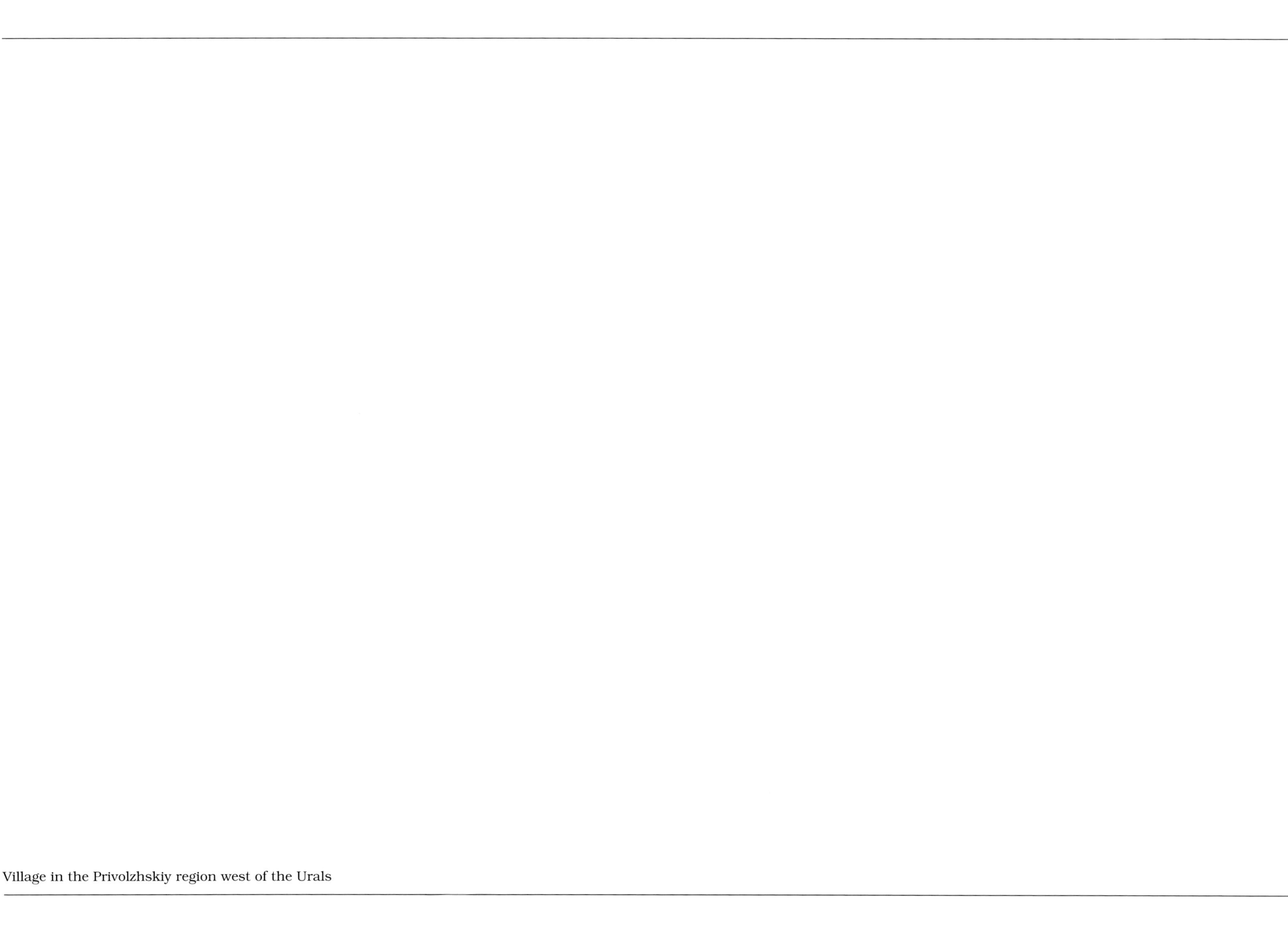

Village in the Privolzhskiy region west of the Urals

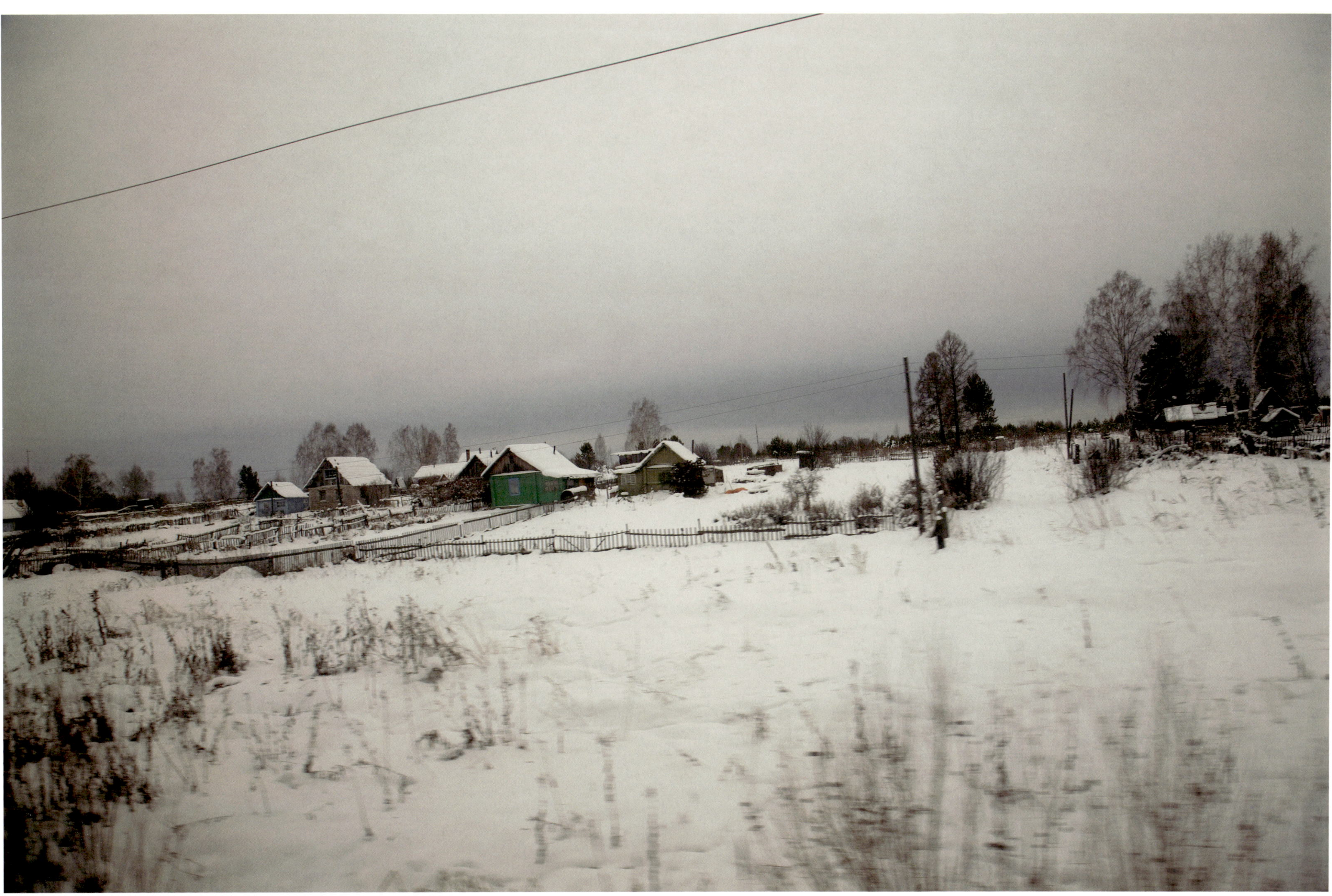

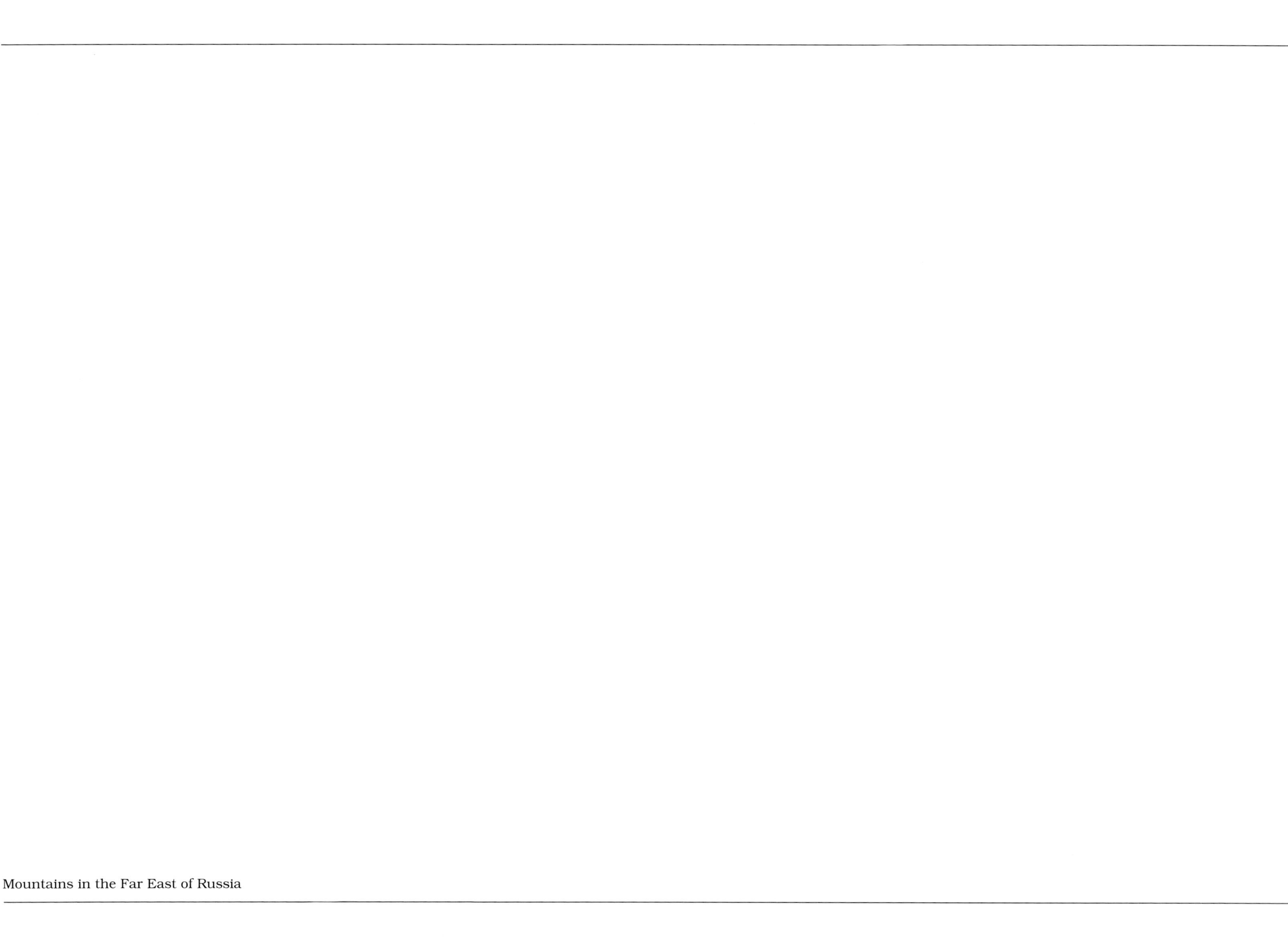

Mountains in the Far East of Russia

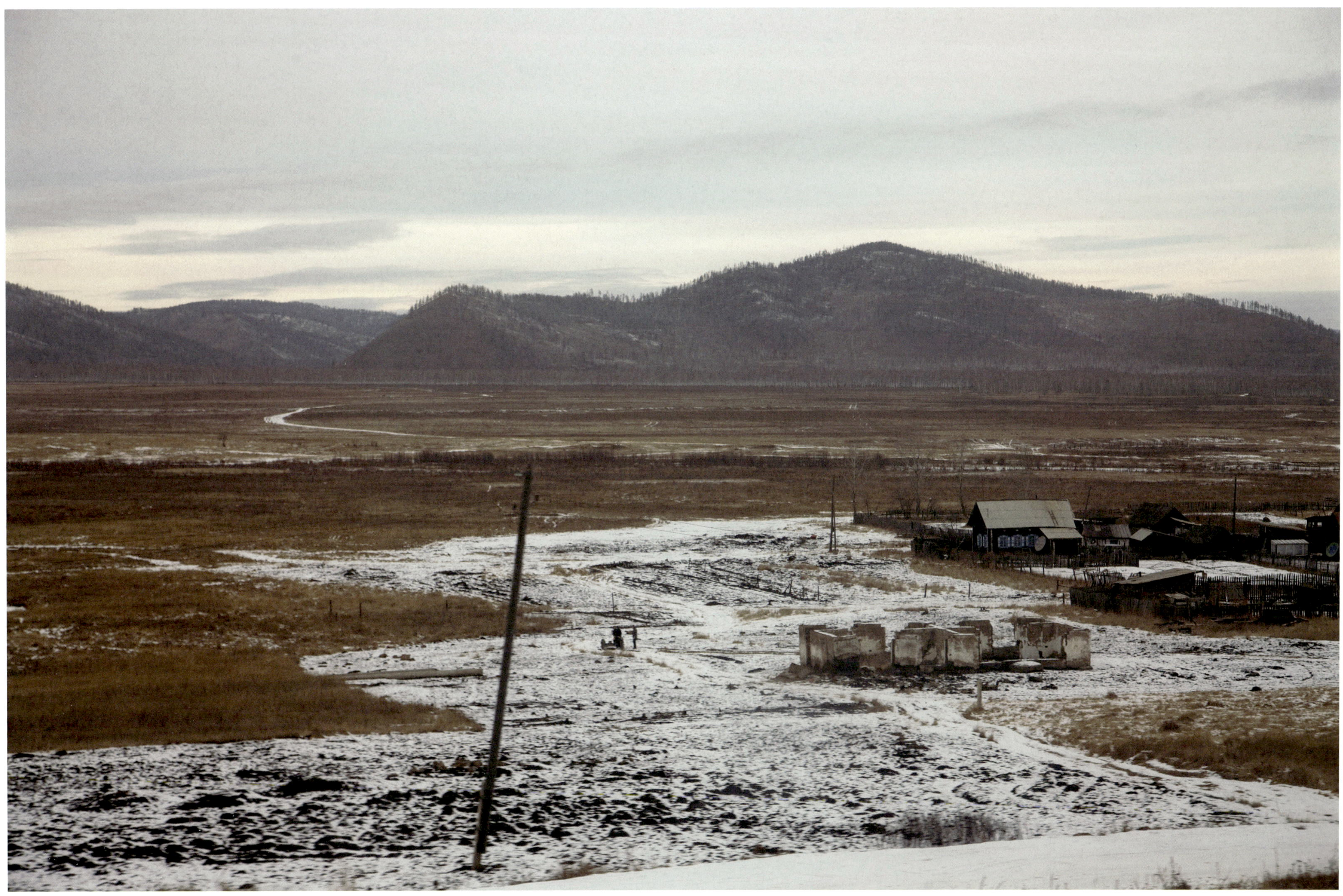

Russia, through revolutions, wars and purges, has seen more people perish on its soil in the past hundred years than perhaps any other country in the world. However, tragedy often engenders resiliency and in turn can unexpectedly lead to greatness. Russia, via the Soviet apparatus, staved off Nazism, became the other superpower, and built one of the biggest empires in the history of the world. However in recent decades it imploded and left its weaknesses and strengths on display for all to view.

Fast forward to today, enfeebled and yet empowered, Russia is still a dynamic paradox, similar and perhaps aptly symbolized, by the relatively slow yet powerful Trans-Siberian Railway. Despite rampant alcoholism, environmental problems, and a lack of democratic transparency amongst a long list of other societal ills, Russia in many ways is remarkably still very powerful and robust. Comprising nearly 6.6 million square miles (nearly twice as large as the USA), Russia constitutes one eighth of the Earth's inhabited land area. Matching its size, Russia has perhaps the greatest abundance of natural resources, including huge reserves of oil and natural gas. Russia's other enormous strength is her nuclear weapons arsenal, to rival the world's lone superpower the USA. Not forgetting Russia has been, and continues to be, a gargantuan cultural force on a global scale with regards to its scientific and technological contribution, as well as with its arts and letters.

Blessed by strength and yet cursed by weakness in both the past and the present, Russia's future trajectory is perhaps best contemplated peering out of the window on the world's longest train ride.